What Art Is Now

What Art Is Now

Creativity in the Age of AI

By Michael E. Jones and Michael Caballes

BLOOMSBURY ACADEMIC
NEW YORK • LONDON • OXFORD • NEW DELHI • SYDNEY

BLOOMSBURY ACADEMIC
Bloomsbury Publishing Inc, 1359 Broadway, 12th Floor, New York, NY 10018, USA
Bloomsbury Publishing Plc, 50 Bedford Square, London, WC1B 3DP, UK
Bloomsbury Publishing Ireland, 29 Earlsfort Terrace, Dublin 2, D02 AY28, Ireland

BLOOMSBURY, BLOOMSBURY ACADEMIC and the Diana logo are trademarks of Bloomsbury Publishing Plc

First published in the United States of America 2026

A catalog for this book is available from the Library of Congress.

ISBN: PB: 979-8-7651-5182-2
HB: 979-8-7651-5176-1
ePDF: 979-8-7651-5192-1
eBook: 979-8-7651-5191-4

Typeset by Deanta Global Publishing Services, Chennai, India

For product safety related questions contact productsafety@bloomsbury.com.

To find out more about our authors and books visit www.bloomsbury.com and sign up for our newsletters.

Contents

Preface

In every era of human history, the creative process has been shaped, challenged, and transformed by new technologies. From the discovery of perspective in the Renaissance to the rise of photography, from the birth of cinema to the digital revolution, artists have constantly adapted, incorporating innovation into their work while redefining the very nature of artistic expression. Today, we stand at another such crossroads, one that is both exhilarating and unsettling—the rise of artificial intelligence as a tool for artistic expression.

Few artists have captured the stakes of this moment as poignantly as rapper J. Cole in his track *cLOUDS* (Cole World, Inc., under exclusive license to Interscope Records 2025), where he writes:

> *"Before long, all the songs the whole world sings'll*
> *Be generated by latest of AI regimes*
> *As all of our favorite artists erased by it scream*
> *From the wayside, 'Ay, whatever happened to human beings?'"*

These lines speak to a growing cultural unease—that in the pursuit of seamless automation and infinite content, we risk erasing the very individuals who make art meaningful. J. Cole's lyrics are not simply a critique of AI, but a warning about what we lose when ownership, authorship, and authenticity are traded for convenience and scale. His poetic concern echoes the larger questions this book sets out to explore: *What happens to creativity when machines generate the music, images, and stories we consume? What happens to us?*

This book emerges from the collision of two perspectives: one rooted in decades of scholarship, academic teaching, and deep engagement with intellectual property law, media, ethics, art, and entertainment law; the other shaped by a digital-first upbringing, steeped in gaming, coding, and the vast possibilities of the metaverse. One of us comes from a family of artists—painters, designers, and visionaries whose work spans generations, including Olympic poster designs and abstract expressionist traditions. The other was raised in a world where pixels, algorithms, and digital environments were not just tools but fundamental elements of creative exploration. Together, our perspectives reflect the broader conversation happening today—between those who have spent lifetimes defining art through human experience and those who see Artificial Intelligence (AI) as a limitless frontier yet to be fully understood.

When Bloomsbury Publishing invited us to write about the meaning of creativity in an AI-driven world, we saw it as an opportunity to explore one of the most urgent and fascinating questions of our time: How does artificial intelligence change the way we create, experience, and define art? This book is not an attempt to provide a single, definitive answer. Instead, it is a journey into the complexities of creative thought, exploring how AI interacts with artistic intent, originality, and human expression.

Throughout the writing of this book, we found ourselves in conversation not only with contemporary artists and theorists but also with the voices of those who have shaped our understanding of art in earlier times. One such voice is that of Arthur Donato, whose posthumously published work *What Is Art* continues to resonate deeply. A revered critic and thinker who taught at Columbia University, Donato's reflections on the cultural, historical, and philosophical dimensions of art provided a critical foundation for this book. His insistence on grounding artistic meaning in context and intention helped illuminate our own inquiries into the role of AI in creative expression. In many ways, *What Art Is Now* can be read as an extension of Donato's thinking—filtered through the digital lens of algorithmic generation, data-driven aesthetics, and the accelerating complexities of authorship in the age of machines.

The questions at the heart of this inquiry are both philosophical and practical. Can AI truly be creative, or is it merely a sophisticated tool of recombination? How do artists, filmmakers, musicians, and designers engage with AI in ways that expand rather than diminish human creativity? What happens to ideas of authorship, ownership, and authenticity when algorithms become collaborators? These questions are not merely academic; they have immense implications for the way we value and protect artistic work in the future.

The purpose of this book is not to take sides in the debate between AI's promise and its potential risks. Rather, it seeks to fill a critical gap for creative professionals, scholars, and anyone curious about how AI is reshaping the artistic landscape. It is for the painter wondering whether AI-generated art undermines traditional skills, for the musician experimenting with machine learning to compose new sounds, for the writer questioning whether AI-generated text is a tool or a threat, and for the broader public grappling with what it means to experience art in an age of deep fakes, synthetic media, and algorithmic aesthetics.

This book also explores the implications of AI-generated art for curators at museums tasked with deciding whether such works merit inclusion alongside traditional masterpieces. How do institutions dedicated to preserving cultural heritage address the blurred boundaries between human creativity and machine output? Auctioneers at galleries face similar challenges—how do they assign value to works that lack the singular signature of an artist declaring, "This is my work"? The absence of clear authorship complicates provenance, authenticity, and the very notion of artistic intent, which has historically driven the visual art market.

For collectives and artist communities, AI-generated art raises questions about collaboration and ownership. Can a collective claim authorship of a piece that is generated largely through algorithms? Does the absence of a human hand diminish the spirit that often defines artistic efforts? And do art critics have any role in shaping perceptions of what constitutes art in this new landscape?

The general public, too, must contend with the rapidly changing nature of art appreciation. As viewers encounter works whose origins are ambiguous, they may find themselves questioning whether a piece is imbued with human intention and tradition or is the product of machine processes and algorithms. This uncertainty challenges long-held beliefs about what constitutes authentic, meaningful art and forces a reconsideration of the emotional and cultural connections we form with creative works.

Through an interdisciplinary approach—drawing on history, law, ethics, philosophy, and technology—we examine how AI fits into the broader arc of artistic innovation. We consider how past technological shifts have altered creative fields and explore whether AI represents something fundamentally different. Does AI challenge the very essence of what it means to be an artist, or is it merely another instrument in the ever-expanding creative toolbox?

Art has long been a subject of philosophical debate, raising the question of whether it is an open concept with no fixed definition or if certain overarching properties make it a universal aspect of the human experience. If anything can be considered art, does that necessarily mean everything is art?

This book embarks on an expedition to explore how art is defined and understood, tracing its evolution through history and examining the ways technology has shaped artistic expression. From the earliest forms of human creativity to the digital era, innovations have continually transformed both the medium, method, and meaning of art. Historically, artistic movements have reflected technological advancements, social change, and shifting cultural values. The invention of paint tubes allowed Impressionist painters to leave their studios and capture light and motion in the open air, just as the development of cameras and photographic techniques redefined realism and paved the way for new artistic explorations.

Marcel Duchamp's readymades, such as *Fountain*, challenged the very notion of what constitutes art, proving that even utilitarian objects could take on new meaning within an artistic context. The transition from realism to abstraction, followed by the rise of conceptual and social commentary art, highlights how changing political and cultural landscapes influence creative expression. Artists like Carrie Mae Weems use photography to address race, gender, and historical narratives, while Andy Warhol's Pop Art interrogates consumer culture and mass production.

Art critics and museum curators have traditionally played a major role in shaping public perceptions of art, determining what is worthy of institutional recognition. However, with the advent of the digital era, these gatekeeping mechanisms are shifting. The widespread availability of smartphones and digital tools means that anyone can capture images, manipulate them, and share their work instantly.

Does this democratization of artistic tools mean that everyone is now an artist? How do we distinguish between artistic intent and everyday digital expression? The impact of new technologies, from Photoshop to AI-generated imagery, continues to redefine artistic boundaries that are explored in the chapters to follow, forcing us to reconsider the relationship between innovation, creativity, and artistic legitimacy.

The history of intelligent machines is crucial to understanding AI's current role in creative processes. We investigate the foundational contributions of individuals like Alan Turing, who theorized the possibility of machine intelligence, and Ada Lovelace, who envisioned computers as tools for artistic expression long before the modern era. Moving forward, we examine today's AI titans—companies and researchers pushing the boundaries of generative AI and even AI's holy grail, Artificial General Intelligence—and how their advancements are transforming creative production in unprecedented ways, challenging our notions of what is art and who is an artist.

Beyond technological advancements, we consider how computational scientists and philosophers view the creative process, questioning whether art is a uniquely human gift, shaped by intuition, lived experiences, and years of practice, or whether machines can truly engage in the act of creation. We also explore the distinction between the process of making art and the final outcome—should the method of creation matter, or is the final product all that counts? We learn that machine-generated art lacks the contextual depth and personal meaning that human-created works carry; does this absence diminish its artistic value, or does it open new, unexplored dimensions of creativity?

These considerations prompt a larger discussion about whether the proliferation of AI-generated works should be a cause for concern or an opportunity to redefine our relationship with art itself. From OpenAI's GPT-4 multimedia text, audio and image generating compositions to AI-assisted music platforms composing symphonies, we discuss how these tools both empower and challenge human artists.

The emergence of AI-generated literature, painting, digital sculptures, and even interactive experiences further complicates questions of authenticity, authorship, and creative value, making it imperative to assess not just what AI can create, but how it redefines the artistic process itself. AI's ability to generate visual and auditory works raises fundamental questions about artistic originality—should AI-generated pieces be considered authentic expressions, or are they merely sophisticated replications of human creativity?

We explore how AI-driven creativity is being utilized in commercial and independent art projects, analyzing its impact on both traditional and digital art spaces. As AI-generated works continue to erase the distinctions between innovation and imitation, we assess whether these tools serve as creative collaborators or disruptors within the artistic landscape.

Further, we analyze the legal and ethical implications of AI scraping data and images from social media platforms and websites, raising questions about intellectual property, authorship, and ownership. AI's methods of training on vast datasets, often culled from online news sources, social media platforms like Instagram and Reddit, and publicly available content, raise serious copyright concerns. Is the automated ingestion of creative works an infringement, or does it fall under fair use?

Courts are now beginning to wrestle with these issues, evaluating whether AI-generated outputs constitute derivative works and, if not, who should be held accountable for potential infringements. Beyond copyright, trademark concerns arise when branded works appear in AI-generated content, particularly in virtual reality environments where brands are replicated without authorization. The European concept of moral rights, which gives authors greater say over how their works are used, presents another layer of legal complexity. Artists worry that AI-generated recreation could misconstrue the meaning of their original work, leading to misrepresentation or reputational harm.

Additionally, cultural appropriation remains a serious challenge, as AI-driven fashion designers and visual artists incorporate sacred symbols and motifs from indigenous and historically marginalized communities without understanding their significance or providing attribution. This raises the question of whether a new form of legal protection is necessary to safeguard cultural heritage and prevent exploitation by AI systems.

We also explore the historical evolution of privacy rights and the growing concerns surrounding the right of publicity in an AI-driven world. Traditionally, individuals have had control over the commercialization of their likeness, name, and personal identity, but AI challenges this notion by scraping vast amounts of personal data from social media and online platforms. Many users, often unaware of the implications of broad terms and conditions agreements, have unknowingly consented to their data being used in AI training models. This has fueled concerns over deepfake technology, where AI can generate hyper-realistic synthetic media that mimics real people without their consent.

These developments pose not insignificant risks to personal and professional reputations, raising ethical and legal debates on consent, misinformation, and identity theft. In response, European regulators have been more proactive in implementing stricter privacy protections, such as the General Data Protection Regulation (GDPR), which aims to limit the misuse of personal data by AI. We examine whether current regulations are sufficient or if new measures are required to address the shifting landscape of privacy and identity in an AI-driven era.

The last chapter concludes with a critical reflection on the future of visual fine arts and creativity in an AI-driven age, considering potential shifts in artistic identity, market valuation, and the evolving relationship between human artists and their algorithmic counterparts. We discuss emerging technologies such as neural networks that can mimic human artistic intuition and the potential of AI as a true creative partner rather than just a tool. We also reflect on how artistic institutions, critics, and audiences might adapt to these transformations, ensuring that the essence of human creativity is preserved in an era increasingly shaped by machines.

The philosopher and mathematician Gottfried Wilhelm Leibniz, writing in 1714 (*Monadology*), takes us to the heart of the problems raised by AI. Leibniz imagined a machine so sophisticated that, if one could walk inside it like a great mill, they would find only mechanical parts pushing against one another—nowhere, he argued, would one find thought or consciousness. This insight, centuries old, remains strikingly relevant as we contemplate AI-generated art. If a machine can replicate the brushstrokes of a master, compose symphonies, or generate poetry that moves us, does that mean it truly creates, or is it merely simulating the patterns it has been trained on? Are we witnessing the emergence of a new form of creativity, or are we simply refining a tool—one more in a long line of technological advancements that have extended the reach of human expression?

As AI becomes increasingly capable of producing works that rival human-made art, we must ask: Does this diminish our own creative capacity, or does it push us toward new frontiers of artistic exploration? Will AI serve as a collaborator, much like the innovations of past centuries that expanded the possibilities of artistic practice, or will it redefine our understanding of what it means to create altogether? These are not just philosophical inquiries but urgent questions for the future of art itself.

We invite you to join us in contemplating these ideas, knowing that while we may not find definitive answers, we will undoubtedly uncover deeper and more profound questions along the way—questions that return us, again and again, to one that J. Cole so succinctly posed: *Whatever happened to human beings?*

Acknowledgments

Michael E. Jones

The creation of *What Art Is Now: Creativity in the Age of AI* has been a profoundly collaborative and interdisciplinary journey. This book would not have been possible without the generous contributions, intellectual challenges, and moral encouragement of a wide-ranging community of artists, scientists, scholars, technologists, legal experts, and students. I am deeply indebted to each of you.

I want to express my gratitude to the visionary computational scientists, ethicists, visual fine artists, legal scholars, inventors, and risk-taking innovators whose groundbreaking work provided the intellectual scaffolding for this book. From early pioneers like **Harold Cohen** and his AARON program to contemporary theorists such as **Margaret Boden, Marcus du Sautoy, Reid Hoffman,** and **Ethan Mollick,** their research has shaped how we understand creativity in the context of machine learning, neural networks, and cognitive science. These thinkers—along with the open discourse fostered through academic publications, podcasts, and digital dialogues—have made it possible to grapple with questions of authorship, sentience, aesthetic value, and agency in art created with and by artificial intelligence. A special note is owed to the late **Arthur C. Danto**, whose lively philosophical meditation *What Art Is* helped inspire the title and reflective spirit of this publication.

A special acknowledgment is due to **Pavel Romaniko**, Director of the Digital Media Program at the University of Massachusetts Lowell, whose leadership created the intellectual space where my students and I could explore the intersections of media, ethics, art, entertainment, and emerging technology. I am also grateful to **Julie Nash**, Senior Vice Provost at the University of Massachusetts Lowell, a longtime champion of my research and teaching, whose steady support has helped sustain my academic efforts. It has been a privilege to teach and learn alongside thousands of students during my time at UMass Lowell—many of whom challenged assumptions, brought fresh Gen Z perspectives, and asked exactly the right questions at the right time.

My deep thanks also go to **Professor Emeritus Steven Lichtenstein**, whose reading of the manuscript and background in law and ethics helped identify subtle tensions in legal reasoning and philosophical framing. His insights helped shape the final articulation of many ideas on these pages.

Among the advanced readers who generously contributed feedback or joined in discussions, whether through public talks or private exchanges, I want to thank:

- **Eric Fritschi**, founder of Ansatz Music Group, for his music industry insights and questions about algorithmic curation and creativity.
- **Michelle Ly**, Microsoft software engineer, former Meta intern and former student of mine, for her technical understanding of generative models and product design.
- **Owen P. Lovely**, passionate gamer and music enthusiast, for raising questions that helped connect digital storytelling, gaming culture, and rap as evolving forms of AI-mediated expression.
- **Bob Korn**, master printmaker, for his historical and aesthetic perspective on visual texture and authorship in the age of digital printmaking.
- **Adam S. Weinberg**, President of Denison University, for his thoughtful reflections on liberal arts, creative freedom, and the responsibilities of academic institutions during a time of rapid change.
- **Ted Cragwell**, Head of Modern Search at Google, and **Katie Cragwell**, graphic designer, offered their thoughtful technical and visual insights, during a lively exchange at the Arts ReMix conference at Denison University.
- **Clarke Doody**, podcaster and conversationalist, for modeling how public discourse about AI can bridge complexity and understanding.
- **Gloria Monaghan**, Professor of Humanities at Wentworth Institute of Technology, whose concern for the ethical and existential implications of AI on humanity has helped sharpen the book's moral lens.
- And especially **Moshe Bar**, cognitive neuroscientist and author of *Mindwandering: How It Can Improve Your Mood and Boost Your Creativity*, who is currently a professor at Bar-Ilan University and was formerly the Director of the Cognitive Neuroscience Laboratory at Harvard University. His research and generous engagement helped

clarify how human mental processes differ from those of AI—and why that difference matters.

I owe a special thanks to the editorial and production team at Bloomsbury Publishing, particularly **Charles Harmon** and **Natalie Plahuta**, whose dedication, editorial acumen, and belief in this project helped refine its ideas and bring it into the world with care and precision. Their high standards of intellectual integrity and production quality reflect the best of academic publishing.

Finally, I extend my deepest appreciation to my family—especially my wife, **Christine M. Jones**—for her enduring love, insightful suggestions, and unwavering belief in this work. Not only did she challenge conventional ideas, but she offered original insights drawn from her perspective as a writer and poet. Her steady support grounded me through the long hours, inevitable doubts, and bursts of inspiration that mark any serious attempt to wrestle with the unknown.

This book is not merely mine—it belongs to all of us striving to make sense of what art means now.

Michael Caballes

It's fitting—and a bit amusing—that I begin my acknowledgments with a reference to *Dota 2*, a game that profoundly shaped my early understanding of artificial intelligence. Growing up in the Philippines, my friends and I spent countless hours in internet cafés after school, immersed in this complex game that mirrors the dynamics of team sports. A turning point came in 2017, when OpenAI's Bot famously defeated Dendi, a legendary *Dota 2* player. Witnessing an AI outperform a human at such a high level opened my eyes to the extraordinary potential of artificial intelligence and sparked my deeper curiosity in the field.

My understanding of AI has since been shaped by the work of many thinkers with diverse perspectives. **Melanie Mitchell's** *Artificial Intelligence: A Guide for Thinking Humans* (2019) provided a strong, accessible foundation. **Yuval Noah Harari**, a masterful storyteller and historian, helped me contextualize humanity's evolving relationship with technology through *Sapiens* (2014), *Homo Deus* (2016), and *Nexus: A Brief History of Information Networks from* *the Stone Age to AI* (2024). His narratives helped trace the arc from early civilization to today's AI-driven world. **Max Tegmark's** *Life 3.0: Being Human in the Age of Artificial Intelligence* (2017) sharpened my sense of urgency with the haunting reminder from the Future of Life Institute: *"Technology is giving life the potential to flourish like never before—or to self-destruct."* This duality resonates with **Mikhail Bakunin's** insight that humanity's creative drive is intertwined with its capacity for destruction.

Despite ongoing debates and concerns surrounding AI, its integration into daily life is accelerating—and I refuse to be left behind. Over the past year, I've immersed myself in online AI and computer science courses, deepening my technical understanding through hands-on coding. Participating in workshops at the University of Rochester, especially discussions with **Professor Adam Purtee** about careers in computer science, has further clarified my path forward.

I am especially grateful to Michael E. Jones for inviting me to contribute to the dialogue on AI and art. I owe deep thanks to my parents, **May** and **Siegfred Caballes**, whose "Go get it" attitude continues to motivate me. And above all, I thank my beloved wife, **Megan Lovely**, for her unwavering support, thoughtful guidance, and quiet wisdom—without which this journey would not have been possible.

One What Art Was

Creativity—and by extension, art—has always been a defining element of human identity, transcending cultural, temporal, and geographic boundaries. It allows us to communicate the inexpressible, explore the complexities of existence, and forge emotional connections. From prehistoric cave paintings to modern digital creations, art has served as a reflection of humanity's hopes, fears, and shifting perspectives on self-awareness. These creative endeavors often mirror the technological advancements and societal transformations of their time. The earliest tools—charcoal, pigments, and primitive chisels—evolved into brushes, printing presses, and cameras, each development broadening the scope of what artists could achieve.

This chapter explores the historical transitions that have shaped art's trajectory, tracing its path from humanity's earliest visual expressions to the provocative pre-digital movements that redefined modern creativity. In its earliest forms, art served as a means of engaging with and documenting the immediate environment. Over time, it expanded to include craftsmanship in sculpture, architecture, and religious iconography—reflecting humanity's reverence for deities, ideals of beauty, and cultural narratives. The classical and medieval periods emphasized form, function, and spiritual devotion, with art often acting as a bridge to the divine.

The Renaissance marked a fundamental shift as humanist philosophy and scientific inquiry elevated art into a celebration of perspective, anatomical precision, and emotional depth. Art became a quest to understand both the physical world and metaphysical truths. By the modern era, artists began experimenting with medium and form in unprecedented ways. Movements like Impressionism, Cubism, and Abstract Expressionism emphasized light, color, space, and emotion over strict representation. These movements questioned traditional notions of perception while addressing broader social issues such as inequality and war.

The rise of consumer culture in the twentieth century introduced new complications within the art world. Pop Art embraced mass production and celebrity culture while challenging distinctions between highbrow art and popular imagery. Conversely, Minimalism and Conceptual Art emphasized intellectual rigor and simplicity by focusing on art's essential elements. By the late twentieth century, Postmodernism examined the commodification of culture while exposing tensions between art as an object for contemplation versus a commercial product.

By situating these historical artistic movements within the broader context of technological advancements, this chapter investigates how creativity has continually adapted to new tools while redefining authorship. It sets the stage for later discussions about pressing questions: What happens to the role of the artist in a world where machines can generate works rivaling human craftsmanship? As artificial intelligence (AI) enters the creative domain, we must ask whether these technologies will serve as collaborative partners that expand artistic possibilities or disrupt traditional ideas about artistic identity.

Through this lens a fundamental question arises: In the absence of human intellect, experience, emotion, and ideas, can AI-generated works truly be considered "art"? Does a machine engage in creativity or merely replicate patterns derived from human input? These concerns echo past anxieties when photography emerged as a new medium—will AI render human artists irrelevant or open new avenues for collaboration? By reflecting on historical intersections between art and technology, we can better understand how digital tools may redefine what it means to create in an increasingly interconnected social media driven world.

Historical Shifts: Evolution of Art and Tools

From Cave Paintings to Contemporary Art

The development of art throughout history demonstrates humanity's continuous drive for innovation and expression. Each historical period has been characterized by its available tools and techniques, which have fundamentally influenced both artistic creation and audience experience. This evolution spans from the basic pigments used in prehistoric cave art to the sophisticated technologies of virtual and augmented reality, reflecting humanity's changing relationship with creativity and self-expression.

Human artistic expression originated more than 30,000 years ago during the Paleolithic era, with consequential examples preserved in the cave complexes of Chauvet and Lascaux in France. These early works demonstrate humanity's basic drive for visual communication and connection through artistic representation. The artists employed naturally occurring materials, including ochre, charcoal, and hematite minerals, to create sophisticated depictions of their world. Their subjects encompassed both naturalistic representations of animals—including horses, bison, and mammoths—and abstract forms such as hand stencils, each carrying profound spiritual and symbolic meaning. These works served multiple functions beyond aesthetic decoration, operating as essential tools for cultural transmission, religious practice, and historical documentation.

The technical sophistication demonstrated by these prehistoric artists merits particular attention. They developed multiple innovative processes for surface preparation, including careful scraping of cave walls to create suitable painting surfaces. The artists displayed a remarkable understanding of their medium, utilizing the natural topography of rock formations to enhance the depth and movement of their images. Their mastery extended to pigment application, employing layering techniques to achieve subtle textural effects. Perhaps most notably, certain works demonstrate an early grasp of perspective, evidenced by overlapping animal figures that create convincing spatial relationships. This integration of artistic vision with technical execution demonstrates the long-standing relationship between creative expression and technological innovation.

The cave paintings provide valuable insights into early human consciousness and social organization. Academic analysis suggests these works served multiple corollary functions within prehistoric communities. The paintings appear to have expressed spiritual beliefs and facilitated connections with divine forces. They likely served as focal points for community gatherings and shared religious practices. The depicted animals transcended mere representation, functioning as sacred symbols or totems, potentially playing crucial roles in hunting rituals and cultural ceremonies. The deliberate placement of artwork in remote cave locations, frequently requiring difficult access, suggests these spaces served as meaningful sanctuaries for significant cultural practices.

Modern art criticism continues to find profound relevance in these ancient works. Pulitzer Prize-winning critic Jerry Saltz offers a particularly insightful interpretation, characterizing cave paintings as "original selfies"—not as expressions of vanity, but as fundamental statements of identity, community, and existence. This analysis suggests these early artists engaged in an enterprise that transcends mere documentation, attempting to understand their world and leave enduring evidence of their presence. Their work demonstrates that the creative impulse represents a constant throughout human history, serving as the foundation for all subsequent artistic innovation.

The prehistoric artists developed an array of effective implements for artistic creation. They fashioned primitive airbrushes from hollow bones and reeds, enabling them to apply pigments with precision and control. For detailed work, they crafted brushes using animal hair and created specialized tools from modified wooden implements. These developments represent early examples of humans adapting natural materials to serve sophisticated creative purposes.

The preparation of pigments involved extensive technical knowledge. Artists sourced minerals such as hematite and manganese oxide to create their fundamental color palette, with hematite providing rich red tones and manganese oxide producing deep blacks. These raw materials underwent careful processing, being ground into fine powders and combined with various binding agents including water, saliva, and animal fat. The resulting paint demonstrated remarkable durability, as evidenced by its preservation over tens of thousands of years within the protective cave environments.

A particularly sophisticated example of prehistoric artistic innovation appears in the hand stencils discovered in Spain's El Castillo cave complex. The artists developed a distinctive technique that involved positioning their hands against the rock surface and carefully blowing pigment around them. This process created striking negative images that served both as personal signatures and as demonstrations of advanced compositional understanding. The technique required precise control of pigment application and an intuitive grasp of artistic principles including contrast and spatial relationships.

The influence of these early artistic innovations extends far beyond their immediate historical context. These works represent humanity's first successful attempts to transform abstract concepts into concrete visual representations. The artists developed methods to capture ephemeral experiences, cultural myths, and emotional responses in permanent form, establishing foundational practices that would influence artistic development across millennia.

The technical and conceptual achievements of these prehistoric artists established essential precedents for subsequent artistic evolution. Just as later generations would employ increasingly sophisticated tools such as chisels and oil paints to explore the human condition, these early practitioners utilized their available materials to articulate their understanding of existence. Their innovative approaches to artistic creation laid the groundwork for the diverse artistic traditions that would emerge across cultures and historical periods.

The endurance of these works, still visible and powerful after tens of thousands of years, testifies to both the technical sophistication of their creators and their unique understanding of artistic principles that continue to resonate in contemporary creative practice.

Evolution of Art: Milestones in Human Creativity

Art's journey across millennia, from the intricate carvings of Mesopotamia to the harmonious landscapes of ancient China and the monumental achievements of ancient Greece and Rome, reveals humanity's enduring drive to create, communicate, and transcend. When we look at art, we are not merely observing forms and materials; we are gazing through them into the collective mind of a culture—its beliefs, struggles, and aspirations. Through pigments, stone, bronze, and ink, these civilizations forged a dialogue that bridges generations, embodying the collective intelligence and spirit of every individual who contributed to these creations.

The ancient Mesopotamians expanded the scope of art by integrating it with governance, religion, and daily life. Cylinder seals, intricately carved with symbols and portrayals, served as both personal identifiers and storytelling devices, while the Stele of Hammurabi combined legal authority with visual storytelling. These artifacts not only conveyed cultural values but also reinforced social hierarchies and divine mandates.

Technological advances such as the invention of the stylus and innovative carving techniques enabled greater detail and permanence. Camille Paglia, in *Glittering Images: A Journey Through Art from Egypt to Star Wars*, sees these works as evidence of humanity's ability to codify complex systems—laws, myths, and identities—into tangible forms, reinforcing the connection between art, power, and culture.

Egyptian art epitomized the interplay of spirituality, technology, and innovation. The frescoes of the *Tomb of Nefertari*, painted with ground minerals like malachite (blue-green) and ochre, showcased technological advancements in pigment preparation, enabling stunning visual effects that have endured for millennia. Monumental sculptures, hieroglyphs, and architectural marvels like the pyramids reflected the Egyptians' obsession with cosmic order, immortality, and the eternal.

In ancient China, art reflected an integral connection to nature, balance, and spirituality. Oracle bones of the Shang dynasty and bronze vessels adorned with *taotie* motifs embodied humanity's relationship with the divine. Ink painting, jade carving, and calligraphy became meditative practices that expressed harmony and philosophical depth. Innovations in alloy compositions for bronze casting and the refinement of ink-making techniques allowed Chinese artists to achieve unparalleled precision and beauty.

Classical Greece ushered in an epic era of art, blending the ideals of realism and idealism to celebrate human potential and the physical form. Advances in marble quarrying and bronze casting allowed sculptors to achieve unprecedented levels of anatomical accuracy and idealized beauty. Artists such as Polykleitos epitomized this synthesis in works like the *Doryphoros* (Spear Bearer), which embodied his canon of ideal proportions and balance.

Greek art extended beyond sculpture to include vase painting, where depictions of mythology and daily life showcased art's capacity for storytelling. These painted vessels, crafted by artists such as Exekias, who created the renowned *Achilles and Ajax Playing a Game*, combined technical skill with intense depth, offering insights into Greek culture and its values.

Renowned sculptors pushed the limits of artistic innovation. Phidias, celebrated for overseeing the *Parthenon's* decoration and creating the colossal statue of *Zeus at Olympia*, epitomized grandeur and divine aspiration. Meanwhile, Praxiteles introduced a softer, more naturalistic approach, redefining the depiction of the human body with works like the *Aphrodite of Knidos*, which marked a groundbreaking representation of the female form in Western art.

Building on Greek foundations, Roman art elevated realism, propaganda, and engineering brilliance to unprecedented heights. The invention of concrete revolutionized construction, enabling architectural marvels such as the *Colosseum*, a grand amphitheater designed for public spectacles, and the *Pantheon*, with its awe-inspiring dome and oculus symbolizing the heavens. Roman artists and architects, including Vitruvius, whose treatise *De Architectura* codified principles of design and proportion, played a pivotal role in shaping this legacy.

Mosaics and frescoes became central to Roman artistic expression, adorning public spaces such as bathhouses and private villas like those in Pompeii and Herculaneum. Renowned mosaicists, although often anonymous, demonstrated incredible skill in creating intricate designs, as seen in the *Alexander Mosaic* from the House of the Faun. Fresco artists, such as those working in the Pompeian styles, brought walls to life with vibrant depictions of mythology, landscapes, and daily life, reflecting the empire's cultural diversity and grandeur.

Roman art's focus on realism is exemplified in portraiture, with busts of emperors like Augustus and ordinary citizens capturing individuality and character. Artists such as Apollodorus of Damascus, who designed the magnificent *Trajan's Forum* and the *Column of Trajan*, demonstrated how art and engineering could serve both aesthetic and partisan purposes, celebrating military victories and imperial power.

These works not only reflected the Roman Empire's cosmopolitan identity and technological prowess but also embodied its ethos of cultural integration and legacy-building, showcasing an art form that sought to immortalize the empire's ideals and achievements for generations to come.

The tools and techniques of antiquity were as varied as the civilizations that employed them. Mesopotamian artists developed styluses for cuneiform writing, Egyptian artisans perfected pigment preparation, and Chinese bronze casters mastered intricate designs. Greek advancements in quarrying and Roman breakthroughs in concrete exemplified how technology and creativity have always been intertwined. These advancements empowered artists to expand the possibilities of their mediums, highlighting the enduring interplay between art and technology that continues to shape creative expression today.

The Renaissance: Rendering the Unseen Seen

The Renaissance marked a poignant shift in the purpose and perception of art. As Toni Morrison eloquently observed, "Art reminds us that we belong here." This sentiment resonates deeply with the works of Renaissance masters who sought not only to depict the divine and the human but to channel intangible emotions, ideas, and aspirations that define the human experience.

Take Michelangelo's *David* as an emblematic example—a biblical tale immortalized in marble. On the surface, the sculpture represents a young shepherd poised to confront the giant Goliath. Yet, its deeper essence—the aesthetic substructure and lifeblood of the piece—transcends its historical roots. Michelangelo's *David* embodies sensuality, beauty, majesty, pathos, and the power of self-determination. The subtle potentiality of movement captured in the tension of *David's* form, the inchoate softness of the marble against its solid grandeur, all resonate as reflections of the human condition. The sculpture is not merely a representation but an invitation to ponder the dynamism and fragility of existence.

Michelangelo's mastery was not achieved in isolation but was facilitated by the technological advances and tools of his time. He used chisels, rasps, and mallets to carve Carrara marble—a material revered for its luminous quality and fine grain, making it ideal for detailed sculpting. These tools, though seemingly rudimentary, were refined through generations of craftsmanship, enabling unparalleled precision. The use of techniques like *pointing machines* to measure proportions and rough out shapes allowed Michelangelo to translate his vision with remarkable accuracy. The technological innovations of the Renaissance elevated the potential of artists, enabling them to create works that redefined the limits of their mediums.

For Renaissance artists, art became an instrument, a medium, and often a miracle—advancing old impressions into new revelations. Through the mastery of perspective, chiaroscuro, and anatomical precision, they explored humanity's place in the cosmos. These innovations were not confined to the medium of paint, stone, or bronze; they were frameworks for understanding and reimagining the world. Art was both a mirror to reflect human potential and a window to envision transcendence.

The Renaissance period transformed artistic creation through advances in materials, techniques, and philosophical approaches. The refinement and widespread adoption of oil paint emerged as a pivotal technical innovation, fundamentally altering artistic possibilities and enabling unprecedented achievements in detail, depth, and color manipulation.

Oil paint's distinct properties, particularly its extended drying time and remarkable versatility, allowed artists to achieve previously impossible effects. Jan van Eyck, renowned for perfecting oil painting techniques, demonstrated the medium's exceptional capabilities in works such as *The Arnolfini Portrait*. Through innovative application of multiple translucent layers, van Eyck created luminous effects and subtle light refractions that established new standards for realistic representation in painting.

Technical advances in painting implements complemented the development of oil paint methods. Artists adopted refined brushes featuring softer bristles crafted from sable and hog hair, providing tools capable of both precise detail work and broad expressive gestures. These improved implements enabled artists to capture intricate textures with extraordinary accuracy, from complex fabric folds to subtle variations in human skin and hair. Leonardo da Vinci exemplified these capabilities in works such as the *Mona Lisa*, where his mastery of the sfumato technique created subtle gradations that imbued his subjects with remarkable vitality.

The expressive potential of oil paint reached new heights through artists like Titian, who demonstrated the medium's capacity for bold artistic statements. His masterwork *Assumption of the Virgin* showcases the dramatic effects possible through layered brushwork and vibrant color application. Titian's dynamic approach created powerful interplays of light and shadow, introducing levels of emotional and physical movement that distinguished oil painting from earlier media such as tempera.

The evolution of oil painting techniques culminated in revolutionary approaches to light and shadow, particularly in Caravaggio's work. His development of chiaroscuro technique, exemplified in *The Calling of Saint Matthew*, demonstrated oil paint's ability to create dramatic contrasts between light and dark. This innovation enhanced the three dimensional quality of painted surfaces while introducing theatrical intensity that influenced generations of subsequent artists.

These combined technical and artistic innovations transformed painting into an extraordinarily versatile medium for creative expression. Artists gained the ability to render minute details with precision while conveying complex emotional states through their work. This advancement in artistic media enabled unprecedented experimentation with perspective and texture, redefining the possibilities for realistic representation in art. The Renaissance development of oil painting techniques represents a crucial turning point in artistic history, establishing foundations that continue to influence contemporary artistic practice.

The Advent of Ready-Made Paint: A New Freedom for Artists

For centuries, visual artists were responsible for creating their own paints by grinding minerals, plant-based dyes, or other natural materials and combining them with oils, egg yolks, or other binders. This labor-intensive process required not only artistic skill but also a deep understanding of chemistry to ensure the right consistency and color stability. The process was time-consuming and often limited artists' ability to experiment freely.

A major technological breakthrough came in the nineteenth century with the invention of pre-mixed paint in tubes by John G. Rand, an American portrait painter. In 1841, Rand patented a collapsible metal paint tube that allowed artists to store and transport pre-mixed paints while preserving their quality over time. This simple yet revolutionary invention transformed artistic practice by eliminating the need for laborious pigment preparation in the studio.

The portability offered by paint tubes was a game-changer for artists. It enabled the rise of plein air painting, where painters could work outdoors to capture natural light and landscapes in real time. This innovation was pivotal for movements like Impressionism, as it allowed artists to leave their studios and paint directly from nature. Additionally, this newfound mobility opened opportunities for women artists, who had historically been excluded from many formal art spaces and training due to societal restrictions. With paint tubes in hand, women could access outdoor settings and participate more actively in emerging movements like Impressionism.

Artists such as Berthe Morisot and Mary Cassatt embraced this freedom, producing works that challenged traditional gender roles in art. Morisot's *Summer's Day* exemplifies the movement's focus on light and spontaneity, while Cassatt's intimate domestic scenes like *The Child's Bath* gained critical acclaim for their emotional depth and technical skill. These women not only contributed significantly to Impressionism but also paved the way for greater acceptance of women in professional art circles.

Moreover, pre-mixed paint tubes democratized art-making by making materials more accessible. Aspiring artists without access to extensive resources or studio facilities could now experiment with a wider range of colors and techniques. This accessibility contributed to the spread of new styles and movements, as painters were no longer constrained by the logistical challenges of pigment preparation.

Technological advancements in paint manufacturing during this period also improved the range and quality of pigments available to artists. Synthetic pigments such as chromium oxide green, cobalt blue, and cadmium yellow offered a broader and more vibrant palette than ever before. These developments enabled iconic works that showcased unprecedented color intensity and dynamic expression, such as Van Gogh's *Starry Night* and Cézanne's *Mont Sainte-Victoire*.

The invention of paint tubes exemplifies how innovation can influence artistic practice. By freeing artists from material constraints and expanding their creative possibilities, this development not only facilitated new artistic movements but also empowered women artists to gain recognition in a field traditionally dominated by men. It laid the foundation for the diversity and experimentation that defined nineteenth- and twentieth-century art movements while continuing to inspire discussions about accessibility and inclusion in art today.

The Printing Press: A Catalyst for Artistic Innovation and Accessibility

The invention of the printing press in the mid-fifteenth century by Johannes Gutenberg marked another turning point in the history of art and culture. While its primary impact was in the dissemination of texts, the printing press also revolutionized the arts by introducing new methods for reproduction and distribution that fundamentally changed how art was created, shared, and consumed.

Before Gutenberg's innovation, text and image reproduction relied on labor-intensive manual processes performed by scribes and woodblock printers. The introduction of movable type and mechanized printing dramatically accelerated production capabilities. This technical advancement quickly expanded beyond text to encompass visual arts through new reproduction methods, including woodcut printing, engraving, and etching. These developments enabled artists to distribute their work to a larger audience.

The printing press allowed artists to reach audiences far beyond their immediate geographic location. For the first time, images could be reproduced on a large scale and circulated extensively, making art more accessible to people outside elite circles. Albrecht Dürer, a German Renaissance artist, is a prime example of how the printing press enhanced an artist's career. Dürer mastered the art of woodcuts and engravings, using them to create detailed prints like *The Four Horsemen of the Apocalypse*. These works were not only artistic masterpieces but also affordable, portable, and widely distributed, establishing Dürer's reputation across Europe.

This commercial element created by the printing press meant that artists could achieve fame and financial success in ways that were previously unattainable. Prints became a democratic medium, allowing artists to appeal to a broader audience, including the emerging middle class. This shift also supported the transition of art from being solely commissioned by the Church or aristocracy to being driven by market demand.

The printing press also facilitated the exchange of ideas among artists. Reproductions of artworks and instructional manuals spread rapidly, enabling artists to study techniques, styles, and subjects from distant regions. For example, prints of Italian Renaissance works reached Northern Europe, inspiring artists like Dürer and Hans Holbein. Similarly, the dissemination of anatomical drawings, such as those by Leonardo da Vinci and Andreas Vesalius, enriched artists' understanding of the human form and influenced the naturalism seen in Renaissance art.

As the centuries progressed, illustrators continued to refine their craft. William Blake seamlessly combined his poetry with visionary illustrations, while Thomas Bewick revolutionized wood engraving in the late eighteenth century, creating detailed and evocative images for natural history books. These contributions highlighted how illustration could enhance textual narratives with visual depth and precision.

The nineteenth century saw the rise of stunning visual interpretations for literary classics, such as Gustave Doré's masterful work for *The Divine Comedy* and *Don Quixote*, which added layers of meaning and emotion to the texts. Frank Merrill followed with his memorable illustrations for Louisa May Alcott's *Little Women*, capturing the warmth and intimacy of the March family with expressive line work. Merrill's art helped solidify the connection between readers and beloved characters, illuminating the power of visual storytelling.

During and after the Civil War, the work of artists at Currier & Ives played a crucial role in informing the public through lithographs. In an era before modern communication technologies, their prints served as a vital source of news and cultural commentary. From capturing historic moments like the death of President Lincoln to depicting battle scenes and social milestones, Currier & Ives' lithographs brought the immediacy of current events to households across America. Their ability to distribute visually compelling representations of national events helped bridge the gap between the public's need for information and the limitations of the day's slower communication systems.

Moving into the late nineteenth and early twentieth centuries, illustrators elevated children's literature with ethereal depictions. Arthur Rackham's interpretations of *Alice's Adventures in Wonderland* and *Peter Pan in Kensington Gardens* enchanted readers with their dreamlike, intricate artistry. Jessie Willcox Smith's tender illustrations for classics such as *Heidi* and *The Water-Babies* further enriched the stories, enchanting young readers with soft, expressive imagery. These works continued the tradition of blending artistic innovation with storytelling, reinforcing the enduring power of illustration as both an artistic and communicative medium.

The early twentieth century saw illustrators expand their influence beyond books to magazines and mass media. Norman Rockwell, one of the most iconic magazine illustrators, captured the essence of everyday American life through his covers for *The Saturday Evening Post*. His illustrations, such as *Freedom from Want* and *The Problem We All Live With*, blended storytelling with social commentary, reflecting and shaping cultural values. Rockwell's ability to combine technical skill with relatable narratives brought art into millions of homes, making illustration a cornerstone of American visual culture.

The printing press contributed to the democratization of art and knowledge. By making both text and imagery widely available, it played a central role in the spread of the Renaissance and later movements like the Reformation. Art was no longer confined to elite patrons but became an integral part of everyday life, seen in religious tracts, educational materials, and even satirical prints.

In the long term, the printing press laid the groundwork for modern concepts of intellectual property and copyright. As artists became more aware of the economic potential of their works, the need to protect original creations and maintain artistic integrity grew, leading to early legal frameworks for intellectual property.

The printing press was not merely a tool for mass production; it revolutionized cultural and artistic practices. By enabling the widespread distribution of art, it elevated artists to new levels of recognition and fostered a shared visual culture that crossed geographic and social boundaries. This groundbreaking technology fundamentally altered the art world, emphasizing the importance of reproduction, communication, and accessibility—principles that continue to shape artistic practices in the digital age.

Photography: Transforming Perception

The nineteenth century introduced photography—a revolutionary medium that fundamentally altered artistic representation and perception. The development of photography was made possible by advancements in optical technology, chemistry, and mechanics. Early cameras, such as the daguerreotype, invented by Louis Daguerre in 1839, used polished silver-plated copper sheets to create highly detailed images. Around the same time, William Henry Fox Talbot, another pioneer, developed the calotype process, which employed paper coated with silver iodide to produce negatives that could be used to make multiple prints. These technological breakthroughs laid the basis for photography's evolution as both a scientific tool and an artistic medium.

Photography's potential to capture reality with precision attracted a range of practitioners, from scientists to artists. Julia Margaret Cameron, one of the earliest art photographers, used soft-focus techniques, dramatic lighting, and staged compositions to create emotive portraits and narrative tableaux. Her approach elevated photography into a fine art, emphasizing its capacity for storytelling and aesthetic innovation rather than mere documentation.

The advent of photography challenged traditional artistic practices, particularly in painting. Photography's ability to document reality with unparalleled accuracy rendered the pursuit of mimetic representation in painting less urgent. In response, painters began to explore abstraction, emotional expression, and new visual strategies that extended beyond realism. For instance:

- Claude Monet and other Impressionists focused on capturing fleeting moments, emphasizing light, color, and atmosphere over meticulous detail. Monet's depictions of landscapes, such as his *Water Lilies* series, illustrate how painters embraced photography's influence while diverging into more interpretive realms.
- Edgar Degas, inspired by photography's framing and perspectives, incorporated techniques like cropping and unusual angles into his compositions. Degas's works, such as *The Dance Class*, reflect his fascination with capturing spontaneous, momentary scenes reminiscent of photographic snapshots.

The interplay between photography and painting catalyzed a wave of radical artistic movements. Photography's ability to capture reality with unmatched precision liberated painters from the need to replicate life exactly, opening the door for experimentation with form, perspective, and abstraction. However, the emergence of photography in the nineteenth century also provoked significant anxiety among visual artists. Many feared that this new technology, with its capacity to depict the world with unparalleled clarity, would render traditional painting obsolete. For some, photography seemed to signal the "death knell" of painting as an essential medium for documenting reality.

This fear was eloquently articulated by French poet and art critic Charles Baudelaire in his essay *The Salon of 1859*. He lamented photography's growing influence, writing, "As it must provide us with every desired detail, photography usurps the place of art in some respects. . . If photography is allowed to supplement art in some of its functions, it will soon supplant or corrupt it altogether." Baudelaire's critique reflected a broader unease about how mechanical reproduction might undermine artistic authenticity and creativity. Interestingly, this apprehension mirrors the concerns of today's twenty-first century artists regarding artificial intelligence (AI) and machine-aided art. Just as nineteenth-century painters questioned whether photography would make them irrelevant, contemporary artists grapple with whether AI technologies will overshadow human creativity or redefine it entirely.

As photography matured—introducing smaller cameras, faster shutter speeds, and advancements in film—it began influencing artists across disciplines. Painters, photographers, and sculptors alike engaged in a dialogue about representation, reality, and the role of technology in art. This interaction between photography and traditional mediums enriched the artistic landscape, fostering a culture of experimentation and interdisciplinary exchange that continues to shape creative practices today.

Art and Societal Shifts: Reflections of Change Through Creativity

The twentieth century marked a period of unparalleled artistic innovation, driven by societal changes, technological advancements, and shifting perspectives on creativity and expression. Artists broke away from classical themes and techniques, experimenting with form, color, and subject matter to reflect the complexities of the modern world. These shifts were not just stylistic but also philosophical, redefining the purpose and boundaries of art itself.

Wassily Kandinsky, one of the pioneers of abstract art, sought to create a "visual music" that used color, shape, and composition to arouse emotion rather than depict recognizable imagery. His works, like *Composition VII* (1913), reflected a desire to transcend traditional representation, paralleling innovations in technology that abstracted human experience, such as the rise of cinema and early experiments in non-representational sound and imagery. Kandinsky's approach also reflected a broader shift toward valuing art as a medium for personal and emotional expression, untethered from realistic depictions.

Pablo Picasso and Georges Braque revolutionized visual art with Cubism, fracturing objects into geometric planes to offer multiple perspectives simultaneously. This innovation mirrored technological advancements like photography and film, which challenged conventional ways of seeing. For example, Picasso's *Les Demoiselles d'Avignon* (1907) deconstructed traditional portraiture, introducing fragmented forms and angular perspectives that echoed the dynamism and disorientation of the industrial age. Cubism redefined art as an intellectual exploration of space, time, and form, aligning with contemporary innovations in science and technology, such as Einstein's theory of relativity, which also questioned fixed perspectives and linearity.

Collage, a technique originating with Cubism and later central to movements like Dada and Surrealism, disrupted aesthetic expression by blending painted elements with pre-existing materials. Georges Braque introduced collage in 1912 with *Still Life with Chair Caning*, incorporating oilcloth to challenge traditional divisions within fine art and invite questions about representation and reality. Pablo Picasso expanded on this innovation, using newspaper clippings, wallpaper, and sheet music to integrate fragments of daily life into art, reflecting the growing influence of mass communication and consumer culture. Technological advancements like the printing press and photography, along with the rise of advertising, further shaped collage by enabling the integration of text and image. Evolving from its Cubist roots, collage became a powerful metaphor for the fragmented modern world, reflecting the tensions between tradition and innovation, the handmade and industrial, and the personal and collective, establishing itself as a dynamic and enduring form of creative output.

Movements like Dadaism emerged as a response to the chaos of the First World War and the mechanization of society. Artists like Marcel Duchamp and Hannah Höch rejected traditional aesthetics in favor of absurdity and chaos. Duchamp's *Fountain* (1917), a ready-made urinal presented as art, exemplified the movement's challenge to conventional norms. These artists used mixed media and ready-made objects to challenge mainstream definitions of art. This shift paralleled innovations in technology that prioritized function over form, such as industrial design and the standardization of production processes.

Surrealism, led by the Spanish artist Salvador Dalí and Max Ernst, also emerged in the aftermath of global wars as a response to the devastation and disillusionment of the era. Drawing on Freudian psychoanalysis, the movement sought to unlock the unconscious mind through dreams, free association, and hidden desires, challenging conventional notions of reality. Dalí's *The Persistence of Memory* (1931), with its iconic melting clocks and barren landscape, symbolized the fluidity of time and the fragility of human existence, using dreamlike imagery to elicit sentient unease and critique the impermanence of human constructs. Employing his "paranoiac-critical activity," Dalí induced hallucinatory states to access irrational thoughts, juxtaposing incongruous elements to create surreal yet emotionally resonant works. Similarly, Max Ernst used techniques like frottage and decalcomania in pieces such as *The Elephant Celebes* (1921) to generate haunting, subconscious imagery that questioned the parameters between the natural and artificial. Artists like George Grosz produced scathing commentaries, as seen in *Eclipse of the Sun* (1926), which depicted the corruption of military and political leaders. Rejecting rationality, Surrealism critiqued the mechanized ideologies that had fueled industrialized warfare, offering an alternative vision that embraced chaos and instability. By embracing the subconscious and irrational, Surrealism redefined artistic expression, turning it into a provocative exploration of dreams, fears, and desires amidst a fractured and fragmented world.

The mechanization of production in the early twentieth century revolutionized art, inspiring movements that embraced industrial materials and processes. Constructivism, born out of post-revolutionary Russia, celebrated industrial design and the transformative potential of technology. Vladimir Tatlin's *Monument to the Third International* (1920), an ambitious design for a spiraling tower, symbolized the fusion of art, engineering, and social progress.

In the United States, the Ashcan School, led by artists like John Sloan and George Bellows, depicted the grit and dynamism of urban life. Their works, such as Bellows' *Cliff Dwellers* (1913), highlighted the human impact of industrialization, portraying bustling city streets and the struggles of the working class. Meanwhile, Charles White offered a powerful narrative of African American laborers, capturing their resilience and struggles within an industrialized society in works like *The Worker* (1944).

Social Realism emerged as a powerful voice for the marginalized. Jacob Lawrence's *Migration Series* (1940–1941) vividly chronicled the Great Migration, capturing the movement of African Americans from the South to urban centers in the North. Through bold colors and dynamic compositions, Lawrence documented systemic oppression, urban transformation, and the resilience of a community striving for a better future.

The struggle for civil rights in the mid-twentieth century brought photography to the forefront of societal change. Black-and-white images captured the immediacy of social movements, amplifying their impact. Rowland Scherman, the official photographer for the 1963 March on Washington, immortalized historical moments, including Martin Luther King Jr.'s "I Have a Dream" speech. His images, published in leading magazines like *Life* and *Look* and republished in the award-winning book *TIMELESS: The Photograph of Rowland Scherman*, conveyed the urgency and dignity of the Civil Rights Movement, galvanizing public support and influencing legislative milestones like the Civil Rights Act of 1964.

Robert Frank, a Swiss photographer, offered a brutally honest examination of everyday American life in his seminal book *The Americans* (1958). With a foreword by Jack Kerouac, *The Americans* combined Frank's stark, unvarnished photographs with Kerouac's poetic sensibilities, creating a portrait of a fragmented nation grappling with identity, inequality, and disillusionment. Frank's images, such as *Trolley—New Orleans* (1955), highlighted racial segregation, economic disparity, and the quiet resilience of ordinary Americans, challenging the myth of a unified "American Dream." This collaboration between the photographer and literary figure underscored the power of visual and written art to provoke societal introspection.

Photographers such as Gordon Parks and Dorothea Lange also used their lenses to shed light on inequality and struggle. Parks' *American Gothic, Washington, D.C.* (1942) juxtaposed a Black cleaning woman against the backdrop of an American flag, challenging perceptions of race and identity. Lange's iconic *Migrant Mother* (1936), capturing a destitute woman during the Great Depression, underscored the power of visual storytelling to inspire empathy and action.

Romare Bearden, through his visionary collages, blended cultural references from African American life, jazz, and popular culture to critique modern identity in a consumer-driven world. Bearden's *The Block* (1971) portrayed the vibrancy and challenges of urban Black communities, offering an introspective perspective on the intersection of culture and consumption for people of color.

Andy Warhol and the Pop Art movement challenged traditional distinctions between "high art" and mass culture, altering the landscape of contemporary art. Works like *Campbell's Soup Cans* (1962) celebrated consumer culture while critiquing its ubiquity and commodification. This movement emerged alongside the rise of mass media and advertising, technologies that reshaped public consciousness and aesthetics. Pop Art embraced the reproducibility of art, reflecting the influence of industrial production and techniques like screen printing, which allowed for mass replication. Warhol's fascination with fame, celebrity, and consumerism highlighted a shift in creativity's role—from crafting unique objects to interrogating the mass-produced images that defined modern life.

Pop artist Roy Lichtenstein subverted mainstream perspectives of originality and artistic technique by appropriating imagery from popular culture like the cartoon images of Mickey Mouse and Donald Duck and the use of Ben-Day dots to mimic the mechanical reproduction of comic books. Among his most famous works are *Whaam!* (1963), a dynamic depiction of an aerial combat scene juxtaposing explosive imagery with detached irony, and *Drowning Girl* (1963), which portrays a crying woman in emotional turmoil, critiquing melodrama through its exaggerated, graphic aesthetic.

Across the Atlantic, British Pop Art paralleled and influenced the movement's development, bringing its own cultural nuances. Richard Hamilton, often referred to as the father of British Pop Art, produced works like *Just What Is It That Makes Today's Homes So Different, So Appealing?* (1956). This collage, a playful yet incisive commentary on post-war consumerism, depicted a surreal domestic scene filled with products and cultural icons, blending humor with critique. Hamilton's exploration of advertising and materialism resonated deeply with the rising consumer culture in Britain.

Peter Blake, another key figure, created *On the Balcony* (1955–57) and *Sgt. Pepper's Lonely Hearts Club Band* album cover (1967) for The Beatles. Blake's works fused pop culture imagery, music, and fine art, encapsulating the spirit of the 1960s. His blending of iconic celebrities, vibrant colors, and layered symbolism reflected the convergence of art and entertainment, cementing Pop Art's relevance in mainstream culture.

These British artists, alongside Warhol and their American counterparts, revolutionized the existing cultural landscape by reflecting and reshaping the public's relationship with consumerism, celebrity, and media. The movement's reliance on emerging technologies, such as screen printing and photographic manipulation, mirrored the industrial and technological changes of the twentieth century. It critiqued the mass production and commodification of culture while also celebrating its visual language.

Redefining Creativity in a Changing World: Pop Art and the Debate on Meaning, Value, and Influence

Clement Greenberg, one of the most influential art critics of the twentieth century, offered a foundational approach for understanding the progression of art and its confrontation with mass culture in his seminal book *Art and Culture*. Greenberg famously distinguished between *high art*—defined by intellectual rigor and aesthetic refinement—and *kitsch*, which he viewed as formulaic, mass-produced works designed for popular consumption and immediate gratification without intellectual depth. For Greenberg, true art demanded active engagement and critical interpretation, encouraging viewers to confront complex ideas and emotions rather than seeking simple entertainment.

Greenberg was a staunch advocate of Abstract Expressionism, particularly the work of Jackson Pollock. He celebrated Pollock's drip paintings as the epitome of modernist purity, emphasizing the medium's flatness and the physical process of painting itself. To Greenberg, Pollock's canvases represented the autonomy of art—painting about painting, devoid of narrative or external references. Pollock's works, with their intricate layers of splattered paint, embodied Greenberg's ideal of an art form that transcended figuration and representation, forcing the viewer to confront the essence of the medium.

However, Greenberg's support for Abstract Expressionism did not extend unconditionally to all its practitioners. He was notably critical of Willem de Kooning's *Woman* series, which reintroduced figurative elements—distorted, primal depictions of women. Greenberg viewed these works as a regression, arguing that they undermined the formal purity of Abstract Expressionism by reintroducing subject matter that could be interpreted through a narrative lens. For Greenberg, de Kooning's depictions straddled the line between raw emotional intensity and a return to traditional figuration, which he believed compromised the modernist ideal of medium specificity.

This strict formalism led Greenberg to dismiss Pop Art entirely. The movement directly challenged his ideals by embracing mass-produced imagery, consumer culture, and celebrity iconography. Works such as Warhol's *Campbell's Soup Cans* and *Marilyn Diptych* straddled the boundaries between high art and commercial kitsch, forcing the art world to grapple with questions of originality, meaning, and cultural value. Unlike Abstract Expressionism's emphasis on the artist's internal world, Pop Art drew its power from external, collective symbols of mass culture, ironically presenting everyday objects as profound commentary on consumerism and the commodification of fame.

For Greenberg, Pop Art's embrace of mass imagery represented the antithesis of artistic autonomy. Rather than transcending popular culture, it mirrored and commodified it, undermining what he saw as art's duty to rise above societal trends and engage viewers in a purely aesthetic experience. Yet, Pop Art's critics argued that the movement revealed a deeper truth: in an age dominated by advertising and consumer goods, could art remain isolated from mass culture? Warhol's work questioned whether the very distinction between art and kitsch was still relevant in a world where images of consumer products and celebrities shaped everyday reality.

As German poet and philosopher Goethe famously said, "Whatever you can do, or dream you can, begin it. Boldness has genius, power, and magic in it." In this spirit, Pop Art boldly confronted the realities of its time, transforming the ordinary into the extraordinary and challenging classical hierarchies of artistic value. By daring to merge the lines between high art and consumer culture, it forced both critics and audiences to reconsider what art could mean in a rapidly modernizing world.

This debate over the role of the artist and the purpose of art continues to shape contemporary discussions on creativity and value. Greenberg's veneration of Abstract Expressionism and his disdain for Pop Art reveal the broader tension between artistic innovation and cultural commentary. As later chapters will explore, this same tension resurfaces in the digital age, as machine-generated art and AI-created works force us to reconsider whether true creativity lies in the mastery of form or in the ability to reflect and critique the world around us. Like Pollock's explosive drip paintings and Warhol's serial reproductions of consumer icons, today's creative technologies challenge us to redefine the boundaries of art, authorship, and meaning in a rapidly maturing cultural landscape.

While Greenberg criticized Pop Art for its perceived lack of depth and originality, other critics offered more expansive and generous interpretations:

- Camille Paglia, in *Glittering Images: A Journey Through Art from Egypt to Star Wars*, describes art as a mediator of cultural, spiritual, and technological forces. For Paglia, Pop Art's embrace of consumerism and mass production reflects its insightful engagement with the human condition in an era defined by commodification and celebrity. She views Warhol's works as cultural artifacts that reveal the anxieties and aspirations of a rapidly modernizing world, while simultaneously describing it as a "death knell" for the avant-garde due to its commercialization.
- Jerry Saltz, renowned essayist, praises Pop Art for breaking down barriers between high and low culture. He sees the movement as a democratizing force, redefining creativity by metamorphosing

everyday objects into subjects of aesthetic inquiry. According to Saltz, Pop Art forces viewers to confront the pervasive influence of media and consumerism, making it deeply relevant to contemporary life.

- Will Gompertz, in *What Are You Looking At?*, highlights Pop Art's pioneering use of technology and materials as a bridge between the radical departure of established forms, techniques, and ideas of art and the mainstream. He credits the movement with challenging traditional hierarchies and expanding the definition of art to include advertising, design, and celebrity culture.
- Lawrence Alloway, credited with coining the term "Pop Art," supported the movement as a legitimate artistic expression of consumerism and societal values. He argued against the dichotomy between high art and kitsch articulated by Greenberg, emphasizing that popular and fine art exist on a continuum. His essay *The Arts and the Mass Media* laid the basis for this perspective.

Pop Art's impact extends far beyond the visual arts. It reshaped advertising, graphic design, fashion, and film, influencing how society views consumer culture and media. It also paved the way for movements like conceptual art and postmodernism, which further obscured the borders among art, culture, and commerce.

The Evolution of Art: Conceptualism and Postmodernism

Conceptual Art: Ideas Over Objects

Conceptual art emerged in the 1960s as a radical redefinition of what art could be. Rejecting traditional notions of art as object-based and focused on aesthetic craftsmanship, conceptualism instead prioritized the intellectual and philosophical underpinnings of artistic creation. Heavily influenced by thinkers like Ludwig Wittgenstein and the field of semiotics, conceptual artists explored fundamental questions such as "What constitutes art?" and "How do we ascribe meaning to art?"

Ludwig Wittgenstein, a renowned twentieth-century philosopher, is best known for his work on the philosophy of language and meaning. His ideas, particularly those in *Philosophical Investigations*, emphasized that the meaning of words and concepts is shaped by their use within specific social and cultural "language games." Applied to art, Wittgenstein's views suggested that the meaning of an artwork depends on the context and the shared practices of those interpreting it. This perspective resonated with conceptual artists who sought to challenge traditional frameworks of interpretation and redefine the role of the viewer in constructing meaning.

Semiotics, the study of signs and symbols and how they create meaning, further influenced conceptual art by highlighting that art, like language, operates through systems of representation. Developed by scholars such as Ferdinand de Saussure and Charles Sanders Peirce, semiotics examines how meanings are constructed through the relationship between *signifiers* (the form of a sign, such as a word or image) and *signifieds* (the concept or meaning it represents). For conceptual artists, this meant that an artwork's significance could lie not in its physical form but in the ideas, associations, and cultural codes it evoked.

By drawing on Wittgenstein's philosophy and the principles of semiotics, conceptual artists questioned the conventional parameters of art. Works by artists such as Joseph Kosuth, whose piece *One and Three Chairs* presents a physical chair, a photograph of the chair, and a dictionary definition of "chair," exemplify this inquiry. Kosuth's work asks viewers to contemplate which representation—object, image, or text—best captures the essence of a "chair" and whether the concept of "chairness" exists independently of these representations.

Conceptual art's embrace of philosophical inquiry and symbolic representation marked a turning point in the art world. It shifted the focus from the creation of objects meant to be admired for their visual beauty to the production of ideas designed to provoke critical reflection. In doing so, conceptual art laid the underpinnings for later debates about authorship, meaning, and the nature of artistic expression—debates that continue today as digital technology and AI challenge long-standing assumptions about creativity and artistic intent.

Sol LeWitt, a leading figure in conceptualism, famously stated, "*When an artist uses a conceptual form of art, it means that all of the planning and decisions are made beforehand, and the execution is a perfunctory affair. The idea becomes a machine that makes the art.*" This approach confronted centuries of artistic tradition, where craftsmanship and aesthetic beauty were paramount. By detaching art from material execution, conceptualism democratized the creative process, suggesting that anyone capable of formulating an idea could be an artist. However, this notion sparked debates about accessibility and elitism, as some critics argued that conceptual art's abstract philosophical frameworks were too esoteric for general audiences.

Artists such as Lawrence Weiner exemplified this shift with works like *A thirty-six" x thirty-six" Removal to the Lathing or Support Wall of Plaster or Wallboard from a Wall* (1968), where language itself became the medium. Additionally, Black conceptual artist Glenn Ligon is renowned for using language to convey powerful ideas, particularly in works like *Untitled (I Am a Man)* (1988), which engages with historical civil rights imagery, and his text-based pieces that explore race, identity, and history. Both artists invited audiences to envision or enact the work, reinforcing the premise that the art resided in the concept rather than its physical form. These artists, in their embrace of non-traditional materials and ideas, support Andy Warhol's assertion that "Art is anything you can get away with," emphasizing that art can challenge conventional definitions and thrive through its audacity.

Conceptual artists also challenged established views of authorship. Yoko Ono's *Instruction Pieces* provided written prompts for viewers to complete, dissolving the distinctions between artist and audience while fostering participatory creativity.

Conceptualism engaged with pressing socio-political issues, using ideas rather than objects to critique the commodification of art in capitalist markets.

- Hans Haacke's institutional critique works exposed the intersections between art institutions, corporate sponsorships, and political power.
- Adrian Piper's performances addressed themes of race, gender, and identity through conceptual frameworks that invited self-reflection from both the artist and audience.

Critics like Lucy Lippard championed conceptualism for its intellectual rigor but also noted its potential elitism due to its reliance on abstract ideas that could alienate broader audiences. She described it as *"the dematerialization of the art object,"* emphasizing how it challenged orthodox definitions of art.

Postmodernism: Deconstructing and Reimagining

Postmodernism emerged later in the twentieth century as a reaction against modernism's utopian ideals and universal truths. Rather than seeking singular narratives or aesthetic purity, postmodernism embraced plurality, irony, fragmentation, and cultural critique. Jean-François Lyotard captured the essence of postmodernism in his assertion that it represents "incredulity toward metanarratives."

Postmodern artists deconstructed established categories, blending high and low culture, and embraced irony and self-reference. This movement critiqued cultural institutions, systemic inequality, and dominant ideologies.

- Jean-Michel Basquiat fused street art, neo-expressionism, and symbolic references to critique the commodification of Black culture and systemic racism. His painting *Boy and Dog in a Johnnypump* (1982) is a chaotic yet exacting exploration of urban life, power, and vulnerability.
- Sherrie Levine's *After Walker Evans* (1981) interrogated authorship and originality by rephotographing Walker Evans' iconic images and presenting them as her own, questioning the nature of ownership and visual history.

Banksy and Shepard Fairey have deeply influenced contemporary street art by embedding political and social commentary into public spaces while threading the tension between activism and commercialization. Banksy, the elusive British artist, uses stencils and graffiti to critique issues such as consumerism, war, and government surveillance. Iconic works like *There Is Always Hope* and *CND Soldiers* convey messages of peace and resilience, making art accessible to the public outside traditional gallery settings. However, despite his anti-establishment ethos, Banksy's art has also gained massive commercial value, with pieces like *Devolved Parliament* selling for millions. This paradox underscores the broader debate on the commodification of street art and the balance between artistic rebellion and market dynamics.

Similarly, Shepard Fairey has harnessed street art as a vehicle for political expression. His OBEY sticker campaign, featuring the face of wrestler Andre the Giant, began as a subversive critique of propaganda and conformity. Fairey gained global recognition with his *Hope* poster for Barack Obama's 2008 presidential campaign, which became a symbol of political optimism and is now housed in the Smithsonian National Portrait Gallery. However, Fairey's mainstream success sparked discussions about whether commercialization dilutes the rebellious spirit of street art, especially after his *Hope* poster drew legal controversy for allegedly infringing on the Associated Press's copyright-protected photograph of Obama.

Technological advancements in media—spanning television, photography, video editing, and digital manipulation—have become central to postmodern artistic exploration. These tools have not only expanded the possibilities for artistic expression but also altered the conventions between reality and representation, a hallmark of postmodernism. The rise of social media platforms and immersive technologies like virtual reality (VR) has further amplified these trends, reshaping how art is created, experienced, and consumed.

- Nam June Paik, the "father of video art," utilized television monitors and digital effects in works like *Electronic Superhighway* (1995) to critique mass media's cultural dominance.
- Barbara Kruger's works, such as *Untitled (Your Body is a Battleground)* (1989), appropriated advertising aesthetics to expose consumerism's influence on identity formation.
- Cindy Sherman's *Untitled Film Stills* (1977–1980) employed photography to deconstruct media stereotypes, casting herself in archetypal female roles from Hollywood films.

Postmodern art frequently addressed issues of identity, power structures, and cultural representation. It often sought to critique dominant narratives by amplifying marginalized voices and exploring the constructed nature of societal norms, such as gender roles, race, and class. Through appropriation, irony, and the incorporation of popular media, postmodern artists challenged traditional hierarchies and redefined authenticity and originality, often sidestepping critical legal and moral issues surrounding attribution and copyright infringement.

Feminist artists like Judy Chicago (*The Dinner Party*, 1979) reclaimed marginalized histories through multimedia installations. While artists from minority backgrounds used postmodern frameworks to critique systemic oppression. Kara Walker's silhouetted installations, such as *Slavery! Slavery!* (1997), overlaid historical Civil War imagery with Black figures in stark contrast to the romanticized originals, forcing viewers to confront the brutality and legacy of slavery.

Similarly, Black feminist photographers such as Lorna Simpson and Carrie Mae Weems utilized historical references and photographic series to deconstruct representations of Black womanhood and interrogate societal narratives. Weems, a leading figure in art and photography, profoundly influenced the field by recontextualizing archival images to critique historical narratives and societal injustices. Her iconic series *From Here I Saw What Happened and I Cried* (1995–1996) exemplifies this approach, using nineteenth-century daguerreotypes commissioned by Harvard scientist Louis Agassiz, who sought to prove racial inferiority. Originally intended to dehumanize African-born Black slaves, these photographs were reimagined by Weems through a red tint symbolizing blood, violence, and suffering, overlaid with text such as "You became a scientific profile" and "You became a lesson." This overlay critiques the objectification and commodification of Black bodies while reclaiming the humanity of the subjects, exposing the brutality of the original context and imbuing the images with new layers of meaning, utilized historical references and photographic series to deconstruct representations of Black womanhood and interrogate societal narratives.

Fredric Jameson, a prominent Marxist literary critic and cultural theorist, described postmodernism as being characterized by pastiche—imitative works devoid of original intent—and cultural fragmentation. Best known for his influential works such as *Postmodernism, or, The Cultural Logic of Late Capitalism* (1991) and *The Political Unconscious* (1981), Jameson criticized how culture becomes commodified under late capitalism. He emphasized the need to analyze cultural images within their historical context to reveal the underlying ideologies shaping them.

In contrast to Fredric Jameson's Marxist criticism of postmodern art, Charles Harrison, a renowned industrial designer and the first Black executive at Sears, Roebuck & Company, argued that postmodernism's qualities of fragmentation and inclusivity enabled art and design to transcend elitist boundaries, making them more accessible to the general public.

Ascribing Meaning: The Viewer as Co-Creator

Both conceptualism and postmodernism shifted interpretive authority from the artist to the audience. Conceptualism asked, "What is art if not an idea?" while postmodernism questioned, "Whose story is being told?" The legacy of these movements endures in contemporary art, especially in the digital age. Social media, augmented reality (AR), and artificial intelligence (AI) have expanded the avenues for participatory and interactive art, as revealed in later chapters.

Together, conceptualism and postmodernism redefined the art world, prompting new dialogues about identity, authorship, and creativity. Their impact persists, reminding us that art is as much about interrogating the systems that define it as it is about visual expression.

Art as a Reflection of Technological Progress

Creativity is the act of bringing something new into existence—whether it's an idea, a work of art, or a solution to a problem. Throughout history, creativity has been shaped and redefined by technological innovations, cultural movements, and societal pressures, all of which contribute to inconsistent definitions of art and its value. The poet and curator Frank O'Hara illustrates how art serves as a mediator of cultural, spiritual, and technological forces, reflecting humanity's collective aspirations and anxieties. In *In Memory of My Feelings: Frank O'Hara and American Art,* O'Hara emphasized that art's role is to capture the fleeting, the intimate, and the interconnected moments of life, making it a medium through which artists interpret their environments and relationships. From the invention of oil paint, which allowed Renaissance artists to achieve unprecedented realism, to the printing press, which democratized access to visual and literary works, each innovation has modified the ways in which art is created, shared, and experienced.

The Industrial Revolution marked a pivotal shift with the introduction of mass production techniques, which made art more accessible but also raised concerns about genuineness and value. Lithography allowed artists like Honoré Daumier to mass-produce politically charged caricatures, turning art into a medium for activism. Francisco Goya's *Los Caprichos* series used etching to expose societal injustices, distributing powerful imagery to a broader audience. Similarly, the development of photography in the nineteenth century challenged conventional perspectives of representation and prompted artists to question whether capturing reality required a painter's brush or a camera lens.

By the time Pop Art emerged in the mid-twentieth century, artists such as Richard Blake and Roy Lichtenstein embraced mechanical reproduction as a statement on modern life, reshaping advertisements, comic strips, and mass-produced goods into cultural icons. Pop Art embraced mass production and celebrity culture while critiquing consumerism, epitomized by Andy Warhol's *Marilyn Diptych* (1962). Numerous cultural observers celebrate Warhol's "proletarian philosophy" of art through impersonal mass production, embodied by his Factory studio, yet critique the commercialization that contributed to the avant-garde's decline. This duality highlights broader questions about who defines art—whether it be artists, critics, cultural institutions, the public, or the market—and how these societal forces influence its meaning and purpose.

Modern technologies have further expanded those nascent moments of creativity. Giclée printing, for instance, enables the production of high-resolution, color-rich reproductions of original works using archival-quality inks and papers. Artists like Chuck Close have used this technique to extend the reach of their work without sacrificing the intricate detail for which they are known. This process preserves the integrity of the original while making fine art more accessible to broader audiences. However, as with previous innovations, giclée printing raises questions about the value of reproductions versus originals and the extent to which technological processes influence perceptions of authenticity and authorship. Conceptual and postmodern art movements have further challenged these notions by shifting the focus from the physical artwork itself to the ideas it represents. Marcel Duchamp's *Fountain* (1917), a mass-produced urinal recontextualized as art, redefined the role of the artist as someone who designates meaning rather than solely creating a unique object of beauty and aesthetics. This redefinition of art opened the door for movements that valued concept over craft, a shift that continues to resonate in contemporary digital and AI-generated art.

The question of who dictates or influences the acceptance of creative movements remains complex. Artists, through their continuous refinements, push the traditional boundaries of what is considered art, but critics, cultural institutions, and the public all play significant roles in shaping artistic legitimacy. Influential critics such as Clement Greenberg championed movements like Abstract Expressionism by framing them within intellectual and aesthetic frameworks, while museums and galleries validated works by curating and preserving them. Public reception can also drive the cultural impact of artistic movements, as seen in the popularity of Shepard Fairey's *Hope* poster during Barack Obama's 2008 presidential campaign, which gained cultural significance through widespread public engagement. The art market further influences what is recognized as valuable art, as the sale of Warhol's *Devolved Parliament* for millions demonstrates. In addition, digital platforms and blockchain technologies, such as NFTs, are reshaping perceptions of ownership and value by creating new marketplaces for digital art, raising concerns about speculation and the commodification of creativity.

Art has long served as a platform for addressing issues of social justice and inequality. Jacob Lawrence's works and ideas capture the struggles and triumphs of the African American experience through bold, narrative-driven paintings such as *The Migration Series*, which vividly portrays the mass movement of Black families from the rural South to the urban North. Similarly, Kara Walker's provocative silhouettes confront the legacy of slavery and systemic racism in works like *A Subtlety*, a monumental, sugar-coated sculpture that critiques historical exploitation. These artists exemplify how art can challenge societal norms and provoke dialogue about pressing cultural issues, while reminding us that art is not always what you see, but what you make others see.

A Continuum of Creation

As we stand at the threshold of the digital age, tools like Photoshop, 3D modeling, and AI-driven programs offer unprecedented opportunities for creativity while raising complex questions about reality, beauty, truth, and authorship. The rise of manipulated digital imagery has blurred the line between creation and deception, sparking ethical and legal debates on how these images are used in contexts ranging from art to propaganda. These advancements compel us to reconsider the definition of art: Is it shaped by the creator's intent, the medium, or the audience's perception? Does an artwork's value lie in its uniqueness, its message, or its cultural resonance?

In the next chapter, we will examine how digital tools are transforming artistic expression and ownership. Who holds creative rights when algorithms or collaborative platforms contribute to a work? How can creators' rights be safeguarded while fostering innovation in a world where replication and reinterpretation are easier than ever? These questions go beyond legal and technical challenges—they probe into the essence of creation and humanity itself. As artists and technologists push the boundaries of imagination, they prompt us to rethink what art is, how it is made, and how it represents our collective identity. In this dynamic era, art becomes more than a product; it is a dialogue between tradition and innovation, humanity and technology, raising far-reaching questions about our values, culture, and aspirations in an interconnected social media driven world.

Works Referenced:

Alloway, Lawrence. "The Arts and the Mass Media." *Architectural Design*, vol. 28, no. 2, 1958, pp. 34–5.

Baudelaire, Charles. *The Salon of 1859.* Translated by Jonathan Mayne, Phaidon Press, 1965.

Blake, William. *In Memory of My Feelings: Frank O'Hara and American Art.* Edited by Russell Ferguson, University of California Press, 1999.

Duchamp, Marcel. *Fountain*. 1917. Porcelain urinal (readymade), signed "R. Mutt 1917". Submitted to Society of Independent Artists, New York, April 1917.

Frank, Robert. *The Americans.* Introduction by Jack Kerouac, Grove Press, 1958.

Gompertz, Will. *What Are You Looking At?: 150 Years of Modern Art in the Blink of an Eye.* Penguin Books, 2012.

Greenberg, Clement. *Art and Culture: Critical Essays.* Beacon Press, 1961.

Hamilton, Richard. *Just What Is It That Makes Today's Homes So Different, So Appealing?* 1956. Collage. Originally created for "This Is Tomorrow" exhibition, Whitechapel Art Gallery, London. Collection of Kunsthalle Tübingen, Germany.

Jameson, Fredric. *Postmodernism, or, The Cultural Logic of Late Capitalism.* Duke University Press, 1991.

Jones, Michael, and Jones, Christine, editor. *TIMELESS: The Photography of Rowland Scherman, Peter E.* Randall Publisher, 2014.

Kosuth, Joseph. *One and Three Chairs.* 1965.

Lawrence, Jacob. *The Migration Series.* 1940–1941.

LeWitt, Sol. "Paragraphs on Conceptual Art." *Artforum,* vol. 5, no. 10, 1967, pp. 79–83.

Lippard, Lucy R. *Six Years: The Dematerialization of the Art Object from 1966 to 1972.* University of California Press, 1973.

Lyotard, Jean-François. *The Postmodern Condition: A Report on Knowledge.* University of Minnesota Press, 1984.

Morrison, Toni. "Memory, Creation, and Writing." *Thought: Fordham University Quarterly,* vol. 59, no. 4, 1984, pp. 385–90.

O'Hara, Frank. *In Memory of My Feelings: Frank O'Hara and American Art.* Museum of Modern Art, 1999.

Paglia, Camille. *Glittering Images: A Journey Through Art from Egypt to Star Wars.* Pantheon Books, 2012.

Saltz, Jerry. "Art at Arm's Length: A History of the Selfie." *New York Magazine (Vulture),* January 26, 2014.

Saltz, Jerry. *Seeing Out Loud: The Voice Art Columns Fall 1998 - Winter 2003.* The Figures, 2003.

Tatlin, Vladimir. *Monument to the Third International (Tatlin's Tower).* 1920. Wooden model exhibited at Petrograd SVOMAS, November–December 1920. Project for headquarters of the Third International (Comintern), St. Petersburg. Known via surviving models and photographs.

Van Eyck, Jan. *The Arnolfini Portrait.* National Gallery, London.

Vitruvius Pollio. *De Architectura [The Ten Books on Architecture].* Translated by Morris Hicky Morgan, Harvard University Press, 1914.

Walker, Kara. *Slavery! Slavery! Presenting a GRAND and LIFELIKE Panoramic Journey into Picturesque Southern Slavery or "Life at 'Ol' Virginny's Hole" (sketches from Plantation Life).* New Museum Contemporary Art, New York, 3 July–19 Oct. 2008.

Warhol, Andy. *Campbell's Soup Cans.* 1962. Synthetic polymer paint on canvas, 32 panels, each 20 x 16 in. Museum of Modern Art, New York.

Weems, Carrie Mae. *From Here I Saw What Happened and I Cried.* Museum of Modern Art (MoMA), 1995–1996.

Wittgenstein, Ludwig. *Philosophical Investigations.* Translated by G.E.M. Anscombe, Basil Blackwell, 1953.

Two Redefining Art in the Digital Age

Art has always advanced alongside technological and philosophical shifts, reflecting changes in how societies define beauty, creativity, and meaning. Following the earlier exploration of art's historical and technological milestones, the intellectual and philosophical origins of aesthetics provide a framework for understanding the nature of beauty and artistic experience. Alexander Baumgarten, an eighteenth-century philosopher, first coined the term "aesthetics" to describe the study of sensory perception and beauty. For Baumgarten, aesthetics was not merely a reflection of taste but a distinct field of inquiry that aimed to capture the complexity of how humans experience art through their senses and emotions. This formalized aesthetics as a discipline focused on the subjective, often emotional dimensions of artistic perception.

Building on these ideas, Immanuel Kant, who ranks among history's most influential philosophers, expanded the theory of aesthetics by proposing a philosophy of the beautiful that continues to shape discussions on art and creativity. Kant argued that true art arises from a dynamic interplay between intellect and imagination, guided by what he referred to as "genius." According to Kant, genius is a rare and innate quality that allows an artist to create works that are both original and exemplary—effortlessly embodying beauty. While technical skill is essential, it is the creative spark that elevates mere craftsmanship into something extraordinary. This positioned the artist as a visionary figure whose work transcends established rules and conventions.

The concept of genius has long shaped how artists and their work are perceived, reinforcing the narrative of the artist as an exceptional individual destined for greatness. Pablo Picasso's anecdotal reflection on his upbringing without any known source illustrates this cultural reverence for innate talent: *"When I was a child, my mother said to me, 'If you become a soldier, you will be a general. If you become a monk, you will end up as the pope.' Instead, I became a painter, and I became Picasso."* This statement not only celebrates personal ambition and creative brilliance but also reflects a broader societal tendency to elevate certain creators as icons of genius.

The late twentieth and early twenty-first centuries ushered in the digital revolution, a seismic shift that markedly reshaped the creative landscape, continuing the legacy of earlier artistic movements. This shift suggests that the concept of genius may now be located not only in human intuition and craftsmanship but also in the emerging technology of digital instruments and creative tools. Digital tools such as Adobe Photoshop, Illustrator, and AutoCAD provided artists with unprecedented precision, flexibility, and opportunities for experimentation. These tools blurred the lines between traditional and digital mediums, offering new ways to manipulate colors, textures, and compositions. Digital art, defined as artwork created or modified using digital technology, spans various forms, including graphic design, digital painting, 3D modeling, and animation. Artists can now produce intricate designs, experiment with virtual textures, and create immersive experiences that transcend the physical limitations of traditional media.

With digital platforms, artists are no longer confined to physical materials; instead, they can explore infinite possibilities within virtual spaces. Trailblazers like David Hockney exemplify how technology can redefine artistic practices while retaining emotional depth and personal expression. Initially celebrated for his traditional works in the 1960s, Hockney began experimenting with iPhones in 2009 and later adopted the iPad as his primary canvas in 2010. This shift marked a pivotal moment in his career and the broader art world.

Hockney's transition from traditional media to digital tools illustrates the changing nature of artistic expression in the digital age. Known for early works like *A Bigger Splash* (1967), which captured California's sunlit swimming pools with acrylic paints, Hockney embraced the Brushes app on the iPhone to sketch everyday scenes—flowers on a windowsill, landscapes from his travels—using only his thumbs. When the iPad became available, its larger screen and stylus compatibility allowed for greater detail and precision. His *Yosemite Suite* depicted scenes from Yosemite National Park with vibrant colors and bold strokes, mirroring the freshness of plein air painting while being executed entirely on a digital device. By blending colors seamlessly and mimicking brushstrokes, Hockney demonstrated that digital art could retain the tactile qualities of traditional painting while expanding creative possibilities.

The digital revolution has democratized creative tools and enabled unprecedented forms of artistic expression while simultaneously raising questions about originality, reality, emotional content, and artistic intent. Early skepticism about digital works—especially those created using tools like the iPad—questioned whether they held the same artistic value as those made with traditional media. However, exhibitions such as *David Hockney: A Bigger Picture* at London's Royal Academy of Arts helped legitimize his digital creations by showcasing their depth and innovation alongside his traditional works. Advancements in printing technology further allowed Hockney to translate his digital sketches into large-scale physical prints without losing resolution or detail.

The philosophical roots laid by early thinkers continue to inform debates about what constitutes art and who has the authority to define it. Digital technologies have erased the distinctions between craftsmanship and innovation, as artists now operate in a social media environment where algorithms, mass reproduction, and audience metrics influence both creative trends and the reception of art. In this new landscape, the idea of genius—once associated with solitary visionaries—must be reconsidered in an age shaped by collaborative digital platforms and multimedia experimentation. Clarity around what defines art and creative authorship must account for both individual expression and the technological tools that shape creative ecosystems.

The values ascribed to art in this digital age are not immutable truths but reflections of cultural shifts and technological advancements. Revisiting foundational concepts such as genius and beauty offers an opportunity to question inherited hierarchies and to reframe art as an evolving discourse rather than a fixed tradition. In this context, statements like Picasso's remind us that while individual brilliance can inspire, the meaning of creativity itself is shaped by collective experiences, technological innovations, and ongoing cultural narratives.

Photoshop: Altering Reality in the Digital Age

In recent decades, digital tools like Adobe Photoshop have revolutionized artistic creation, offering unparalleled precision and flexibility in image manipulation. With its ability to layer and edit non-destructively, Photoshop provides a limitless digital canvas for experimentation, freeing creators from the constraints of physical materials or irreversible processes. Tools such as the clone stamp, liquify filters, and AI-driven neural filters allow artists to enhance colors, adjust lighting, and merge disparate elements, crafting everything from hyperrealistic portraits to surreal dreamscapes that defy traditional artistic boundaries. This versatility has made Photoshop a transformative medium for visual storytelling.

Photoshop's capacity to alter reality has expanded artistic possibilities and fundamentally altered how imagery is perceived in everyday life. Artists can heighten emotional impact, turning ordinary photographs into striking visual statements or constructing intricate compositions that challenge viewers' understanding of truth and fiction. For instance, digital artist Erik Johansson seamlessly merges multiple photographs to create fantastical scenes, such as staircases leading into clouds or cities unraveling into fabric. These works blur the line between photography and painting, showcasing Photoshop's potential to push creative boundaries and redefine artistic expression.

However, this power to manipulate reality raises consequential ethical questions about authenticity and trust. In the realm of photography, heavily edited images can misrepresent events or perpetuate unrealistic beauty standards, sparking debates about transparency and truthfulness. Similarly, in fine art, the ease of creating digital works sometimes provokes skepticism about craftsmanship and originality. Critics question whether Photoshop-produced art loses some of the tactile and emotional depth associated with traditional mediums.

Using Photoshop responsibly involves understanding the ethical implications of image manipulation, particularly in contexts where altered visuals could mislead, deceive, or manipulate public perception. Cultural critics like Susan Sontag have argued that photography—and by extension, manipulated imagery—bears a responsibility to truth, emphasizing that images shape how reality is understood. Media scholar Fred Ritchin, in *After Photography*, warns that the ability to alter photographs undetectably undermines their reliability, stating, "The photograph can no longer serve as an evidentiary document if it can so easily be altered without leaving a mark." These concerns highlight the risks of using Photoshop to fabricate events or distort reality for political, cultural, or social purposes.

The consequences of manipulated imagery are evident in cases where altered photos have been used in propaganda or misinformation campaigns. During protests or conflicts, doctored images have circulated online, amplifying tensions without clear indicators of their inauthenticity. This has led to calls for watermarking or labeling altered images, particularly in journalism and documentary contexts, to ensure transparency and preserve public trust.

In the art world, responsible use of Photoshop also means maintaining conceptual integrity. Manipulation should deepen a work's message rather than mask a lack of creativity or authenticity. Media critic John Berger's insights in *Ways of Seeing* remain relevant: art should provoke thought and enhance meaning, not obscure reality. The power of altered imagery lies in its ability to elevate the narrative and conceptual elements of a piece, ensuring that the manipulation serves a purpose beyond aesthetic appeal.

By balancing technical skill with ethical consideration and conceptual depth, artists can harness Photoshop to craft works that captivate and provoke while contributing to a constructive cultural dialogue. This requires not only a mastery of the tool but also an acute awareness of the societal impact of their creations, ensuring that their work enhances understanding rather than perpetuating harm or misinformation. In this way, Photoshop continues to redefine the possibilities of art in the digital age while demanding thoughtful engagement with its transformative capabilities.

Procreate and the New Canvas: Redefining Digital Artistry

Another widely used digital tool that has boldly impacted artistic creativity, societal acceptance, and cultural narratives is Procreate—a powerful digital illustration app embraced by both amateurs and professional artists. Like Photoshop, Procreate offers artists the ability to create intricate digital paintings, manipulate textures, and simulate traditional art techniques such as watercolor, oil painting, and pencil sketching. This tool has transformed not only how artists create but also how they share their work, often blurring the boundaries between physical and digital media.

Leading digital art experts highlight Procreate's role in redefining creative experiences. Illustrator and designer Lisa Congdon has noted, "Procreate's intuitive design makes it possible for artists to draw anywhere and experiment without limits, allowing creativity to flow more freely." Similarly, art critic Christopher Knight has observed that tools like Procreate challenge traditional notions of permanence, stating, "Digital art apps shift the focus from fixed, final works to evolving, fluid pieces that can be iterated upon endlessly. This reimagines not only the creative process but also what society accepts as complete or authentic art."

Moreover, Procreate's widespread availability on tablets and iPads has democratized digital art in significant ways. Emerging artists who once faced barriers to entry due to the high cost of traditional materials or specialized training now have access to professional-level tools that enable them to produce high-quality, exhibition-ready work. This accessibility, however, raises important questions about artistic authorship and authenticity. Some critics argue that preloaded brushes and templates may reduce the perceived individuality of digital creations, while others contend that such tools expand the potential for personalized innovation.

Procreate, much like Photoshop, forces a reconsideration of traditional aesthetic categories. Non-Fungible Tokens (NFTs), which are unique digital assets verified using blockchain technology, have further complicated this redefinition. NFTs allow artists to assign ownership to digital works, making it possible to buy, sell, and trade art that exists solely in digital form. Proponents argue that NFTs empower artists by creating new revenue streams and protecting digital ownership, while critics question the speculative nature of the NFT market and its environmental impact due to the energy-intensive blockchain processes.

As digital paintings created on Procreate are displayed in major exhibitions or sold as NFTs, debates arise regarding whether these works fit within classical definitions of fine art. This tension mirrors broader societal shifts where technology-mediated creativity continues to challenge long-standing hierarchies. Ultimately, Procreate and the integration of NFTs exemplify how digital tools not only reshape the act of creation but also prompt society to rethink what it means for art to be original, personal, and enduring.

3-D Printing: Precision Meets Innovation

Digital technology has profoundly transformed the art of sculpture, taking a form of expression that has long been defined by tactile materials like mud, clay, wood, and metal into an era where digital processes and 3D printing have redefined creative boundaries. Traditionally, sculpture was an art form rooted in direct human contact, where every chisel mark or molded surface bore the trace of the artist's hand. Ancient civilizations crafted sculptures from materials like stone and bronze to commemorate gods, leaders, and mythic stories, while later movements explored abstract forms in mediums such as marble, plaster, and cast metals. The tactile manipulation of these materials gave sculpture its revered status as both labor-intensive and expressive of human emotion and creativity.

The advent of digital tools, particularly 3D modeling software and 3D printing, has expanded the possibilities of sculpture beyond traditional materials and methods. This technological evolution has introduced a new paradigm for sculptors, enabling them to conceptualize and execute works with unprecedented precision and complexity. Programs such as Blender, Rhino, ZBrush, and Autodesk Maya allow artists to design intricate digital forms down to the finest detail. These virtual designs can then be brought into physical reality through 3D printing technologies or remain as purely digital creations in virtual or augmented reality spaces. This shift has led to what some call the "post-tactile" era of sculpture, where creation begins not with physical interaction but with a digital blueprint. Artists like Antony Gormley have embraced digital frameworks to explore themes such as the relationship between the human body and space. Gormley's works often integrate complex geometric structures that would be difficult to achieve without computational tools. Similarly, Anish Kapoor has collaborated with engineers to produce monumental installations that push the boundaries of scale and form—achievements that would be nearly impossible using traditional sculptural techniques.

One of the most transformative aspects of this digital revolution is 3D printing. This technology has introduced remarkable precision and opened new material possibilities for sculpture. Robotic arms and multi-material printers enable artists to fabricate sculptures using a variety of substances, including metals, resins, polymers, ceramics, and even biological materials like living cells. This innovation allows for the creation of forms that were previously inconceivable due to limitations in traditional carving or casting techniques. For example, artist Joshua Harker uses 3D printing to create intricate lace-like sculptures with astonishing detail—designs that would be nearly impossible to carve by hand. His work exemplifies how digital tools can redefine the boundaries of what is achievable in sculpture while raising philosophical questions about authorship: does artistic genius reside in the conceptual design or in the physical object itself? Similarly, Neri Oxman's work at the intersection of art, design, and science explores biomimicry through 3D-printed sculptures made from organic materials like glass or silk.

Despite these advancements, many argue that the human hand remains an essential part of the sculptural process. As artist and critic David Pye observed, "The handmade is the antidote to the anonymous." Even when a sculpture is fabricated by a robot or printer, it is ultimately guided by human vision, intent, and creativity. Olafur Eliasson's studio exemplifies this philosophy; while employing cutting-edge technology to create immersive installations and sculptures, Eliasson emphasizes that machines are tools serving creativity rather than replacing it. He asserts: "Machines don't make art—people do." This perspective underscores an important truth: while technology can extend an artist's capabilities, it cannot replace their role as a creator. The essence of sculpture lies not only in its physical form but also in its capacity to convey ideas, emotions, and meaning—qualities that remain inherently human.

Digital technology has also expanded the definition of sculpture itself from static objects fixed in physical space to dynamic experiences that can be interactive, immersive, or even ephemeral. VR allows artists to create sculptures that audiences can "walk through," experiencing them as fully immersive environments. AR overlays virtual sculptures onto real-world settings, blending physical and digital spaces in ways that challenge traditional notions of materiality. For instance, contemporary artists are increasingly exploring virtual installations where viewers engage with sculptures through VR headsets or mobile devices. Such works blur the line between tangible art objects and experiential media. This evolution raises profound questions about permanence: Can a virtual sculpture hold as much significance as one carved from stone? What does it mean for a work to exist only temporarily in an augmented reality setting?

While digital tools have democratized access to advanced sculptural techniques—allowing more artists to experiment with complex forms—they also present challenges. The reliance on technology introduces concerns about accessibility (due to cost), sustainability (given energy-intensive processes), and authenticity (as machine fabrication becomes indistinguishable from handmade works). Furthermore, as algorithms increasingly play a role in design processes through generative art or AI-driven tools, questions arise about authorship: How much credit belongs to the artist versus the software? At the same time, these technologies offer unparalleled opportunities for innovation. Artists can now collaborate across disciplines—working with engineers, architects, scientists, and technologists—to create works that transcend traditional artistic boundaries. These collaborations have led to groundbreaking projects such as bio-art sculptures grown from living organisms or kinetic installations powered by artificial intelligence.

The Role of NFTs, Blockchain, and Cryptocurrency in the Digital Art Revolution

In addition to Procreate and Photoshop, NFTs and blockchain technology have emerged as pivotal elements in the evolving digital art landscape. NFTs are unique digital assets stored on blockchain networks that verify ownership and authenticity. Unlike traditional cryptocurrencies such as Bitcoin, which are interchangeable, NFTs are distinct, one of a kind items representing digital art, music, videos, and even collectibles. This innovation has allowed artists to secure and sell their work in ways previously impossible in digital formats.

Blockchain technology ensures that each NFT has an immutable record of provenance, providing transparency and security for digital creators and collectors. This framework has introduced new avenues for monetization, as artists can embed smart contracts within their NFTs to receive royalties each time their work is resold. Digital art markets such as OpenSea, Rarible, and Foundation have grown exponentially, enabling creators to showcase and sell their works globally. However, as noted by art critic Jason Farago, "NFTs have introduced a paradoxical permanence to digital art—a field once defined by its ephemeral nature—by attaching it to the blockchain."

Cultural institutions have approached NFTs with caution, yet some museums and galleries have begun experimenting with digital exhibitions. The Uffizi Gallery located in Florence, Italy, for example, tokenized a digital reproduction of Michelangelo's *Doni Tondo*, demonstrating how traditional institutions are beginning to embrace blockchain technology. However, the question of how to display digital art remains a challenge. Unlike physical paintings or photographs, NFTs often exist within digital wallets, online platforms, or virtual galleries. Curators have employed digital screens, VR experiences, and interactive installations to bridge the gap between virtual ownership and tangible display.

Proponents, including prominent artists like Beeple, who sold his digital collage *Everydays: The First 5000 Days* for $69 million at Christie's auction house, argue that NFTs validate digital art as a legitimate and valuable form of cultural expression. Celebrities, musicians, and athletes, including Grimes, LeBron James, and Snoop Dogg, have also embraced NFTs to create and distribute digital collectibles, further legitimizing the medium. In particular, Grimes—a Canadian musician, visual artist, and producer known for her experimental music—sold her *WarNymph* collection of digital art as NFTs, earning approximately $6 million. The collection featured futuristic, otherworldly imagery that reflected her exploration of digital aesthetics and identity. Grimes praised NFTs for giving artists more control and opportunities, stating, "I see this as a way to empower creators in a system that often devalues digital work." These high-profile sales have brought mainstream attention to digital art and increased its cultural and financial value.

On the other hand, critics raise ethical concerns regarding the environmental impact of blockchain technology. The energy-intensive process of validating transactions through proof-of-work protocols has contributed to concerns about the carbon footprint of NFT transactions. Art historian Claire Bishop warns, "The allure of blockchain permanence cannot come at the cost of ecological devastation, which remains a stark concern." Additionally, the speculative nature of the NFT market has led to concerns about volatility and exploitation, with some viewing it as a financial bubble rather than a sustainable platform for artistic innovation.

Despite these criticisms, many artists continue to explore the potential of NFTs as a means of self-sufficiency and creative autonomy. By bypassing traditional galleries and auction houses, artists gain more direct control over their work and revenue. However, this also introduces challenges related to oversaturation in digital marketplaces and the risk of art becoming commodified as investment assets rather than celebrated for its intrinsic cultural and aesthetic value.

The integration of NFTs, blockchain, and cryptocurrency into the art world exemplifies the complex relationship between technology and creativity. As the digital art market expands, the dialogue surrounding the role of these technologies will continue to shape the future of artistic expression, challenging both artists and audiences to redefine what it means to create and experience art in the digital age.

Digital Media's Role in Video Games and Film as Artistic Expression

Video games and film represent some of the most dynamic intersections of digital media and artistic expression, utilizing cutting-edge technology to create immersive, narrative-rich experiences. Video games have evolved into complex storytelling platforms that combine visual art, sound design, and interactivity. Games such as *The Last of Us* and *Journey* are often cited as examples of games that transcend entertainment, becoming amazing artistic ventures that engage players emotionally and aesthetically. Game designers, like Hideo Kojima, view their work as a form of digital cinema, where every scene, sound, and interaction contributes to an overarching artistic vision. Kojima, often hailed as a visionary, once remarked, "Art is storytelling, and video games are an interactive way to experience that story in a way other mediums cannot replicate."

Similarly, filmmakers have leveraged digital technologies to push the boundaries of cinematic art. From CGI (computer-generated imagery) to virtual production techniques like those used in *The Mandalorian*, digital tools have become integral to creating believable yet fantastical worlds. The introduction of tools like Unreal Engine, originally designed for video game development, has extinguished the line between cinema and gaming. Virtual sets allow directors to control entire environments digitally, creating scenes that would be impossible or prohibitively expensive to achieve practically.

The economic benefits of collaboration between producers, writers, and digital media professionals have been substantial, fostering a new era of independent content creation. Indie developers and filmmakers can now use affordable tools like Unity, Blender, and crowdfunding platforms to launch projects with minimal overhead costs. For example, the critically acclaimed game *Hollow Knight* was developed by a small team using open-source software and became a commercial and artistic success, demonstrating the potential for start-up creative teams to achieve global recognition. In film, creators can use digital tools to design entire sets, produce visual effects, and edit with unprecedented flexibility, enabling small production teams to compete with major studios.

Moreover, digital platforms such as Steam, YouTube, and Vimeo provide accessible spaces for independent creators to distribute their work, allowing niche films and games to find devoted audiences. By bypassing traditional gatekeepers, creators have more opportunities for creative freedom and direct profit. However, this democratization of the industry also raises concerns about market saturation and the sustainability of creative livelihoods in an environment where visibility often depends on algorithmic promotion.

Organizations like the Screen Actors Guild-American Federation of Television and Radio Artists (SAG-AFTRA) have expressed concerns over the use of AI and motion capture technology in video games and film, particularly regarding performers' rights and compensation. SAG-AFTRA President Fran Drescher has stated, "We must ensure that digital likenesses and AI-generated performances do not replace the heart and soul that human artists bring to their craft. Technology should enhance, not exploit, our contributions." These concerns highlight the delicate balance between technological advancement and ethical labor practices.

Video games have also become a crucial platform for interactive art installations and cultural exhibitions. Museums such as the Smithsonian American Art Museum have recognized video games as legitimate artistic works, curating exhibitions like *The Art of Video Games* to showcase the medium's evolution and cultural significance. Additionally, indie developers have used platforms like itch.io to distribute narrative-driven games that challenge traditional notions of gameplay and function as immersive digital artworks.

Despite their growing acceptance, debates about whether video games and CGI-heavy films fit within traditional definitions of art persist. Critics argue that technological spectacle can sometimes overshadow narrative and emotional depth, prioritizing hyperrealistic graphics over substantive storytelling. However, proponents contend that the fusion of technology and creativity enables entirely new forms of expression that redefine the boundaries of art.

As digital media continues to evolve, its role in video games and film will likely expand further, incorporating artificial intelligence, augmented reality, and virtual reality. These advancements invite discussions not only about artistic innovation but also about ethical considerations, such as data privacy and representation within digital worlds. Ultimately, video games and film exemplify how digital technologies can serve as both tools for artistic creation and catalysts for reimagining what art means in an increasingly interconnected, virtual society.

Social Media Platforms: Building Visibility and Engagement

Social media platforms like Instagram, TikTok, Pinterest, and DeviantArt have revolutionized how artists share their work. These platforms provide a visual-first approach that allows artists to display their portfolios, share behind-the-scenes content, and engage directly with followers.

- **Instagram:** With its visually driven format and features like Stories, Reels, and IGTV, Instagram is a favorite among artists. It enables them to showcase their work to a global audience while using hashtags and the Explore Page to reach potential buyers. According to Statista, 74 percent of art buyers use Instagram to discover and purchase art, making it a powerful tool for both exposure and sales. Artist Danny Casale, known for his quirky animated characters, stated, "Instagram gave me a stage to showcase my work without needing gallery approval. It changed everything."
- **TikTok:** This platform's short-form video format allows artists to create time-lapse videos of their work, participate in trending challenges, or share creative processes. TikTok's algorithm helps content go viral quickly, providing immense visibility even for emerging artists. Illustrator and TikTok creator Devon Rodriguez, who gained millions of followers for his subway portraits, said, "TikTok gave me direct access to an audience that traditional galleries couldn't offer."
- **Pinterest:** Known for its thematic boards and discovery features, Pinterest is ideal for driving traffic to an artist's website or online store. It allows users to curate collections of artworks while offering insights into audience preferences and trends. Artists often use Pinterest to display mood boards and creative inspiration, fostering deeper connections with their audience.
- **DeviantArt:** As one of the oldest online communities tailored specifically for artists, DeviantArt provides a space for showcasing artwork, receiving feedback, and selling prints through its integrated marketplace. The platform has cultivated niche communities where digital illustrators, photographers, and mixed-media artists can thrive.

Additionally, platforms like YouTube allow artists to share tutorials or time-lapse videos of their creative process, building a loyal community while monetizing content through ads or sponsorships.

Specialized Online Marketplaces

Beyond social media platforms, specialized online marketplaces like Etsy, Redbubble, Society6, and Saatchi Art have made it easier than ever for artists to sell their digital work directly to buyers worldwide.

- **Etsy:** Known for its focus on handmade and unique items, Etsy is a popular choice for artists selling original works or prints. It provides tools for listing products, managing payments, and handling shipping logistics. Artists can also use print-on-demand services like Gelato or Printify to create high-quality reproductions without maintaining inventory.
- **Redbubble & Society6:** These print-on-demand platforms allow artists to upload designs that can be printed on various products like clothing, home décor items, or stationery. Artists earn royalties on each sale while the platform handles production and shipping.
- **Saatchi Art:** This curated platform connects contemporary artists with high-end buyers worldwide. Its reputation as a marketplace for serious collectors offers exposure to a more exclusive audience.
- **Fine Art America:** As one of the largest global art platforms, Fine Art America enables artists to sell prints, framed works, and other products featuring their art. Its extensive network helps creators reach international buyers with ease.

For those seeking more control over branding and profits, e-commerce platforms like Shopify allow artists to create personalized online stores. These stores can integrate with social media channels for seamless promotion and sales.

Interactive Digital Art Installations

In addition to online sharing and selling, digital art installations are redefining how audiences experience creativity. Interactive works like teamLab's *Flowers and People—Dark* or Chris Milk's *The Treachery of Sanctuary* immerse viewers in dynamic environments that obscure the boundaries between physical spaces and virtual experiences. TeamLab's immersive exhibitions use digital projections, motion sensors, and real-time data to create constantly shifting visual landscapes that respond to the audience's movements. In *Flowers and People—Dark*, for example, flowers bloom, wither, and regrow as visitors move through the space, creating a sense of interactivity that makes the audience an integral part of the artwork.

Chris Milk's *The Treachery of Sanctuary* is another signature example of how technology can merge with narrative storytelling to create evocative artistic experiences. The installation invites viewers to interact with a triptych of digital panels, where their silhouettes transform into flocks of birds or dissolve into abstract forms. Milk, a strong advocate for virtual reality as a medium for storytelling, has described his work as "a way to evoke empathy and connection in ways that static art cannot." This emphasis on interaction shifts the role of the audience from passive observers to active participants, reinforcing the collaborative nature of digital creativity.

Interactive installations also highlight the importance of audiovisual synchronization and environmental design. Works by collectives such as Meow Wolf combine digital projections, sculptures, and soundscapes to create multisensory environments that blur the lines between virtual and physical spaces. Meow Wolf's *House of Eternal Return*, for example, offers visitors an immersive, nonlinear narrative experience where every room contains interactive digital elements embedded within physical art pieces.

By using AR apps and VR headsets, creators are extending the reach of these installations beyond museum walls and into everyday spaces. For instance, digital artist Nancy Baker Cahill's *4th Wall* app allows users to view large-scale digital art overlays in public spaces through their smartphones, fostering a dialogue about the convergence of art, place, and technology.

These innovations highlight the potential of technology not just as a tool for creation but also as a medium for interaction and collective engagement. They raise questions about the ownership of digital experiences and the role of audience participation in defining artistic value.

By using social media platforms, online marketplaces, and interactive experiences, artists today have unprecedented opportunities to share, sell, and create art that transcends traditional boundaries. This interconnected ecosystem not only alters the way art is consumed and appreciated but also raises questions about the nature of creativity in the digital age. Market dynamics and social media engagement increasingly drive artistic recognition, often superseding traditional validation from museums, galleries, and art critics. For instance, digital artists gaining prominence through NFT sales or viral social media posts may achieve substantial commercial success without the conventional approval of cultural institutions or scholarly critique. Art critic Jerry Saltz notes this shift in his essay "The Last Days of the Art World," observing that "the market has become the message, drowning out critical discourse with the sound of counting money." This phenomenon echoes concerns raised by Arthur Danto, longtime art critic for *The Nation* magazine and professor of philosophy at Columbia University, who warned that "the art market has become less about artistic merit and more about speculation and social media metrics." The rapid rise of digital art platforms like OpenSea and Foundation demonstrates how market forces can establish artistic legitimacy independently of traditional cultural gatekeepers, leading some observers to question whether monetary value has supplanted critical evaluation as the primary measure of artistic significance.

New Tools, New Possibilities

Digital tools have expanded the artist's creative palette beyond the limits of traditional materials. These innovations have opened avenues for artistic exploration and expression that were previously unimaginable:

- **Vector Graphics**: Software like Adobe Illustrator introduced vector-based designs, allowing for infinitely scalable images without any loss of quality, a significant advantage for graphic designers and commercial artists. The precision of vector graphics has also become integral to branding, animation, and digital illustrations for platforms like video games and web design.
- **Simulated Traditional Media**: Programs such as Corel Painter mimic traditional techniques like watercolor, charcoal, or oil painting, offering artists the ability to experiment without the physical limitations or costs of traditional media. Artists like Kyle Lambert use these tools to create hyperrealistic portraits and scenes that rival traditional oil paintings.
- **3D Modeling and Rendering**: Tools like Blender and Autodesk Maya allow artists to create detailed three-dimensional models and

environments. This technology is widely used in film, animation, and video game design, enabling creators to build lifelike characters and immersive worlds. For example, films like *Avatar* relied heavily on digital modeling to create their rich, otherworldly landscapes.

- **Animation for Beginners**: Platforms like Procreate offer accessible animation tools on devices like iPads, making it easy for beginners to create looping GIFs or polished animations. Cartoon Animator 4 simplifies 2D animation with motion templates and motion capture technology, while Moho Pro's smart bone system enhances fluid character movements.
- **Interactive Media**: Digital platforms have also enabled the creation of interactive art, where audiences can influence or participate in the artwork itself. Tools like TouchDesigner allow artists to design immersive installations that react to viewer input, blending art and technology in real-time experiences. The Dalí Museum in Saint Petersburg, Florida, exemplifies this innovation with its "Dalí Lives" exhibit. This interactive AI experience allows visitors to engage with a digital re-creation of Salvador Dalí himself, who appears on-screen to share insights about his life and art. Visitors can also interact with Dalí's works in virtual reality through *Dreams of Dalí*, a VR installation that immerses participants in the surreal landscapes of his paintings, offering a new way to experience the complexity and depth of his imagination.

Accessibility and Democratization

One of the most transformative impacts of digital tools is their ability to democratize art creation, breaking down traditional barriers and making artistic expression more inclusive, affordable, and globally connected. By reducing the need for expensive materials, specialized training, or dedicated studio spaces, digital platforms have empowered creators from all walks of life to share their vision and participate in the global art community.

- **Inclusivity:** Digital tools have made art accessible to individuals with physical disabilities, opening new pathways for creative expression. Adaptive technologies like eye-tracking software or voice commands enable artists to create intricate digital works without relying on traditional physical tools. For example, the EyeWriter project, developed for graffiti artist Tony Quan (who suffers from ALS), allows users to draw using only eye movements. Similarly, platforms like Procreate and Adobe Fresco offer touch-based interfaces that accommodate a wide range of accessibility needs, ensuring that physical limitations do not restrict creativity.

- **Affordability:** The cost of traditional art supplies—canvas, paints, brushes, or sculpture materials—can be prohibitive for many aspiring artists. Digital platforms like Canva, Blender, and GIMP (a free alternative to Photoshop) provide affordable or even free access to powerful tools for graphic design, 3D modeling, and digital painting. Subscription-based programs like Adobe Creative Cloud allow artists to access professional-grade software at a fraction of the cost of physical materials, democratizing access to advanced creative resources. For example, emerging illustrators can use Procreate on an iPad to produce high-quality digital art without needing a full studio setup.
- **Global Reach:** The internet has fundamentally changed how art is shared and consumed. Artists can now publish their work online, reaching a worldwide audience instantly through platforms like Instagram, DeviantArt, or ArtStation. This global accessibility fosters collaboration and cultural exchange on an unprecedented scale, enabling artists from diverse backgrounds to learn from and inspire one another. Digital marketplaces like Etsy and platforms like Patreon also allow creators to monetize their work directly, bypassing traditional gatekeepers like galleries or publishers.
- **Community Building:** Digital tools and platforms have also facilitated the creation of artist communities that transcend geographic and cultural boundaries. Forums, Discord servers, and virtual workshops provide spaces for collaboration, mentorship, and peer feedback. Projects like The Sketchbook Project encourage artists worldwide to contribute to a collective archive of creativity, bridging gaps between professionals and amateurs alike.
- **Expanded Mediums:** By making advanced tools accessible, digital platforms enable experimentation in mediums that were once out of reach for most artists. Aspiring filmmakers can create animations or short films using tools like DaVinci Resolve or Blender, while musicians

can compose, produce, and share tracks using free digital audio workstations like Audacity. VR and AR platforms, such as Tilt Brush or Adobe Aero, allow creators to craft immersive experiences, pushing the boundaries of traditional art forms.

Concerns Over Cultural Appropriation and Intellectual Property

While digital platforms have opened new opportunities for artistic expression, they have also raised serious concerns about the ethical and legal implications of digital creativity. Many creators use copyrighted materials, trademarks, and personal images without permission or attribution, raising issues of cultural appropriation and intellectual property infringement. Digital artists may unintentionally or deliberately draw from cultural symbols, traditional art, or pre-existing works, sparking debates about ownership, exploitation, and respect for cultural heritage.

Cultural appropriation occurs when digital creators incorporate elements from marginalized cultures without understanding their historical or symbolic significance. This practice can perpetuate stereotypes or commercialize sacred imagery for profit. Historically, even renowned artists like Pablo Picasso and other members of the Cubist movement drew inspiration from African masks and traditional sculptures, incorporating these elements into their works without crediting their origins. While once seen as part of artistic innovation, this practice is now viewed through a more critical lens as cultural norms have evolved to emphasize ethical representation and respect for cultural heritage. Similarly, digital artists today have been criticized for using Indigenous symbols, African patterns, or religious motifs without attribution or compensation to the communities they come from, echoing unresolved issues of ownership, exploitation, and cultural integrity.

Moreover, legal frameworks governing intellectual property struggle to keep pace with the rapid evolution of digital media. The recent US Supreme Court decision involving Andy Warhol's use of a black-and-white photograph of Prince by celebrity photographer Lynn Goldsmith highlights the complexities of fair use in the digital era. Warhol had transformed the photograph into a stylized, bold-colored silkscreen image that was later used by *Condé Nast* magazine on its cover after Prince's death. Despite Warhol's argument that his work constituted fair use due to its transformative nature and different message, the court ruled in favor of Goldsmith, stating that Warhol's commercial licensing of the image did not meet the criteria for fair use. This case underscores the ongoing debates about what constitutes "transformation" and the importance of protecting the rights of original creators in an age where digital tools enable rapid appropriation and remixing.

Fair Use Doctrine, a legal principle in the United States, allows creators to use portions of copyrighted works for purposes such as education, criticism, and parody without seeking permission. However, fair use is subject to interpretation and may not protect all types of digital appropriation. Public domain works—those no longer protected by copyright—are permissible to use freely, while Creative Commons licenses provide a structured way for artists to share their works with attribution requirements, granting permission upfront for certain types of use.

Sage experts like Professor Lawrence Lessig, a key advocate for Creative Commons, argue that the movement "fosters a culture of collaboration and remixing while respecting the original creator's rights." However, even within Creative Commons, creators face ethical dilemmas about proper attribution and boundaries. For example, some digital creators use Creative Commons images as foundational elements but heavily modify them to the point of unrecognizability—raising questions about whether the final product still requires credit.

The conversation around digital appropriation has led to calls for more robust education on copyright law and the ethical responsibilities of digital creators. Organizations such as the Electronic Frontier Foundation and cultural advocacy groups have emphasized the need for clearer guidelines and protections, both for those creating derivative works and for communities whose cultural heritage is at risk of misappropriation.

Ultimately, the democratization of art creation through digital tools has expanded opportunities for expression and accessibility, but it also necessitates a deeper dialogue about the implications of appropriation, ownership, and authorship in the digital age. As technology continues to redefine artistic boundaries, bridging the intersection of creativity and ethical responsibility will remain a critical challenge for digital creators and cultural institutions alike.

Global Regulatory Frameworks and the Contest for Digital Governance

The global contest over the regulatory frameworks that govern digital technologies has serious implications for artists and creative expression. As Anu Bradford outlines in her analysis of global digital power dynamics in *Digital Empires*, the United States, Europe, and China have each adopted distinct approaches to regulating digital platforms, which in turn shape how artists create, distribute, and share their work.

- **The American Market-Driven Model:** The US approach prioritizes innovation and free market dynamics, with minimal regulatory oversight. This model fosters a competitive environment where artists can leverage social media platforms, marketplaces, and crowdfunding tools to reach global audiences. However, this same model can lead to issues such as the commodification of art and unchecked exploitation of creative content. Digital creators often face challenges related to algorithm-driven visibility and data privacy concerns, as platforms collect and monetize user-generated content. Independent creators such as digital painter Beeple and animator Emily Yang (*pplpleasr*) have thrived in this model, using NFTs and decentralized platforms to bypass traditional gatekeepers. However, their success also underscores the volatility of a system where financial speculation can overshadow artistic value.
- **The European Rights-Based Model:** The European Union's regulatory framework emphasizes privacy, data protection, and platform accountability. Regulations such as the General Data Protection Regulation (GDPR) and the Digital Services Act aim to balance innovation with the protection of individual rights. For artists, this model provides greater control over their digital footprints and intellectual property. It also establishes stronger protections for moral rights, which recognize an artist's enduring connection to their work. These rights include the right to be credited (paternity), the right to prevent unauthorized alterations (integrity), and the right to object to uses that could damage the artist's reputation. However, strict regulations on data usage and content moderation can limit certain forms of artistic and political expression, raising questions about censorship and the potential stifling of provocative art.

The expansive view of moral rights in Europe contrasts with the United States, where such protections are more limited and often overridden by commercial interests. For example, the estate of French artist Jean-Michel Folon once invoked moral rights to prevent unauthorized alterations to his public sculptures. Similarly, European visual artists have successfully leveraged these rights to challenge unauthorized reproductions and adaptations of their works. Meanwhile, artists like Banksy, who maintain anonymity, face challenges navigating these rights, particularly when their unauthorized public art is digitized and distributed without consent. While Banksy's works are celebrated globally, the European emphasis on "authorship" raises questions about how moral rights apply to anonymous or pseudonymous creators.

The case of Banksy's shredded artwork *Love is in the Bin*, which self-destructed partially after being auctioned, highlights the ongoing debate about how digital reproductions and transformations impact moral rights. This event, celebrated as a statement about commodification, also sparked discussions about whether such acts of destruction or reinterpretation could be protected under moral rights law in different jurisdictions. These differences demonstrate how the European regulatory model can both empower artists and introduce legal complexities.

- **The Chinese State-Centric Model:** China's regulatory framework is characterized by strict state control over digital platforms, content, and online behavior. Artists in China must operate under complex censorship laws that restrict political dissent and enforce narratives aligned with government interests. Despite this, influential artists such as Ai Weiwei have used digital media to subvert these restrictions. Ai Weiwei, who is openly critical of the Chinese government and advocates for human rights, faced intense surveillance and harassment. His outspoken activism, combined with his art, led to his arrest in 2011 and a period of detention. Eventually, he was forced to leave China and has since continued his work in exile, addressing themes of displacement, oppression, and resilience.

  Ai Weiwei's work often incorporates symbolic imagery and digital storytelling to critique government policies. His 2010 piece *Sunflower Seeds*—an installation of millions of hand-painted porcelain seeds symbolizing mass production and individuality—gained global recognition partly due to its digital promotion and virtual exhibitions. However, his social media presence has been repeatedly censored, illustrating how the state-centric model imposes crushing creative constraints and forces artists to find new ways to connect with global audiences. Ai Weiwei has highlighted the challenges of digital censorship, stating, "Censorship is not only about the deletion of information; it is about the control of memory and narrative."

Each of these regulatory models impacts free will, creativity, and artistic expression in different ways. In the United States., digital platforms may encourage commercial and viral content over meaningful artistic commentary. In Europe, the focus on protecting privacy and combating misinformation can unintentionally suppress experimental or controversial art. In China, the blending of surveillance and state-sponsored narratives has prompted both innovation and restriction, with some artists using emerging technologies like virtual reality and augmented reality to create immersive works that navigate the boundaries of permissible expression.

The work of Bradford and other scholarly commentators emphasizes the importance of understanding these global regulatory models, as they not only shape digital creativity but also influence political and commercial commentary through images, videos, and interactive media. In an increasingly harmonized social media world, it is crucial for artists, cultural institutions, and commentators to remain aware of the differing senses of aesthetics, cultural values, and regulatory expectations that exist globally. Recognizing these variations helps artists channel cross-border collaborations and avoid cultural missteps while fostering more respectful and informed exchanges of creative expression.

However, when regulatory restrictions conflict with an artist's personal convictions and values, an element of civil or artistic disobedience may be called for. This can take the form of creating works that subtly challenge censorship or address social injustices, echoing the efforts of figures like Ai Weiwei and other dissenting voices who use art as a form of resistance. Not unlike the earlier responses of artists such as Carrie Mae Weems, who has used her photography and installations to protest racism and social injustice, or artists like Barbara Kruger and the Guerrilla Girls, who decades earlier have challenged sexism and institutional biases, civil and artistic disobedience can serve as a powerful tool for advocacy, dialogue and change.

A Continuum of Innovation

The digital revolution represents the latest chapter in the ongoing evolution of art as a reflection of technological progress. Like the printing press and photography before it, digital technologies have expanded the possibilities of creative expression while simultaneously raising universal questions about the nature and purpose of art itself. These innovations have lowered barriers to entry, democratized artistic creation, and fostered an unprecedented inclusivity, ensuring that art remains accessible to creators across all backgrounds and circumstances.

Former Tate Gallery director Will Gompertz, in his book *Think Like an Artist*, emphasizes that innovation and failure are central to the creative process. According to Gompertz, true creativity is rooted in curiosity and the willingness to break rules, reject existing frameworks, and look beyond the obvious. Artists, he argues, thrive on experimentation, using failures not as setbacks but as opportunities to push boundaries and explore new possibilities. In this context, digital technologies serve as both a catalyst and a collaborator in the creative process, enabling artists to challenge conventions and reimagine the limits of what is possible.

Pablo Picasso once said, "Every act of creation is first an act of destruction." This perspective underscores how innovation in art often involves dismantling old ideas to build new ones, a process mirrored in the integration of digital tools into creative practices. Digital technologies allow artists to reimagine traditional forms while exploring novel mediums, fostering a transformative environment where boundaries between art, technology, and the audience are continually redefined.

This progression aligns with earlier philosophical inquiries into aesthetics, beauty, and genius. Baumgarten's study of sensory perception, Kant's delineation of artistic genius, and Picasso's assertion of self-determination all highlight a throughline in artistic history: that the artist remains at the center of creation, using available tools to express emotions, intuition, and imagination. In the digital age, the artist is still the director and creative progenitor, wielding new technological instruments to continue this tradition of storytelling and exploration.

As we look to the future, the interplay between technological innovation and artistic experimentation will continue to drive the evolution of creativity.

By embracing the failures and possibilities that come with breaking rules and reinventing frameworks, artists ensure that art remains a dynamic and transformative force, capable of reflecting and shaping the world around us. This ongoing continuum of innovation highlights the enduring power of art as a space for curiosity, reinvention, and the boundless exploration of human potential—now profoundly influenced by the latest technological revolution: artificial intelligence.

Work Referenced

"A Bigger Picture." *Exhibition, Royal Academy of Arts*, London, 21 Jan.–9 Apr. 2012.

Andy Warhol Foundation for Visual Arts, Inc. v. Goldsmith, 598 U.S. 2023.

Baumgarten, Alexander. *Aesthetica*. Impensis I.C. Kleyb, 1750.

Berger, John. *Ways of Seeing*. Penguin Books, 1972.

Bishop, Claire. *Artificial Hells: Participatory Art and the Politics of Spectatorship*. Verso Books, 2012.

Bishop, Claire. "Digital Divide: Contemporary Art and New Media." *Artforum*, vol. 51, no. 1, 2012, pp. 434–42.

Bradford, Anu. *Digital Empires: The Global Contest to Govern Technology*. Oxford University Press, 2023.

Danto, Arthur. "The Art World." *The Journal of Philosophy*, vol. 61, no. 19, 1964, pp. 571–84.

Danto, Arthur. *The Transfiguration of the Commonplace: A Philosophy of Art*. Harvard University Press, 1981.

"Dreams of Dalí." *Exhibition, The Dalí Museum*, Saint Petersburg, FL, 2016.

"Everydays: The First 5000 Days." *Christie's Auction House*, 11 Mar. 2021.

Farago, Jason. "The NFT Gold Rush." *The New York Times*, 12 Mar. 2021.

"From Dream to Reality: My Creative Process." *Digital Photography Review*, 2019.

Gompertz, Will. *Think Like an Artist: ...and Lead a More Creative, Productive Life*. Penguin Books, 2015.

Hockney, David. *David Hockney: A Bigger Picture*. Royal Academy of Arts Exhibition Catalogue, 2012.

Johansson, Erik. *Imagine: Surreal Photography and Digital Manipulation*. Text by Göran Segeholm, Bokförlaget Max Ström, 2016.

Kant, Immanuel. *Critique of Judgment*. 1790. Translated by Werner S. Pluhar, Hackett Publishing, 1987.

Knight, Christopher. "Art Review: Digital Art Comes of Age." *Los Angeles Times*, 15 Jan. 2020.

Lessig, Lawrence. *Free Culture: How Big Media Uses Technology and the Law to Lock Down Culture and Control Creativity.* Penguin Press, 2004.

Milk, Chris. *The Treachery of Sanctuary.* Installation, 2012.

Oxman, Neri. "Design at the Intersection of Technology and Biology." *TED Conference*, 2015.

Pye, David. *The Nature and Art of Workmanship.* Cambridge University Press, 1968.

Ritchin, Fred. *After Photography.* W.W. Norton & Company, 2008.

Saltz, Jerry. "The Last Days of the Art World." *New York Magazine*, Apr. 2020.

Sontag, Susan. *On Photography.* Farrar, Straus and Giroux, 1977.

teamLab. *Flowers and People—Dark.* Installation, 2015.

"The Art of Video Games." *Exhibition, Smithsonian American Art Museum*, Washington, DC, 16 Mar.–30 Sept. 2012.

Weiwei, Ai. *Sunflower Seeds.* Installation, Tate Modern, London, 2010.

Three The Creative Divide Human Vs. Machine

If we accept that art is shaped by culture, we must also recognize that we create our reality—whether through the cut of a chisel, the stroke of a paintbrush, the hum of a melody in our head, the weaving of a tapestry rich with stories, or the innovations of the latest technological inventions. In this way, we contribute to reality and possess the power to change it. Despite rising concerns about the development, growth, and influence of artificial intelligence (AI) in our daily lives, this perspective is inherently empowering. It frames us as active participants in shaping our world, rather than passive observers.

But what does it mean to be truly creative? As AI-generated art, music, and writing become increasingly prevalent, society is grappling with new questions: Where does inspiration end and imitation begin? How do we distinguish between a work of innovation and one that merely assembles the fragments of preexisting creations? These questions are at the heart of debates about human versus machine creativity.

In this chapter, we will explore the essence of creativity by examining its core components—inspiration, imitation, and innovation—and consider how they intersect with, and diverge from, along with exploring the hallmarks of creativity, the different types of creativity, and the capabilities of artificial intelligence. By reflecting on these dimensions, we aim to understand how human creativity, with all its flaws and flashes of genius, differs from the algorithmic output of machines.

Creativity as Cultural Expression

Art has always served as both a mirror and a catalyst—reflecting societal values while simultaneously reshaping them. From the ancient printmaking tools discovered in South African caves to today's cutting-edge digital canvases, art chronicles humanity's collective imagination, fears, and aspirations. It has the unique power to connect individuals, fostering a shared sense of identity by revealing how one person's inner world resonates with another's. Throughout history, technological advancements have deeply influenced artistic expression: the printing press democratized literature, photography revolutionized portraiture, and digital tools have unlocked new realms of creative possibility. Yet, at its heart, creativity transcends technology. It remains deeply rooted in human emotion, intent, and the cultural context that shapes our understanding of the world.

Human creativity is inherently both personal and cultural, intertwining individual experiences with the broader currents of society. When artists draw from their lived experiences, emotions, and societal influences, they create works that not only express their unique perspectives but also contribute to the ongoing evolution of culture. For instance, Edvard Munch's *The Sick Child* is deeply infused with the grief he endured after losing family members to illness. The raw, expressive brushstrokes in the painting capture his emotional turmoil in a way that feels profoundly human—something no machine could replicate, as it lacks the capacity for personal loss or emotional depth.

As Joyce Carol Oates, American literary critic and novelist, observed, "Creative work, like scientific work, should be greeted as a communal effort—an attempt by an individual to give voice to many voices, an attempt to synthesize and explore and analyze." This insight underscores the collaborative essence of artistic creation. While an artist's work may emerge from personal experience, it often resonates with universal themes and emotions that connect individuals across time and space. In this way, the creative process becomes a synthesis of the personal and the collective—a dialogue between the artist's inner world and the shared human condition.

Similarly, Picasso's *Les Demoiselles d'Avignon* exemplifies how creativity synthesizes diverse artistic influences. Drawing inspiration from African tribal masks, Iberian sculpture, and the Post-Impressionist works of Paul Cézanne, Picasso created a revolutionary composition that redefined modern art. His genius lay not in inventing entirely new forms but in reinterpreting existing visual languages in a way that shattered traditional perspectives. This process was not mere imitation but an act of radical transformation, reimagining familiar elements to evoke new meanings and challenge artistic conventions.

Beethoven's symphonies and Steve Jobs' iPhone serve as additional examples of transformative creativity. Beethoven built upon classical structures but infused them with unprecedented emotional intensity, while Jobs combined existing technologies into an entirely new user experience. This ability to innovate with intent and purpose distinguishes human creativity from machine-generated outputs.

Kirby Ferguson's *Everything is a Remix* YouTube series echoes this sentiment, emphasizing that human creativity thrives on remixing existing ideas into novel expressions. However, Ferguson critiques AI-generated art for lacking true creativity because it cannot innovate with intent or awareness. As Ferguson notes, "AIs know nothing whatsoever about the images and words they generate . . . Art is the voice of a person." This distinction underscores why human art resonates deeply: it emerges from lived experiences of love, loss, and identity that machines cannot comprehend.

In the age of AI, questions arise: Can machine-generated art contribute to culture as profoundly as human-created works, or will it remain an echo of human creativity? David Eagleman and Anthony Brandt, authors of *The Runaway Species*, remind us that while "every idea is a remix," the depth and meaning behind the remix depend on intention. At the same time, emerging research and data suggest that AI systems are increasingly capable of producing images that rival human creations in complexity, emotional resonance, and cultural impact, challenging traditional notions of artistic authorship and creativity. By exploring how humans and machines engage with cultural expression, we can better understand the enduring uniqueness of human creativity, while recognizing the possibilities of a different kind of creativity.

AI-generated art has made remarkable strides in mimicking human styles and producing visually stunning results. Tools like ChatGPT and MidJourney can illustrate intricate works based on text prompts alone. However, AI operates on patterns and probabilities derived from vast datasets—it lacks subjective experience or emotional intention. While an algorithm might generate a painting reminiscent of Van Gogh or compose music akin to Bach, its "inspiration" is mathematical rather than experiential. Eagleman and Brandt emphasize that while AI can recombine patterns in novel ways, it lacks the ability to "bend" ideas with purpose or "break" conventions with intent. For example, when Georgia O'Keeffe drew inspiration from natural forms and abstracted them into vivid compositions in *Red Canna,* she redefined how viewers perceive flowers, converting them into powerful representations of emotion and perspective. AI lacks this capacity for intentional disruption because it does not understand the norms it appears to challenge. Critics like Ferguson further underscore that AI art is fundamentally derivative by design and inventive only by chance. It cannot grapple with complex themes like mortality or social justice because it lacks the consciousness to understand these concepts.

The Role of Emotion and Imperfection

Human art often derives its emotional power from imperfections—those raw brushstrokes, uneven textures, or subtle inconsistencies that reflect an artist's struggles, vulnerabilities, and lived experiences. These imperfections are not flaws but features that make human creativity deeply relatable and emotionally resonant. Machines, in contrast, excel at precision but often produce work that feels overly polished and sterile, lacking the "human touch" born of personal insight and emotional depth.

This distinction is critical in understanding how viewers perceive and value art created by humans versus artificial intelligence (AI). A recent study led by Theresa Rahel Demmer and published in *Computers in Human Behavior* sheds light on this phenomenon. The study found that while people can attribute emotions and intentions to both AI- and human-created artworks, they tend to report stronger emotional responses to art they know was made by humans. Participants frequently ascribed emotional intentions to AI-generated works but still felt more connected to human-made pieces, suggesting that the perceived authenticity of human intention plays a central role in shaping emotional reactions.

Interestingly, the study also revealed that participants' emotional responses were influenced by "priming"—whether they were told beforehand if the artwork was AI- or human-made. When participants believed a piece was created by a human, they rated it more positively and reported stronger emotions, even if the artwork was AI-generated. Conversely, when told an artwork was AI-made, participants were more likely to describe it as lacking emotional depth or intentionality.

In an earlier study similar outcomes were reached. David Cope, a musicology professor at the University of California, Santa Cruz, gained notoriety for his pioneering yet controversial work in algorithmic composition. Cope developed computer programs capable of composing intricate musical works, including concertos, chorales, symphonies, and operas. His first creation, EMI (Experiments in Musical Intelligence), was designed to emulate the compositional style of Johann Sebastian Bach. It took Cope seven years to perfect the program, but once completed, EMI could generate 5,000 chorales in Bach's style in a single day—a feat that astounded both computer scientists and music enthusiasts.

Cope arranged for several of EMI's chorales to be performed at a music festival, where the audience responded with glowing praise. Some listeners described how the performance touched their innermost emotions. However, when Cope revealed that the music had been composed by a machine rather than by Bach himself, the audience's admiration quickly turned to outrage. This revelation sparked widespread debate and brought hostility from classical music aficionados who viewed Cope's work as a threat to the sanctity of human artistry. Critics decried EMI's output as mere mimicry, devoid of the soul and depth that defines truly great music.

The controversy escalated when Professor Steve Larson from the University of Oregon issued a challenge to Cope. Larson proposed an experimental performance in which professional pianists would play three pieces—one by Bach, one by EMI, and one by Larson himself—without identifying the composer of each piece. The event took place at a packed concert hall at the University of Oregon, attended by faculty, students, and music fans. At the end of the performance, the audience was asked to identify which composer corresponded to each piece. In a surprising twist, the audience overwhelmingly believed EMI's composition was an authentic Bach chorale, attributed Bach's actual piece to Larson, and mistakenly thought Larson's composition was machine-generated.

Despite these results, critics continued to argue that EMI's music, while technically brilliant, lacked something essential—what they described as emotional authenticity or "soul." Skeptics maintained that computer-generated compositions were too precise, too perfect, and therefore incapable of the spontaneity and vulnerability that make human music resonate so deeply. Yet, paradoxically, when audiences were unaware of the origins of EMI's even later works, they frequently praised the compositions for their emotional depth and resonance, often attributing profound spiritual meaning to them.

David Cope's EMI project offers a striking example of how machine-generated compositions can challenge our assumptions about creativity and intelligence. When audiences mistook EMI's chorales for authentic Bach, it was as if the program had passed a "musical Turing Test," producing art so convincing that listeners attributed human creativity and emotional depth to it. This raises a fundamental question: should the ability to imitate human expression be treated as proof of genuine creativity, or is it simply sophisticated mimicry?

The Turing Test, originally proposed by Alan Turing in 1950, was designed to evaluate a machine's ability to exhibit intelligent behavior indistinguishable from that of a human. While the original focus was on conversational intelligence, the test's broader implications resonate with artistic expression as well.

Turing Test Relevance to Art and Creativity:

1. **Defining Creativity:** The core premise of the Turing Test—indistinguishability—applies directly to the arts. If audiences cannot tell the difference between machine-generated and human-created art, does that mean the machine is genuinely creative? Or does creativity require subjective intent, emotional experience, and the ability to engage in self-expression?
2. **Machine Learning in Art:** Programs like EMI challenge traditional views of the creative process by generating music that can evoke genuine emotional responses from listeners. However, whether these responses indicate the machine's "understanding" of emotional significance or merely reflect its ability to replicate familiar patterns remains contested.
3. **The Value of Human Creativity:** The controversy surrounding EMI highlights the deeper issue of what makes human artistic expression distinctive. Is it the imperfections, emotional vulnerability, or the unique cultural and personal context embedded in human creations? If machines can replicate style and form but not subjective experience, does that distinction matter—or is it irrelevant to the artistic experience?

These examples also highlight a subtle but persistent bias: even when AI art is visually indistinguishable from human art, viewers tend to devalue it due to preconceived notions about its origin. This preference seems tied to the belief that human art carries a sense of effort, narrative, and personal meaning—qualities that viewers associate with the artist's lived experience.

For culture to continue valuing human-made art and preserving its distinctiveness from machine-generated creations, transparency is crucial. One potential approach is to adopt clear identification practices, like the wall labels found in museums and galleries that provide the artist's name, an artist statement, the medium, and the context of the work. These labels not only inform viewers but also frame their interpretative experience by highlighting the artist's vision and the personal or cultural narrative behind the creation.

In a world where AI-generated works are increasingly sophisticated, this kind of transparency helps audiences discern the human element that enriches art with intentionality and lived experience. By clearly labeling the origins of a piece—whether human-made or AI-generated—viewers can engage with the art on a more informed level, appreciating the technical mastery of AI without conflating it with the emotional and existential depths often associated with human creativity. This practice preserves the cultural significance of human art by reinforcing the context in which it was created.

Moreover, such transparency may foster a deeper appreciation for both forms of expression. Instead of diminishing the value of AI-generated works, honest labeling could encourage audiences to explore new questions: What role does authorship play in our emotional connection to art? Does knowing the artist's journey enhance our experience? British art critic Tom Lubbock, in *Great Works*, often approached artists' biographies as stories worth telling—ones that enriched our understanding rather than reducing their lives to routine facts. For example, when analyzing a painting by Vermeer, Lubbock wrote, "Painting was perhaps not Vermeer's main job. He had a line as an innkeeper." By offering these kinds of insights, Lubbock reframed the artist's life in a way that brought new texture to the work itself. Similarly, engaging with the background of human-made and AI-generated art can deepen our appreciation by prompting us to consider the creator's—or the process's—role in shaping meaning.

By engaging with these questions, viewers can better understand how and why human-made art continues to hold an irreplaceable place in cultural discourse, even as machine learning reshapes creative landscapes. As Lubbock's work suggests, understanding context—whether it is Vermeer balancing painting with his innkeeping business or a photographer marshaling a historic event—helps us see art not just as an outcome but as part of a story, inviting us into a richer, more layered experience.

Inspiration: The Spark of Imagination

Inspiration is often described as a sudden flash of insight or a slow-building sense of purpose sparked by external influences—a poem, a landscape, a conversation, or even silence. Human inspiration can be unpredictable, deeply personal, and shaped by emotional and psychological experiences. It can arise from an immersive moment of awe in nature, such as watching the sunrise over the Grand Canyon, or from a mundane but contemplative walk through a familiar neighborhood or a beachfront. These moments weave together memory, emotion, and external stimuli to form the catalyst for creation.

Historical examples abound of artists crediting their inspiration to specific experiences. For instance, Mary Shelley conceived *Frankenstein* after a night of storytelling and a vivid dream, while Beethoven found solace and inspiration for his *Pastoral Symphony* during walks in the countryside. In literature, Virginia Woolf described her writing process as capturing fleeting "moments of being"—intense, vivid experiences that reveal deeper truths. These examples underscore that human creativity is often sparked by moments of intense emotional resonance.

As Eagleman and Brandt note, "Innovation doesn't come from generating something out of nothing—it comes from transforming what exists." This insight invites a provocative question: Does the absence of lived experience undermine or enhance AI's ability to inspire and create? Proponents of AI art often point to its capacity for collaboration, such as Scott Eaton's "Artist+AI: Figures & Faces" series, where he works with AI algorithms to craft lifelike digital portraits. By training models on vast datasets of facial features, Eaton generates unique interpretations of human faces, blending traditional artistry with machine learning. Through this collaborative process, AI acts as a creative partner, expanding the possibilities of artistic exploration and challenging conventional notions of creativity.

Another compelling example is the work of Sougwen Chung, who collaborates with robotic arms in her project *Drawing Operations Unit Generation (DOUG)*. In this interactive performance, Chung and the robot co-create drawings, blurring the lines between human and machine creativity. This partnership explores the concept of shared agency, challenging traditional notions of authorship and creativity while demonstrating how AI can augment human expression rather than replace it. These works emphasize the synergy between human imagination and machine intelligence, showcasing how AI can elevate artistic visions by offering new tools for exploration.

However, critics argue that without emotional stakes or personal interpretation, AI's contributions remain derivative. The poetry generated by machines may mimic meter and metaphor but often lacks the layered emotional weight of human introspection. Philosopher Hannah Arendt provides a compelling framework for understanding this distinction.

In *The Human Condition*, Arendt emphasizes that true inspiration and creativity stem from the uniquely human capacity to reflect on the condition of existence—a process deeply rooted in memory, imagination, and narrative. Creativity is not merely about producing objects but about engaging with the world in a way that transforms fleeting experiences into something enduring and meaningful. This act of creation is tied to what she calls "natality," the human ability to initiate something new through thought and action.

Arendt also highlights the importance of "world-building" in human creativity—the process of crafting durable works that transcend the ephemeral nature of daily life. Art, in her view, is a means of preserving human experience and offering permanence amidst life's impermanence. This durability is not just physical but symbolic, as art embodies the narratives, emotions, and cultural meanings that define humanity.

For example, photojournalist Rowland Scherman's first major assignment was to cover the March on Washington for the United States Information Agency (USIA). In the book *TIMELESS: The Photography of Rowland Scherman*, he reflects on the experience, writing that when Martin Luther King Jr. delivered his iconic "I Have a Dream" speech, it was a day filled with powerful songs and impassioned speeches. "The songs, as the crowd was gathering, enhanced the mood that prevailed: the people of this country wanted change. Echoing the classic, can-do spirit that we all thought and believed America was founded upon, we marched." Scherman's mission as a photographer was clear: to capture the scope and majesty of the historic event for the millions of Americans who couldn't witness it firsthand. "I was young enough to move everywhere," he recalled, "and I had an official US government pass that allowed me to cover it all. I worked pretty hard that day."

Scherman's photographs do more than document a moment in time—they reveal how the event was experienced on a deeply personal level. These are not static images meant for detached observation. They draw viewers in, placing them amidst the energy of the march. The photographs are imbued with purpose, guiding the viewer on a visual journey aimed squarely at the shared goal of equality, jobs, and freedom.

AI, lacking subjective experience and the capacity for introspection, can show us a view or scene, but it cannot show us how a self experiences the world. While it may generate aesthetically pleasing works by synthesizing data patterns, it does so without the reflective dialogue that Arendt sees as central to human creativity—the "silent conversation" between an individual and their inner world.

This philosophical distinction raises profound questions: Can meaning truly be conveyed without lived experience? Arendt would likely argue that creativity inherently requires a connection to personal or collective memory because it is through this connection that art gains its depth and resonance. Without the ability to grapple with existential questions or draw from the richness of human experience, AI's outputs remain surface-level imitations rather than authentic expressions of the human condition.

As Arendt notes, art transforms "sense-objects into thought-things," embedding them with layers of meaning derived from an artist's unique perspective. AI may replicate form, but it cannot replicate this depth of meaning because it lacks both the "natality" to initiate new ideas and the reflective capacity to imbue them with significance. Thus, while AI can serve as a tool for expanding creative possibilities, its contributions are ultimately limited by its inability to engage in the deeply human processes of reflection, memory, and narrative construction. Arendt's insights remind us that true creativity is not just about technical skill or innovation but about the ability to make sense of our shared existence—a capacity that remains uniquely human.

Ultimately, the contrast between human inspiration and machine recombination illuminates a deeper truth about creativity: while machines may process patterns and rearrange data, humans derive meaning from context and narrative. This connection to purpose and experience shapes art that resonates across generations, inviting empathy and emotional engagement.

Imitation: The Foundation of Learning

Imitation has always been a cornerstone of the creative process. Many of history's greatest artists, musicians, and writers began their journeys by closely studying and replicating the masters who preceded them. This process allowed them to internalize techniques, styles, and frameworks, which they later transformed into their own unique voices. For example, Michelangelo studied classical sculptures to refine his understanding of anatomy, while The Beatles drew heavily on American rock and roll and rhythm and blues before developing their signature sound.

Art schools reinforce this foundational process by teaching students composition, line, space, tension, atmosphere, color and anatomy through direct engagement with the works of great masters. Students are often encouraged to visit museums, sketch notable works, and even replicate iconic pieces as part of their training. This approach mirrors Marcel Duchamp's assertion: "I don't believe in art. I believe in artists." By immersing themselves in the study of one artist at a time and building an understanding of their techniques and innovations, students gradually develop their own artistic voice. This method encourages not blind replication but a deep engagement with and reinterpretation of artistic practices.

Will Gompertz, in *Think Like an Artist*, emphasizes that imitation is not only natural but essential for creative growth. He argues that successful artists are those who absorb influences from a wide range of sources and then filter them through their personal lens to create something distinct. Gompertz writes, "Great artists copy, but they don't just copy—they adapt, transform, and make it their own." This highlights the potential of imitation as a stepping stone toward originality.

Austin Kleon echoes this sentiment in *Steal Like an Artist*, where he reframes imitation as a form of creative apprenticeship. Kleon encourages creators to "steal" ideas from their influences—not in a literal sense but by deeply engaging with their work and reinterpreting it in new ways. He writes, "You don't want to look like your heroes; you want to see like your heroes." For Kleon, imitation is not about replication but about understanding the thought processes behind great works and using them as inspiration for one's own creations.

AI systems also rely heavily on imitation—training on massive datasets of existing works to understand style, composition, and form. However, while human artists imitate as a means of discovery and personal growth, AI imitates as an end in itself. Its outputs often feel derivative because they lack the intentionality and emotional depth that come from personal experience. As Gompertz notes, "Art is not just about technical skill; it's about having something to say."

This distinction raises important ethical and philosophical questions about authenticity and originality in an era when machines can replicate human styles with stunning precision. It also invites reflection on how meaning and authorship are constructed.

Moreover, the process of imitation in human creativity is often messy and subjective. A painter may mimic brushstrokes learned from their teacher but introduce imperfections that reveal their inner emotions. A writer may adopt structural elements from a favorite novel but weave in personal memories and cultural references. This subjective infusion of meaning underscores why imitation for humans often leads to innovation, rather than mere replication. As the artist Saul Steinberg remarked, "What we respond to in any work of art is the artist's struggle against his or her limitations." He suggested that it is often what an artist chooses to leave out that makes the art interesting—what is not shown versus what is.

An example of this theme is found in the absence of the human figure in Walker Evans's untitled photographs of urban architecture. These images capture the strong lines of bridges and skyscrapers in a formally reduced language, almost abstract but still recognizable, lacking the presence of the crowds who flocked to the cities during the bustling decades of the 1920s and 1930s. Yet, their very emptiness makes a statement, emphasizing the human imprint through what is left unseen.

Innovation: The Leap Beyond

Innovation is often regarded as the pinnacle of creativity—the moment when an artist or thinker transcends conventions to produce something groundbreaking. Whether it's James Joyce revolutionizing literature with *Ulysses*, Miles Davis inventing new musical genres with *Kind of Blue*, or Jackson Pollock breaking artistic norms with his drip paintings, innovation shifts paradigms and opens new frontiers.

Gompertz highlights that innovation is rarely a sudden leap but rather the result of incremental experimentation built on a foundation of imitation. He argues that great innovators are those who take risks, challenge norms, and embrace failure as part of the creative process. For instance, he points to Claude Monet's evolution toward Impressionism as a deliberate progression—drawing from his studies of light, Japanese woodblock prints, and his observations of nature—to develop a radically fresh approach that defied traditional academic standards.

Austin Kleon similarly emphasizes that innovation often emerges from remixing existing ideas in unexpected ways. He writes that "nothing is completely original," but originality lies in how creators combine influences into fresh forms. He uses the metaphor of a "creative family tree," where every artist is connected to those who came before them but branches out in unique directions.

In the context of AI, innovation occupies a space that is both promising and ambiguous. Proponents argue that machines could eventually surpass human creativity by discovering new artistic languages or forms unbound by human biases or traditions. Freed from conventional limitations, AI has the potential to explore territories that human artists might overlook, offering novel perspectives and reshaping how we understand art itself. This potential excites many who see AI as a tool to expand creative possibilities beyond what humans alone can achieve.

However, skeptics caution against conflating complexity with creativity. While AI-generated works may astonish with their intricate designs and unexpected combinations, there remains a fundamental debate about whether such creations constitute genuine innovation or merely sophisticated recombination of existing ideas. True innovation, they argue, requires more than novelty; it demands purpose—a sense of why something matters within its cultural or emotional context. Without the ability to imbue work with meaning, AI risks producing art that is technically impressive but emotionally hollow.

Austin Kleon echoes this sentiment, warning against mistaking technological sophistication for genuine creativity. He writes that "machines can make things faster or more efficiently, but they can't make meaning." Innovation, in this view, is deeply tied to human experience—our emotions, intuition, and ability to ask questions about the world around us. It's not just about what is created, but why it is created and how it resonates with others. Algorithms, no matter how advanced, lack the lived experience and emotional depth that underpin truly meaningful art. This tension between efficiency and meaning underscores the precarious balance AI occupies in the creative realm, leaving open the question of whether machines can ever truly innovate in the fullest sense of the word.

As we maneuver through this new era, the task lies not in choosing between human and machine creativity but in understanding their intersections and boundaries. Rather than viewing AI as a replacement for human artistry, we can approach it as a tool that complements and expands creative possibilities.

Ultimately, the essence of creativity may reside not solely in the act of producing something new but in the meaning we derive from the process itself. By reflecting on inspiration, imitation, and innovation, we can better appreciate the unique ways in which art—whether created by human hands or digital algorithms—continues to shape and be shaped by the ever-evolving story of humanity.

Hallmarks of Creativity in the Age of AI

Creativity has long been celebrated as one of the defining traits of human ingenuity, characterized by the blending of imagination, intuition, and insight to produce inspirational ideas. Jackson Pollock, the hero of post-war American art, embodied this ideal—a mythic figure of violent bohemian outsider turned celebrity casualty. Emerging from these influences, he created unprecedented works: canvases laid flat on the studio floor, with paint dripping and pouring onto them in dense, layered webs, executed in a frenzied dance of activity as he proclaimed, "I am nature." His genius, as British art critic Tom Lubbock noted, was to make human artifacts that possessed the raw fascination of natural phenomena—until he succumbed to alcoholism and tragically crashed his car.

As machine learning and artificial intelligence systems continue to develop, they have entered the conversation as potential partners—or challengers—in the creative process. This section offers a comprehensive exploration of the hallmarks of creativity, incorporating philosophical insights, cognitive science perspectives, and examples that illuminate both the promise and limitations of AI-driven creativity.

Defining Creativity: Beyond Simple Innovation

Creativity involves generating ideas that are novel, meaningful, and valuable within their context. According to Margaret Boden, Research Professor of Cognitive Science in the Department of Informatics at the University of Sussex, creativity spans three main types: exploratory, transformational, and combinational, each requiring distinct cognitive engagements. Boden argues that true creativity emerges when existing constraints are transcended in meaningful ways, leading to groundbreaking shifts in understanding.

Exploratory Creativity: Expanding Within Boundaries

Exploratory creativity involves working within an established conceptual space, testing its boundaries, and iterating on existing ideas. Boden emphasizes that this form of creativity accounts for an overwhelming 97 percent of all human creative activity, making it the most common type. It is particularly effective in domains where incremental improvements or variations yield valuable results. Boden likens exploratory creativity to navigating a "conceptual map" where the rules and constraints of the space are known, but new possibilities emerge through systematic exploration. In art, Agnes Martin's meditative grid paintings exemplify exploratory creativity. Her works, such as *Untitled #5* (1984), demonstrate a meticulous refinement of geometric abstraction. By repeatedly exploring the interplay between grids, color, and line, Martin created subtle variations that evoke tranquility and introspection. Her adherence to a single format—a six-foot-square canvas—enabled her to dive deeply into the nuances of her chosen conceptual space, producing works that resonate with emotional depth despite their simplicity.

Martin's process reflects how exploratory creativity allows artists to expand possibilities within a defined framework while maintaining coherence. Boden also highlights how exploratory creativity thrives in scientific contexts, such as iterating chemical compounds to discover new treatments. Similarly, AI excels in this domain by generating and evaluating countless variations at scale. For example, AI programs like AARON can produce thousands of line drawings in a particular style, mimicking the exploratory process of artists.

However, Boden's premise is that while AI can replicate patterns and generate novel combinations within a predefined space, it lacks the intuitive insights and emotional resonance that human creators bring to their work. The implications of Boden's observation that exploratory creativity dominates human activity are significant. It suggests that much of what we consider "creative" is rooted in disciplined practice and iterative refinement rather than radical breakthroughs. This reinforces the value of persistence and mastery in artistic and scientific endeavors while highlighting the complementary role AI can play as a tool for exploration.

Transformational Creativity: Redefining Boundaries

Transformational creativity occurs when an individual fundamentally alters or transcends an existing conceptual space, creating entirely new frameworks or paradigms. Boden describes this as the rarest and most revolutionary form of creativity because it requires reimagining the rules themselves rather than working within them. Transformational creativity often leads to groundbreaking innovations that redefine entire fields. Kazimir Malevich's *Black Square* (1915) serves as a quintessential example in art. By reducing painting to its most elemental form—a black square on a white background—Malevich rejected centuries of representational art and introduced Suprematism, a movement focused on pure feeling rather than depiction.

Malevich described his work as the "zero point" of painting, symbolizing a radical departure from tradition and the birth of non-objective art. This act of transformation not only challenged viewers' perceptions but also laid the groundwork for modern abstraction. Boden compares transformational creativity in art to Einstein's theory of relativity in science—both represent paradigm shifts that alter how we understand reality.

However, she notes that transformational creativity is exceedingly difficult for machines to achieve because it requires not just processing data but fundamentally rethinking the constraints of a conceptual space. While AI can simulate exploratory processes or generate novel combinations (combinational creativity), it struggles to produce genuinely transformative ideas because it operates within predefined parameters. The implications are significant: transformational creativity underscores the uniquely human capacity for radical innovation driven by intuition, imagination, and cultural context. It also highlights why such breakthroughs are celebrated—they represent leaps into uncharted territory that reshape our understanding of art, science, and society.

Expressive Creativity: Conveying Personal Truths

Expressive creativity is deeply personal and emotional, rooted in an individual's subjective experiences and inner world. Boden emphasizes that this form of creativity involves more than technical skill; it requires conveying meaning through works imbued with personal narrative and emotional depth. Louise Bourgeois's sculptures exemplify expressive creativity. Her works often draw on childhood trauma, memory, and identity to create pieces that resonate on an intensely psychological level.

For instance, her iconic spider sculptures symbolize both protection (a maternal figure) and vulnerability (the fragility of life). Bourgeois's ability to translate her inner emotional landscape into tangible forms demonstrates how expressive creativity connects deeply with audiences by evoking shared human experiences. In contrast, AI-generated art often lacks this emotional resonance because it cannot draw from personal experience or intention. While algorithmic portraiture or generative designs may be aesthetically compelling, they lack the layered narratives and intentionality that define expressive creativity.

For example, AI can mimic Bourgeois's style or create visually similar sculptures but cannot replicate the psychological complexity embedded in her work. Boden's insights into expressive creativity highlight its intrinsic connection to human emotion and lived experience. This distinction raises critical questions about authenticity in AI-generated art: Can machines ever truly "express" without subjective experience? The answer reinforces why expressive works remain uniquely tied to human creators—they reflect not just technical skill but also the depth of individual perspective.

Margaret Boden's framework provides a comprehensive lens for understanding different types of creativity and their implications for both human and AI-generated art. Exploratory creativity dominates human activity by expanding possibilities within existing frameworks; transformational creativity redefines those frameworks entirely; and expressive creativity conveys deeply personal truths tied to emotion and experience. While AI excels at exploratory tasks by generating variations at scale, it struggles with transformational breakthroughs or expressive depth due to its lack of intuition, cultural context, and subjective experience. These distinctions underscore why human creativity remains irreplaceable even as AI becomes an increasingly powerful tool for artistic exploration.

Marcus du Sautoy, in *The Creativity Code*, reinforces the idea that creativity is a delicate balance between constraints and freedom—a process where breaking the rules often leads to innovative leaps. He argues that while algorithms can generate surprising outputs, they lack the personal stakes and introspection that define human creativity. For example, Beethoven's symphonies, shaped by his personal hardships and eventual deafness, are imbued with emotional grandeur and a narrative of triumph over adversity. AI may compose harmonious pieces or mimic Beethoven's style, but it cannot replicate the meaning derived from such lived experiences.

Du Sautoy also introduces the concept of the "Lovelace Test," named after Ada Lovelace, often regarded as the first computer programmer. This test challenges whether machines can truly transcend their programming to create something genuinely novel and valuable—not simply recombinations of pre-existing patterns or data inputs. Unlike the Turing Test, which focuses on whether machine outputs are indistinguishable from human outputs, the Lovelace Test demands that a machine generate work so original and unexpected that even its creators cannot fully explain how or why it came into being.

Du Sautoy argues that while AI-generated works can indeed surprise audiences with their sophistication, the absence of intentionality, subjective experience, and emotional context often renders these creations less impactful on a deeper level. For example, an AI may compose a beautiful symphony or craft a visually stunning painting, but without a lived history of struggle, triumph, or personal introspection, its "choices" remain rooted in algorithmic probabilities rather than an emotional or existential narrative.

This distinction underscores the importance of human experience as a foundational element of creativity, particularly in art forms like literature, painting, and music, where individual history, cultural context, and intent shape the meaning of the work. The Lovelace Test, therefore, reframes the debate: it is not simply about whether a machine can produce output that resembles human creativity, but whether it can imbue its work with a sense of purpose, originality, and value that is independent of its programmed directives—qualities often seen as quintessentially human.

Moments of creativity often include the "Aha!" experience—a flash of insight that cognitive scientists liken to unconscious problem-solving reaching conscious realization. Arthur I. Miller, Professor of History and Philosophy of Science at University College London, compares these moments to the resolution of cognitive tension, describing them as pivotal breakthroughs in both science and art. He cites Georges Braque's innovations in Cubism as an artistic example, where Braque's collaboration with Picasso redefined visual representation by breaking traditional perspectives. Similarly, Rosalind Franklin's X-ray crystallography image of DNA's double helix structure represents a scientific epiphany born of years of meticulous work followed by a moment of clarity. Miller emphasizes that these breakthroughs are not isolated events but emerge from prolonged immersion in a field combined with moments of spontaneous insight. He further argues that while AI can simulate this process through combinatorial creativity—rearranging existing elements into new configurations—it struggles to replicate the emotional resonance or deeper meaning tied to human epiphanies.

Intuition and Emotional Depth

Human creativity frequently draws upon an intuitive understanding of complex ideas, informed by emotions, cultural context, and lived experiences. Paul Klee's observation, "We construct and construct, but intuition is still a good thing," highlights the indispensable role of intuition in the creative process. Cognitive scientists describe intuition as the rapid, unconscious synthesis of knowledge accumulated over time, enabling creators to make seemingly irrational yet groundbreaking connections. This capacity for intuitive leaps often leads to innovation that transcends logical reasoning or strict adherence to established frameworks.

Jackson Pollock's action painting exemplifies this principle. His works, such as *No. 5, 1948*, emerged from a process that relied heavily on spontaneity and instinct rather than premeditated design. Pollock's method of dripping and splashing paint onto a canvas was not guided by traditional techniques but by his ability to trust his intuition and respond to the moment. Each chaotic yet intricate layer of paint reflects a deeply personal engagement with his inner world, creating art that resonates on an emotional level. This process demonstrates how human intuition allows artists to break free from conventional norms and produce works that connect with viewers in profound ways.

The issue of whether machine learning can replicate such intuitive creativity raises important questions. For example, AlphaGo, the AI program developed by DeepMind, offers a compelling case study in algorithmic decision-making that mimics some aspects of intuition. During its famous match against Go champion Lee Sedol in 2016, AlphaGo made a move so unconventional that experts initially dismissed it as a mistake. However, as the game progressed, the move revealed its strategic brilliance, leading to AlphaGo's victory. David Silver, one of AlphaGo's developers, noted that the program had "taught itself" this strategy through reinforcement learning—playing millions of games against itself and refining its approach over time.

This raised the provocative question: could AI develop beyond its training data to achieve something akin to human intuition? While AlphaGo's move appeared intuitive, Marcus du Sautoy argues that such surprises are not born of genuine intuition but emerge from probabilistic modeling and vast computational training. Unlike Pollock or other human creators who draw on emotional depth and cultural context and, perhaps, a little alcohol consumption, AlphaGo's decisions are rooted in algorithmic optimization rather than experiential insight. The system operates within predefined parameters and lacks the subjective experience necessary for true creative leaps.

As du Sautoy notes, while AI can generate outputs that surprise even its developers, these outputs lack the intentionality and emotional resonance that define human creativity. Creative breakthroughs also require symbolic meaning and cultural context—elements deeply tied to human intuition.

Martha Graham's modern dance choreography offers another example of how intuition drives transformational creativity. Her piece *Lamentation* redefined storytelling through movement by using starkly minimalist gestures to evoke both personal grief and universal themes of loss. Graham's ability to connect her inner emotional world with broader human experiences demonstrates how intuition enables creators to synthesize knowledge, emotion, and lived context into works that resonate deeply with audiences.

Similarly, Wassily Kandinsky's abstract paintings were guided by what he called "inner necessity," an intuitive process rooted in his belief that art should express spiritual truths rather than merely depict physical reality. Kandinsky's use of color and form as tools for emotional expression pushed the boundaries of visual language, creating works that continue to inspire viewers with their symbolic depth.

These examples highlight the limitations of AI-generated creativity compared to human creativity. While systems like AlphaGo or generative AI tools can produce novel outputs by recombining existing data in innovative ways, they lack the emotional grounding and cultural understanding necessary for true intuitive breakthroughs.

The question remains whether future advancements in machine learning could enable AI to transcend its reliance on data-driven processes and develop something closer to human-like intuition. Some researchers speculate that unsupervised learning—where machines explore possibilities without predefined outcomes—might allow AI to discover entirely new ideas beyond human-imposed constraints.

However, even in such scenarios, machines would still lack the curiosity, frustration, and inspiration integral to human creativity. Ultimately, intuition is not simply rapid or efficient thinking but a deeply human synthesis of knowledge, emotion, and lived experience. It allows creators like Pollock or Graham to navigate ambiguity, break conventions, and imbue their work with symbolic meaning that transcends mere technical execution. While AI can augment human creativity by generating surprising outputs or exploring new possibilities at scale, it remains tethered to imitation rather than innovation—unable to replicate the deeply personal insights that define transformative artistic expression.

Thoughtfulness and Intent

Creativity often involves deliberate exploration and purpose—a thoughtful construction of themes, symbols, and meanings. Claude Debussy once remarked, "Works of art make rules; rules do not make works of art." His words emphasize that creativity is an active process of shaping rules, not merely following them. A filmmaker crafting a narrative about resilience, for example, may meticulously structure each scene to evoke reflection and empathy. This intentionality imbues human creativity with symbolic complexity and layered meaning.

Arthur Koestler, in *The Act of Creation*, introduces the concept of "bisociation," where creative breakthroughs occur at the intersection of two unrelated frames of reference. This process, he argues, is central to both scientific discoveries and artistic innovations. The Renaissance itself exemplifies bisociation, as classical knowledge from antiquity intersected with emerging scientific methods and artistic techniques to produce groundbreaking works.

For instance, Renaissance painters like Leonardo da Vinci combined mathematical precision with emotional storytelling, creating masterpieces that transcended their time by blending technical innovation with profound human expression. Similarly, modern innovations like the smartphone embody this principle by integrating previously unrelated technologies—such as telecommunication, computing, and photography—into a single device that addresses multiple human needs.

Steven Johnson, in *Where Good Ideas Come From*, expands on this idea by emphasizing the importance of "liquid networks" in fostering creativity. He argues that great ideas often emerge from environments where diverse perspectives interact over time, allowing for the exchange and recombination of ideas. Johnson cites historical examples like coffeehouses during the Enlightenment, which served as hubs for intellectual exchange and spurred advancements in science and philosophy. In contemporary terms, Johnson's insights suggest that collaborative environments—whether physical or digital—are essential for nurturing thoughtfulness and creativity. These networks create opportunities for bisociation by bringing together individuals from different disciplines to share knowledge and spark new connections.

Koestler's and Johnson's perspectives align in highlighting how creativity stems from both reflection on existing knowledge and the ability to synthesize seemingly unrelated ideas into novel solutions. For example, the creation of the paperclip—a simple yet indispensable invention—can be seen as an act of bisociation that reduces complexity to its core function while addressing a universal need.

Similarly, Koestler's concept applies to modern design breakthroughs like the electric car, which integrates advancements in battery technology with sustainable energy practices to address contemporary environmental challenges. Both Johnson and Koestler also underscore the interplay between tradition and innovation in producing enduring works of art and science. Just as Renaissance painters built upon classical techniques while introducing new perspectives, modern innovators rely on foundational knowledge while pushing boundaries to create transformative solutions. Whether through the integration of diverse technologies or the cultivation of collaborative networks, these processes demonstrate that creativity thrives at the intersection of existing frameworks and bold new ideas.

In literature, T.S. Eliot's *The Waste Land* illustrates deliberate complexity, layering references to mythology, religion, and modern despair, requiring readers to engage deeply with its intent to fully appreciate its meaning. Similarly, in science, Charles Darwin's use of metaphor in *On the Origin of Species* shaped the reception of evolutionary theory by creating accessible yet symbolic narratives of survival and adaptation. His *Tree of Life* metaphor, for instance, provided a vivid illustration of how species branch out from common ancestors, diverging and evolving over time. This imagery not only helped readers visualize the interconnectedness of all life forms but also underscored the dynamic, ever-changing nature of evolution, making an abstract scientific concept more relatable and easier to grasp.

Artistic intention shapes not only the creation but also the reception of a work. As BYU professor Collin Bradford notes, understanding an artist's intent enriches our experience of their work by providing critical context. Consider Felix Gonzalez-Torres's *Perfect Lovers*, which features two synchronized clocks gradually falling out of sync—a poignant metaphor for love and mortality. Without knowledge of the artist's intent, viewers might dismiss it as mundane or purely decorative. However, understanding its conceptual underpinnings transforms it into a deeply moving piece. Similarly, Walead Beshty's shattered glass boxes gain significance when one learns they were intentionally designed to break during transit, symbolizing how objects acquire meaning through movement and context.

In contrast, AI-generated content—while sometimes impressive in scope and coherence—lacks intrinsic purpose or an understanding of why certain choices matter. Language models like GPT-4 produce compelling prose based on probabilistic associations within vast datasets but lack the reflective process that imbues creative work with personal and cultural meaning. Critics argue that AI cannot emulate the intentionality that drives human creativity. As Felix Gonzalez-Torres noted about his own work, art is often about leaving a mark that says: "I existed: I was here. . . I had an idea and I had a good purpose." This sense of purpose is absent in AI-generated works because machines lack consciousness, emotions, or lived experience.

Serendipity and Unpredictability

Some of history's greatest creative breakthroughs have emerged from serendipitous moments. Alexander Fleming's accidental discovery of penicillin and Helen Frankenthaler's "soak-stain" technique in abstract expressionism illustrate how chance, combined with an openness to the unexpected, can lead to transformative innovation. Serendipity often arises from human curiosity and the ability to embrace mistakes or randomness as opportunities for growth.

In the world of science, Henri Poincaré described a moment of sudden clarity when stepping onto a bus, realizing the geometric relationships that would become a cornerstone of chaos theory. Similarly, Barbara McClintock's discovery of "jumping genes" in maize came after she noticed unexpected patterns and allowed intuition to guide her analysis. In mathematics, Andrew Wiles's proof of Fermat's Last Theorem was marked by a moment of serendipity when he revisited an old idea that suddenly connected previously unrelated concepts.

In the arts, the spontaneous scribbles that Pablo Picasso added to early drafts led to the revolutionary development of Cubism, and John Cage's experimentation with randomness in music—such as using the I Ching (the ancient Chinese Book of Changes), where elements of chance were left to chance to determine notes—demonstrated how relinquishing control could result in groundbreaking compositions.

Steven Paley, author of *The Art of Invention*, emphasizes that creative individuals often reinterpret mistakes or unexpected outcomes as opportunities for innovation. For example, the invention of the Post-it Note at 3M illustrates how serendipity and adaptability can transform failure into success. Spencer Silver, a 3M scientist, was attempting to create a strong adhesive when he instead developed a uniquely repositionable, low-tack adhesive with no immediately obvious application. However, Art Fry, another 3M scientist, recognized its potential as a bookmark that could stick temporarily to paper without damage, leading to the creation of the now-iconic Post-it Note.

This process highlights how human creativity thrives on the ability to assign new meaning to unforeseen results, turning "failed" experiments into groundbreaking products. Similarly, Thomas Edison's famous remark, "I have not failed. I've just found 10,000 ways that won't work," underscores the value of persistence and reframing failure as part of the creative process.

Mistakes are not merely setbacks but steppingstones toward innovation when approached with a growth mindset and vision. In contrast, AI systems can introduce variability through randomization algorithms but are inherently bound by predefined parameters and lack the cognitive flexibility to reinterpret errors meaningfully. While machine learning models like reinforcement learning agents can simulate exploration by incorporating randomness into their decision-making processes, they lack the intentionality and reflective capacity that humans bring to serendipitous discoveries.

Arthur I. Miller notes that even in machine learning's exploration of randomness, serendipity remains constrained by mathematical rules rather than genuine openness to reinterpretation. For instance, while randomized algorithms in AI can enhance robustness and diversity—such as in generative adversarial networks (GANs)—within a framework designed for optimization rather than discovery through error. However, researchers are exploring ways to incorporate exploration-based reinforcement learning to simulate serendipitous breakthroughs. Techniques like curiosity-driven learning or inverse reinforcement learning aim to mimic human-like exploration by encouraging AI systems to seek out novel states or solutions. While promising, these approaches still fall short of replicating the human ability to assign symbolic meaning or emotional resonance to unexpected outcomes.

The concept of "AI serendipity" offers another intriguing avenue for addressing this limitation. Scholars like Dr. Christian Busch, in *The Serendipity Mindset: The Art & Science of Creating Good Luck*, argue that fostering serendipity in AI requires designing systems that balance relevance with randomness, enabling algorithms to surprise users with unexpected yet meaningful discoveries. Busch emphasizes that true serendipity is not merely about chance but about creating conditions where unexpected connections can spark meaningful outcomes.

For instance, recommendation systems that introduce controlled variability—like Netflix's shuffle feature—can nudge users toward unexplored content while maintaining contextual relevance. However, Busch also notes that serendipity often stems from our personal openness and interpretive flexibility, which machines struggle to replicate. Human serendipity arises from unique combinations of memory, emotion, and curiosity, which influence how we recognize something as meaningful. Thus, while AI can simulate serendipitous moments by widening the range of possibilities, it cannot yet fully replicate the human ability to ascribe deeper personal meaning to these surprises.

This insight suggests that while AI-generated "discoveries" may expand creative horizons, they remain tethered to their programmed parameters. In contrast, human serendipity often results from navigating uncertainty and adapting to unforeseen circumstances—a process enriched by subjective experience. Busch's work reinforces the idea that true creativity, including artistic breakthroughs, is not just about randomness or recombination but also about recognizing and seizing moments of meaningful connection—a capacity that remains distinctly human.

Where AI Excels

Computer scientists, as discussed throughout this chapter, highlight that AI excels at pattern recognition, iteration, and the generation of creative outputs by leveraging vast datasets and computational power. Through layered neural networks that mimic certain aspects of human cognition, AI systems can identify intricate patterns, generate novel combinations, and refine outputs through repeated processes. However, while AI may appear to "think," its operations are fundamentally rooted in encoded instructions and probabilistic modeling rather than conscious reasoning or intent. It refines outputs through trial and error, much like how neurons fire and adjust in the human brain, but without the subjective awareness or emotional depth that defines human thought.

This process echoes Ada Lovelace's prescient observation that "The Analytic Engine weaves algebraic patterns just as the Jacquard loom weaves flowers and leaves." Lovelace recognized that while machines could manipulate symbols and produce complex outputs, they lack the originality and intentionality of human creators. The Jacquard loom, for instance, could create intricate textile designs by following pre-programmed punch cards, yet it was a tool entirely dependent on the creativity of its human operators. Similarly, modern AI systems can weave intricate "patterns" of data—whether generating text, images, or music—but these outputs are shaped by the training data provided by humans and the goals set by programmers. The creativity lies not in the machine itself but in how it is used as a tool to augment human imagination and exploration.

The roots of computer-generated art trace back to the pioneering work of Georg Nees, who showcased his algorithmic drawings at the Technische Hochschule Stuttgart in 1965. Nees used mathematical algorithms to create pieces like *Schotter* ("Gravel"), where random variables disrupted structured grids to create images transitioning from order to chaos. This early demonstration of generative art laid the groundwork for today's AI-driven creativity, demonstrating that machines can participate in aesthetic exploration while guided by human intent.

Mathematics remains central to this creative partnership. Descartes' Cartesian geometry revolutionized visual representation by mapping shapes to algebraic equations, providing a foundation for computational graphics and enabling artists and scientists to systematically explore geometric forms. This innovation paved the way for fractals, discovered by Benoit Mandelbrot, which describe infinitely complex patterns found in nature. Fractals became essential tools in entertainment, enabling realistic landscapes in films like *Doctor Strange*, where complex, kaleidoscopic dimensions folded and shifted with mathematical precision, creating visually stunning alternate realities.

Loren Carpenter, a pioneering computer graphics researcher and co-founder of Pixar, revolutionized film with his application of fractal algorithms. His groundbreaking work at Boeing and later at Lucasfilm demonstrated how mathematical models of chaos could generate naturalistic planetary surfaces, most notably in the Genesis planet sequence in *Star Trek II: The Wrath of Khan*. Carpenter's innovations laid the groundwork for procedural generation techniques, which continue to influence modern visual effects and animation by allowing filmmakers to simulate vast, realistic worlds with unprecedented detail and coherence.

Fractals have since played a pivotal role in shaping Pixar's cinematic worlds, where fractal-based textures are used to render lifelike details in virtual environments, from rocky cliffs and tree branches to sweeping distant landscapes. These techniques not only enhance visual realism but also contribute to the emotional and narrative depth of the films by creating immersive, believable settings. Beyond cinema, fractal generation has become integral in gaming and virtual reality (VR), where it helps build expansive, interactive worlds that would be impossible to create manually. For instance, games on platforms like PlayStation and PC frequently use fractal-based noise functions to procedurally generate complex terrains and ecosystems, enhancing both realism and gameplay interactivity. These applications underscore how mathematical principles extend beyond visual aesthetics to drive narrative and experiential depth in modern storytelling, bridging the gap between technology and creative expression.

This mathematical language underpins AI systems like DeepDream and GANs. DeepDream, developed by Google engineers, works by enhancing and amplifying patterns detected in images, creating surreal compositions that resemble dreamlike hallucinations. The system visualizes what neural networks "see" by iteratively enhancing the features they detect, making familiar objects morph into fantastical, fractal-like structures. This process raises questions about how machines interpret visual data and the creative potential of revealing machine perception.

GANs, pioneered by Ian Goodfellow, operate differently by using two competing networks—a generator and a discriminator—to create new, realistic images. The generator creates images from random noise, while the discriminator evaluates them and provides feedback, pushing the generator to improve its outputs. This adversarial process enables GANs to simulate creative processes, producing outputs that range from photorealistic portraits to abstract art forms.

Together, these advancements in mathematical modeling, AI, and procedural design illustrate the profound ways in which mathematics drives creativity across disciplines. Whether rendering fantastical movie scenes, crafting immersive game worlds, or revealing the hidden layers of neural networks, mathematical frameworks continue to expand the boundaries of human and machine-made art, enriching the storytelling experience in diverse ways.

Gerhard Richter's *4900 Farben*, a series of paintings constructed from randomized colored grids, exemplifies how human artists also explore chance and structure. Richter, known for his mastery in both abstraction and photorealism, often challenged the boundaries between control and spontaneity. *4900 Farben* reflects his fascination with color theory and randomness, as he meticulously arranged the grids using a systematic yet unpredictable process to create unique visual experiences. Each composition invites viewers to contemplate the relationship between order and chaos, showing that even within randomness, human agency remains central. By contrast, AI's engagement with randomness is more mechanical, following programmed parameters and repeating processes without the contemplative intent that characterizes Richter's approach to meaning and form.

AI's strengths in creative fields can be categorized as follows:

- Combinatorial Creativity: AI excels at combining pre-existing elements in novel ways by identifying patterns across massive datasets. For example, music generation software can blend genres to create hybrid compositions, assisting composers in uncovering new musical possibilities. AI-generated musical collaborations, such as those involving Amper Music, show how the fusion of human direction and machine capabilities can lead to unexpected harmonies.
- Generative Creativity: Systems like GANs simulate creative processes and produce original visual art based on learned styles. This technology has been used in gaming and film to generate prototypes and immersive visuals. GAN-generated scenes in virtual reality applications create dynamic worlds by continuously improving upon randomized input data, enabling more realistic and surreal visual environments. Similarly, DeepDream enhances and amplifies the patterns detected in images to create dreamlike, kaleidoscopic visuals that invite questions about perception and representation.
- Pattern Discovery: AI is highly effective at detecting patterns and solutions that human creators may overlook. In *How AI Ate the World*, Chris Stokel-Walker highlights how AI-assisted tools in architecture and film editing generate templates that allow creators to refine their artistic vision. For example, in architectural design, tools like

Spacemaker use AI to suggest efficient layouts for urban projects, freeing architects to focus on aesthetics and user experience.

However, du Sautoy cautions that despite their capabilities, AI systems lack the serendipitous leaps and emotional resonance that define human creativity. While AARON, the AI painting program created by Harold Cohen, produces vibrant compositions by following encoded artistic rules, and *The Painting Fool* attempts to simulate artistic behavior with randomness and contextual prompts, their outputs remain reflections of the parameters set by their programmers rather than autonomous artistic intent. These systems excel at producing aesthetically interesting works but struggle with conveying the personal narrative and purpose that define human creativity.

Brad Smith, president of Microsoft, and Harry Shum, former executive vice president at Microsoft, argue in *Tools and Weapons* that coders are modern artists, crafting digital canvases with algorithms that push aesthetic and functional boundaries. They emphasize that while AI can expand creative possibilities, its autonomy is often overstated. Human oversight shapes every system, and ethical principles must guide its development to ensure accountability and societal benefit. Smith and Shum highlight the need for transparency and fairness in AI systems, warning against the risks of bias or misuse if these technologies are left unchecked. Their perspective underscores the duality of AI as both a tool for innovation and a potential source of harm if not responsibly managed.

Scholars like Ethan Mollick and Mustafa Suleyman build on these concerns by exploring the limitations of AI in fostering true innovation. Mollick, a professor at the Wharton School, University of Pennsylvania, argues that while AI can assist creators by automating repetitive tasks and generating drafts, it lacks the intuition required to disrupt creative paradigms. He emphasizes that AI's reliance on historical data often reinforces existing conventions rather than challenging them. For example, while generative AI can produce art or music in the style of past masters, it struggles to break free from inherited patterns to create something genuinely transformative. Mollick also warns that effective collaboration with AI requires human oversight to ensure outputs align with ethical standards and societal values.

Mustafa Suleyman, co-founder of DeepMind and author of *The Coming Wave*, adds that AI's dependence on historical data poses risks beyond artistic stagnation—it can perpetuate cultural biases embedded in its training sets. He explains that while AI systems are adept at synthesizing existing knowledge, their outputs are inherently shaped by the data they consume. This raises concerns about whether AI can ever achieve true originality or whether it will remain constrained by the limitations of its programming. Suleyman also introduces the concept of "the containment problem," emphasizing the importance of maintaining control over increasingly powerful AI tools to prevent unintended societal consequences.

Both Mollick and Suleyman highlight the need for human involvement not only in guiding AI's outputs but also in shaping its purpose. As Mollick notes, effective use of AI requires humans to remain "in the loop," providing critical oversight to prevent errors or biases from undermining its utility. Similarly, Suleyman argues that fostering innovation with AI demands a balance between leveraging its capabilities and addressing its limitations. This includes designing systems that encourage exploration while ensuring they align with human values and ethical considerations.

Together, these perspectives emphasize that while AI has immense potential to augment human creativity and productivity, it remains fundamentally dependent on human intention and oversight. Coders may be modern artists crafting digital tools, but their creations require careful stewardship to ensure they serve society responsibly rather than reinforcing existing inequalities or stifling innovation. As Smith and Shum remind us, the future of AI lies not in its autonomy but in how humans choose to shape and direct its capabilities.

This duality—AI as both a tool and a constraint—raises important questions about the future of art. Will AI remain a sophisticated studio assistant, refining human visions, or could it evolve into a collaborator that challenges creators to think in new ways? The concept of a "studio assistant" is not new; throughout history, master artists have relied on apprentices and assistants to execute portions of their work, often blending collective labor with individual genius. For example, Renaissance masters like Michelangelo and Raphael employed teams of assistants to help paint large frescoes, with apprentices often entrusted with background elements or detailed finishing work.. Similarly, in the Baroque era, Peter Paul Rubens maintained an extensive workshop where assistants contributed to the grandeur of his large-scale commissions.

In these historical contexts, the master artist maintained creative control, guiding the overall vision while relying on their assistants' craftsmanship to achieve scale and precision. Today, AI functions in much the same way—enhancing efficiency, producing iterations, and even suggesting stylistic variations. However, as AI systems grow more sophisticated, they are increasingly capable of producing outputs that diverge from direct instructions, introducing unexpected patterns and interpretations.

By reflecting and remixing artistic traditions, AI may push artists to reconsider assumptions about form, meaning, and innovation. Just as the historical use of studio assistants allowed for the exploration of grander narratives and complex compositions, AI could open new avenues for artistic experimentation, prompting creators to embrace randomness, collaboration, and even co-authorship.

Interestingly, AI's engagement with past styles may have an unexpected benefit: it forces human artists to reflect more deeply on their own assumptions about form and meaning. By encountering works generated by machines—pieces that echo familiar forms but lack intentionality—artists may be inspired to push boundaries in new directions. This dynamic mirrors historical moments when technological advances spurred artistic revolutions, such as the invention of photography prompting Impressionist painters to explore light and movement in unprecedented ways.

For example, when IBM's Watson created a trailer for the horror movie *Morgan*, it analyzed thousands of existing trailers to identify patterns in pacing, music, and imagery before assembling its own version. While Watson's trailer was effective at evoking suspense, it also highlighted how formulaic certain elements of filmmaking had become—prompting filmmakers to reconsider their reliance on conventional tropes. This reinforces the idea that AI may not only generate content but also encourage human creators to reassess their creative instincts, potentially leading to new artistic breakthroughs.

The integration of artificial intelligence into the creative process has sparked a debate about whether it will serve as a valuable collaborator or inadvertently lead to the erosion of human creativity. Remo Pareschi, a scholar and author of *Centaur Art: The Future of Art in the Age of Generative AI*, envisions a future where humans and AI collaborate symbiotically, with AI augmenting human creativity rather than replacing it. This "centauric intelligence," as he describes it, could enable artists to transcend traditional limitations and explore entirely new forms of expression.

Critics, though, warn of potential pitfalls. Anne Ploin, a researcher at the Oxford Internet Institute, notes that while machine learning tools can assist artists in exploring new techniques, they may also disrupt traditional skill-building processes, leading to a decline in manual proficiency over time. This "laziness paradox," as described by Cash Myers, an innovation theorist and speaker on technology and creativity, suggests that the convenience of AI might tempt creators to rely too heavily on algorithms, diminishing their own creative input and critical thinking skills.

Moreover, some fear that AI could devalue human creativity altogether. Zhao Tingyang, a keynote speaker on art and AI ethics, warns that AI's ability to imitate established styles threatens the artistic identity of creators whose unique approaches risk being diluted in an AI-saturated market. This concern is echoed by cultural theorist Tallon Austin, who points out that AI's feedback loops—where models are trained on increasingly homogenized datasets—could limit diversity and experimental art forms.

While proponents argue that AI offers unprecedented opportunities for experimentation and collaboration, skeptics caution that over-reliance on these tools could lead to complacency among artists or even a loss of the uniquely human drive for self-expression. The challenge lies in finding a balance: leveraging AI as a tool to inspire and enhance creativity while preserving the intuition, emotional depth, and cultural context that define human artistry.

As Pareschi, an accomplished researcher and creative technologist known for his work at the intersection of computational creativity and media arts, suggests, as do many other research experts, the true potential of AI lies not in replacing human creativity but in complementing it—enabling artists to push boundaries while maintaining their essential role as the primary creative force. Pareschi has been instrumental in developing AI-driven systems that serve as creative partners rather than mere tools, focusing on how machine learning can be harnessed to enhance rather than overshadow human ingenuity.

Blending Human and Machine Creativity

These conversations pose a provocative and timely question: Are coders our new artists? By designing algorithms capable of generating music, literature, and visual art, programmers are undeniably reshaping the creative landscape. OpenAI's GPT models, for example, have written poetry and prose that blur the line between human and machine authorship. Yet we know these outputs are inherently constrained by the data they are trained on, reflecting humanity's collective knowledge rather than introducing entirely new ideas. This raises profound philosophical questions about the nature of creativity: Is art merely the recombination of existing patterns, or does it require breaking rules and inventing paradigms—as Marcel Duchamp did with his readymades or Stravinsky with atonal music? Can an algorithm ever achieve this level of innovation, or is it destined to remain a tool for exploring variations within established frameworks?

The future of creativity no longer hinges on a binary choice between humans and machines but is unfolding as a thoughtful collaboration. Artists across disciplines are already using AI as a partner in their creative processes, amplifying their potential rather than replacing it. Visual artists incorporate AI-generated textures and color palettes as inspiration, writers employ AI tools to brainstorm plot ideas or refine language, and architects rely on generative algorithms to prototype innovative designs before infusing them with their personal vision and meaning. In this evolving model, AI acts as a catalyst for human ingenuity, offering new perspectives while empowering creators to shape the final product.

However, meaningful breakthroughs in creativity require more than technological augmentation—they demand emotional depth, intuition, and a willingness to take existential risks. These uniquely human qualities remain central to transformative artistry. Ethan Mollick and Mustafa Suleyman echo this sentiment, emphasizing that true originality often emerges from grappling with ambiguity, failure, and uncertainty—experiences that machines cannot replicate.

The ethical and philosophical implications of this collaboration cannot be ignored. Brad Smith and Harry Shum argue that coders act as digital visionaries by shaping algorithms capable of producing aesthetic outputs. However, their role raises critical questions about ownership and responsibility. Who deserves credit when an AI-generated masterpiece emerges—the coder who designed the algorithm? The user who provided the prompts? Or should the work be considered a collective product of humanity's shared knowledge? Attribution becomes even more complex when considering the training data used to develop these systems. Many generative models rely on datasets scraped from copyrighted works or culturally significant materials without consent or acknowledgment. This practice not only raises legal concerns about intellectual property infringement but also ethical questions about fairness and respect for cultural heritage. Without clear guidelines for transparency and accountability, AI risks becoming a disruptor in ways that undermine trust in creative industries.

A Shared Future

The future of creativity will likely be defined by collaboration—a dynamic interplay between human intuition and machine precision. By harnessing the strengths of both humans and machines, society can push the boundaries of innovation while preserving what makes creativity uniquely human: its capacity for insight, emotional connection, and transformative meaning-making. However, this partnership demands vigilance and thoughtful stewardship. Machines must not merely replicate existing patterns or reinforce biases; they must challenge creators to think differently, inspire new perspectives, and respect ethical principles of fairness, accountability, and transparency.

Scholars and innovative thinkers emphasize that prompt engineers and coders already now play pivotal roles in shaping the creative landscape. These individuals act as intermediaries between human intention and machine execution, effectively defining what society views as "creative." This influence places significant responsibility on those designing algorithms to ensure that AI systems foster exploration, diversity, and originality rather than stagnation or homogenization. Coders must consciously guide their creations to challenge conventions, confront biases embedded in training data, and expand the possibilities of artistic expression.

The integration of AI into creative fields also raises profound philosophical questions about the nature of art itself. If creativity involves breaking rules and inventing paradigms—as seen in the revolutionary works of Marcel Duchamp or Stravinsky—can a machine ever achieve such innovation? Or will its outputs always remain constrained by the parameters set by its human designers? These questions provoke deeper reflection on the essence of creativity: Is it defined by the novelty of the output, the process of creation, or the intent behind it?

As AI continues to evolve, these debates will shape how we understand not only art but also humanity's role in an increasingly machine-influenced world.

While AI systems have demonstrated remarkable capabilities in assisting with creative tasks—generating images, composing music, or drafting literature—they are not replacements for human ingenuity. Instead, they are tools that can amplify human potential when used responsibly. For instance, visual artists might use AI-generated textures as inspiration for their work, writers may employ AI to refine language or brainstorm ideas, and architects could rely on generative algorithms to prototype designs before infusing them with personal vision. In this way, AI becomes a collaborator that enhances human creativity rather than undermining it. However, collaboration with AI is not without risks. Over-reliance on algorithmic processes could lead to a homogenization of artistic expression, where efficiency is prioritized over originality. Furthermore, algorithms trained on historical data may perpetuate cultural biases or reinforce conventional norms unless creators consciously intervene to challenge these patterns.

Ethical guidelines and legal frameworks must evolve alongside AI technologies to address issues such as authorship, attribution, intellectual property rights, and cultural appropriation. Transparency in how AI systems are trained and deployed will be essential for ensuring fairness and accountability. Whether seen as tools, collaborators, or co-creators, AI systems have the potential to reshape art—not by replacing humanity, but by inspiring it to reach new heights.

This partnership between humans and machines echoes historical moments when technological advancements—such as the invention of oil paints in tubes or digital editing software—expanded creative possibilities without diminishing the role of human creators. Similarly, AI has the capacity to enrich artistic expression by broadening the scope of what is possible, empowering creators rather than making them obsolete.

Creativity will remain a distinctly human endeavor, defined by qualities such as intuition, emotional depth, serendipity, and intentionality—attributes that machines can illuminate through collaboration but cannot fully replicate. By approaching this relationship with care and responsibility, society can ensure that AI serves as a catalyst for innovation while preserving the integrity of human expression.

Ultimately, creativity transcends mere output; it is about meaning-making, personal expression, and intentionality. While AI can assist in generating novel and aesthetically pleasing results or exploring new possibilities within existing frameworks, it lacks the intrinsic ability to imbue creations with purpose or emotional resonance. This evolving partnership between humans and machines offers an unprecedented opportunity to redefine creation in the twenty-first century—a chance to push artistic boundaries while safeguarding the uniquely human capacities for insight, emotion, and authenticity.

To fully harness AI's potential, its development and use must be guided by ethical principles that prioritize equity, diversity, and respect for individual creators and cultural traditions. Establishing clear norms around transparency, attribution, and responsible use will ensure that AI serves as a collaborator rather than a disruptor or diminisher of human creativity. By embedding these values into the creative process, we can ensure that this new era of art preserves the essential qualities that make it a profound reflection of our shared humanity.

Works Referenced

Arendt, Hannah. *The Human Condition.* University of Chicago Press, 1958.

Boden, Margaret A. *The Creative Mind: Myths and Mechanisms.* 2nd ed., Routledge, 2004.

Bourgeois, Louise. *Spider.* Tate Modern, 1997.

Bradford, Collin. "Artistic Intention and Context.' *BYU Studies Quarterly*, vol. 58, no. 1, 2019, pp. 45–67.

Bradford, Collin. "Understanding Artistic Intent." *BYU Studies Quarterly*, vol. 56, no. 4, 2017.

Brandt, Anthony, and David Eagleman. *The Runaway Species: How Human Creativity Remakes the World.* Catapult, 2017.

Busch, Christian. *The Serendipity Mindset. The Art & Science of Creating Good Luck.* Penguin Random House, 2020.

Cope, David. *Experiments in Musical Intelligence.* A-R Editions, 1996.

Demmer, Theresa Rahel, et al. "The Impact of Artificial Intelligence on Art Perception." *Computers In Human Behavior*, vol. 122, 2021.

Duchamp, Marcel. *The Writings of Marcel Duchamp.* Edited by Michel Sanouillet and Elmer Peterson, Da Capo Press, 1989.

du Sautoy, Marcus. *The Creativity Code: Art and Innovation in the Age of AI.* Harvard University Press, 2019.

Eagleman, David. "Creativity and the Brain." *Nature Neuroscience*, vol. 14, no. 2, 2011, pp. 137–39.

Evans, Walker. *Untitled [Urban Architecture Series].* 1928–1930, Museum of Modern Art, New York.

Ferguson, Kirby. "Everything is a Remix." *YouTube Series*, 2010–2021, www.everythingisaremix.info. Accessed 13 Feb. 2025.

Frankenthaler, Helen. *Helen Frankenthaler: Paintings on Paper (1949–2002).* Edited by Karen Wilkin and Elizabeth Smith, Skira Rizzoli Publications, 2013.

Gompertz, Will. *Think Like an Artist: and Lead a More Creative, Productive Life.* Penguin Books, 2015.

Gonzalez-Torres, Felix. *Perfect Lovers.* 1991, Museum of Modern Art, New York.

Johnson, Steven. *Where Good Ideas Come From: The Natural History of Innovation.* Riverhead Books, 2010.

Kleon, Austin. *Steal Like an Artist: 10 Things Nobody Told You About Being Creative.* Workman Publishing, 2012.

Koestler, Arthur. *The Act of Creation.* Hutchinson, 1964.

Lovelace, Ada. "Notes on the Analytic Engine." In *Ada Lovelace: The Making of a Computer Scientist* (pp. 26–66), edited by Christopher Hollings et al., Bodleian Library Publishing, 2018.

Lubbock, Tom. *Great Works: 50 Paintings Explored.* Frances Lincoln, 2011.

Malevich, Kazimir. *Black Square.* 1915, State Tretyakov Gallery, Moscow.

Martin, Agnes. *Untitled #5.* 1984, Solomon R. Guggenheim Museum, New York.

Miller, Arthur I. *The Artist in the Machine: The World of AI-Powered Creativity.* MIT Press, 2019.

Mollick, Ethan. "Artificial Intelligence and the Future of Work." *Harvard Business Review*, 2023.

Mollick, Ethan. "AI and Creativity." *Journal of Business Innovation*, vol. 34, no. 3, 2024.

Munch, Edvard. *The Sick Child.* 1885–86, National Gallery, Oslo.

Myers, Cash. "The Laziness Paradox: AI and Creative Decline." *Technology and Society Review*, vol. 12, no. 2, 2024.

Oates, Joyce Carol. "On Writing as a Communal Act." *The New York Review of Books*, vol. 45, no. 8, 1998.

O'Keeffe, Georgia. *Red Canna.* 1924, High Museum of Art, Atlanta.

Paley, Steven. *The Art of Invention: The Creative Process of Discovery and Design.* Prometheus Books, 2010.

Pareschi, Remo. *Centaur Art: The Future of Art in the Age of Generative AI.* MIT Press, 2024.

Picasso, Pablo. *Les Demoiselles d'Avignon.* 1907, Museum of Modern Art, New York.

Pollock, Jackson. *No. 5.* 1948, Private Collection.

Richter, Gerhard. *4900 Farben.* 2007, Serpentine Gallery, London.

Rowland Scherman: The Photography of Timeless. Loring Art Museum Exhibition Catalog, 2019.

Smith, Brad, and Harry Shum. *Tools and Weapons: The Promise and the Peril of the Digital Age.* Penguin Press, 2019.

Stokel-Walker, Chris. *How AI Ate the World.* HarperCollins, 2023.

Suleyman, Mustafa. *The Coming Wave: Technology, Power, and the Twenty-first Century's Greatest Dilemma.* Crown, 2023.

Turing, Alan M. "Computing Machinery and Intelligence." *Mind*, vol. 59, no. 236, Oct. 1950, pp. 433–60.

Four Beyond the Algorithm
The Essence of AI

The history and evolution of artificial intelligence (AI) reflect a fascinating journey from ancient myths to modern technological marvels. This trajectory is marked by the contributions of pioneering figures and groundbreaking companies that have transformed AI from a conceptual dream into a world-shaping force. It is a story of scientific curiosity, philosophical ambition, and societal transformation.

The conceptual origins of AI can be traced to ancient philosophical questions about whether machines could emulate human reasoning. However, the modern foundation was laid by Alan Turing, often called the "father of AI." In his seminal 1950 paper *Computing Machinery and Intelligence*, Turing posed the provocative question, "Can machines think?" To explore this, he proposed the "imitation game," later known as the Turing Test, as a way to evaluate machine intelligence. In this game, a human interrogator interacts with two unseen entities—one human and one machine—through text-based communication. If the interrogator cannot reliably distinguish which is which; that is, the machine's output is considered indistinguishable from that of a human, then the machine is said to have demonstrated "intelligent" behavior. The test shifted the focus from abstract definitions of "thinking" to a practical, behavior-based assessment of whether machines could convincingly replicate human responses.

Turing's imitation game was groundbreaking because it bypassed metaphysical debates about the nature of consciousness and instead framed intelligence as observable performance. This approach influenced not only early computer science but also sparked discussions about the potential for machines to engage in more creative, abstract thought. While the Turing Test was initially applied to areas like language processing and problem-solving, its implications for creativity emerged over time. The idea that a machine might one day "fool" a human into believing it authored a poem, composed a symphony, or painted a picture aligns with contemporary debates about AI-generated art and literature.

Modern applications of Turing's ideas extend beyond mere imitation of human conversation. Generative AI models like Stable Diffusion, ChatGPT, and Google Imagen are, in a sense, heirs to the imitation game, as they are designed to produce outputs that humans might mistake for creative works made by people. Turing's test thus remains relevant today, not only as a measure of machine intelligence but also as a philosophical touchstone for assessing whether machines can create in ways that resonate with human emotion, originality, and intent.

The official birth of AI as a distinct field came in 1956 at the Dartmouth College Conference, a landmark event organized by John McCarthy, Marvin Minsky, Claude Shannon, and Nathaniel Rochester. This conference was a pivotal moment in the history of computing, as it brought together mathematicians, cognitive scientists, and computer engineers who believed that human-like intelligence could be replicated in machines. John McCarthy, who coined the term "artificial intelligence," envisioned the development of machines that could reason, learn, and solve complex problems autonomously. He foresaw a future where machines could process information and make decisions in a way comparable to human cognition.

Marvin Minsky, a co-founder of MIT's AI Lab and one of the most influential figures in early AI research, contributed immensely to fields such as neural networks, robotics, and knowledge representation. Minsky was a strong advocate for symbolic AI, an approach that relied on encoding knowledge as symbols and rules. His work laid the groundwork for the development of expert systems, which could replicate human decision-making in specialized fields. Meanwhile, John McCarthy developed Lisp, a programming language that became foundational to AI research. Lisp's importance stemmed from its ability to handle symbolic data and its support for recursion—a process where a function calls itself to solve smaller instances of a problem, making it especially useful for tasks like mathematical computations and data structure manipulation. Lisp's flexibility made it the programming language of choice for many early AI systems and remains influential in modern AI research.

Despite the optimism surrounding the Dartmouth College Conference, early AI systems soon encountered notable limitations. Initial successes, such as Allen Newell and Herbert Simon's *Logic Theorist*, demonstrated that machines could prove mathematical theorems using symbolic reasoning. This program was hailed as a "thinking machine" capable of replicating human problem-solving processes. Another milestone was Joseph Weizenbaum's *ELIZA*, a program that simulated conversation by responding to text inputs with pre-programmed scripts designed to mimic a psychotherapist's questions. While *ELIZA* was an early example of natural language processing and captivated the public's imagination, it was also limited in its capabilities—it did not "understand" the conversation but instead relied on pattern matching and scripted responses.

The limitations of these early systems stemmed from their reliance on rigid, rule-based approaches. These systems lacked the ability to adapt, generalize, or learn from new information beyond their predefined rules. They excelled in narrow domains but failed when presented with ambiguous or unexpected inputs. For example, the *Logic Theorist* could solve mathematical proofs but could not apply its reasoning to broader, less-structured problems. Similarly, *ELIZA* could simulate therapeutic dialogue but failed to engage meaningfully with deeper, context-dependent questions. These shortcomings highlighted the need for more flexible, learning-based approaches to AI, setting the stage for the eventual development of machine learning and neural networks that moved beyond symbolic AI's constraints.

By the 1970s, the limitations of symbolic AI—the approach that relied on explicitly programmed rules and logic—became apparent, leading to what became known as the "AI winter." This period of stagnation was marked by unmet expectations, as early AI systems failed to achieve the ambitious goals set by their creators. Researchers had promised machines that could reason and learn as humans do, but symbolic AI struggled with tasks that required adaptability, intuition, and learning from real-world environments. When AI systems encountered scenarios outside their programmed knowledge base, they were prone to errors and often incapable of generalization. As a result, enthusiasm waned, funding for AI projects was cut, and research momentum slowed as skepticism about AI's potential grew. The "AI winter" highlighted the gap between theoretical aspirations and practical limitations, forcing the field to reconsider its foundational methods.

However, the 1980s and 1990s saw a resurgence of interest in AI, driven by major breakthroughs in both technology and theory. One key factor in this revival was the rise of expert systems—computer programs designed to mimic the decision-making abilities of human specialists within narrow domains. Edward Feigenbaum's *Dendral* exemplified this approach, becoming the first successful expert system used in scientific research. Developed for chemical analysis, *Dendral* could predict molecular structures based on spectrometric data, outperforming human experts in some cases. This success demonstrated AI's potential to excel in specialized tasks where structured data and domain-specific rules could be leveraged effectively. The commercial applications of expert systems in fields such as medicine, engineering, and finance fueled renewed investment and optimism in AI.

In parallel, advancements in neural networks provided a new direction for AI research. Unlike symbolic AI, which relied on explicitly defined rules, neural networks were designed to mimic the architecture of the human brain by using interconnected nodes (artificial neurons) to process information. A breakthrough came with the development of the backpropagation algorithm by Geoffrey Hinton and his colleagues. Backpropagation enabled neural networks to learn from data by adjusting their internal weights based on errors in their predictions, a process analogous to how humans learn from mistakes. This algorithm allowed networks to identify complex patterns in large datasets, opening the door to applications in image recognition, speech processing, and other fields that required adaptive learning.

During this period, AI research began exploring the potential for machines to engage in creative imitation within the arts and creative fields. Projects like Harold Cohen's *AARON*, an early example of a computer program designed to create original artwork, pushed the boundaries of what AI could achieve creatively. *AARON* was not merely an expert system applying predetermined rules; it could generate abstract paintings by making decisions about shapes, forms, and colors based on its programming and its "understanding" of artistic composition. Cohen's goal was not to replicate human art exactly but to explore whether a machine could exhibit behaviors some would describe as "creative." This was a significant departure from traditional symbolic AI and demonstrated that machines could imitate creative processes rather than merely producing static outputs.

Similarly, in the late 1990s, another technological breakthrough rocked the art and design world with IBM's *Deep Blue*, the chess-playing supercomputer that defeated world champion Garry Kasparov. While primarily seen as a triumph of machine learning in gaming, *Deep Blue* symbolized something greater—it was a system capable of strategic "creativity" in its play. Kasparov himself remarked that some of the moves made by *Deep Blue* during the match seemed startlingly "human" in their unpredictability and brilliance. This challenged the notion that creativity is solely the domain of artistic pursuits and illustrated that even within structured activities like chess, creativity could emerge as the ability to make unconventional, surprising decisions. *Deep Blue*'s victory became a cultural moment, showing the world that machines were not only catching up to humans in computational power but also in their capacity to make decisions that mirrored human ingenuity.

A little over a decade later, machine learning once again demonstrated its prowess in a different intellectual arena when IBM's Watson competed on *Jeopardy!*, defeating two of the game's greatest champions, Ken Jennings and Brad Rutter. Unlike chess, where moves follow a rigid set of rules, *Jeopardy!* required Watson to interpret natural language, understand puns, and retrieve the most relevant answer with astonishing speed. Watson's victory highlighted how AI could navigate human language and knowledge, further expanding the boundaries of machine intelligence.

The convergence of expert systems, neural networks, and creative AI projects demonstrated the potential for hybrid approaches, combining domain-specific expertise with data-driven learning and imitative creativity. However, these advancements also underscored the complexity of defining creativity itself—was creativity merely the recombination of known elements, or did it require novelty and intent that machines lacked? This period of experimentation in creative AI showed that while machines could convincingly imitate certain forms of artistic expression, their "creativity" was still a reflection of the data and parameters provided by human designers.

The 2010s marked a turning point with the advent of deep learning. Pioneered by researchers like Geoffrey Hinton, Yann LeCun, and Yoshua Bengio—known collectively as the "godfathers of deep learning"—this approach revolutionized natural language processing, computer vision, and generative models. Deep learning models, powered by vast datasets and advanced neural network architectures, made it possible for machines to not only recognize patterns but also generate new content that closely mimicked human creativity. Companies like Google, OpenAI, and DeepMind scaled these technologies to global significance, embedding AI into everyday life through voice assistants, recommendation systems, and creative tools.

One of the most groundbreaking examples of AI creativity during this period was DeepMind's *AlphaGo*, which made headlines in 2016 by defeating world champion Lee Sedol in the complex game of Go—a game renowned for its reliance on intuition and creativity rather than brute-force calculation alone. The match captivated global audiences, as *AlphaGo* made surprising, unconventional moves that stunned even experienced players, demonstrating that reinforcement learning algorithms could exhibit forms of strategic creativity that appeared uniquely human.

In 2024, AI's creative potential was showcased through a project at UC Merced that transformed photographs into Cubist-style artworks inspired by Pablo Picasso and Georges Braque. Led by Professor Miguel Á. Carreira-Perpiñán, the research team used advanced machine learning algorithms to deconstruct and reimagine images into the fractured geometric forms characteristic of Cubism.

The project analyzed visual elements such as shapes, colors, and spatial relationships within photographs, then reassembled them into abstract compositions capturing the essence of early twentieth-century Cubist art. The outputs included surreal reinterpretations of iconic subjects, such as a scenic landscape transformed into a fragmented mosaic of angular planes and a portrait of Albert Einstein reimagined as a Cubist masterpiece.

These works not only paid homage to the artistic innovations of Picasso and Braque but also demonstrated how AI could bridge historical art movements and contemporary technology. The project sparked discussions about AI's role in preserving cultural traditions while simultaneously creating new forms of data-driven or algorithmic art.

In music, projects like OpenAI's *MuseNet* and *Jukedeck* demonstrated that AI could compose original pieces in various styles, from classical to jazz, blending notes and rhythms in ways that surprised and delighted listeners. Similarly, tools like OpenAI's *DALL-E* erased the line between text and image generation by producing vivid, imaginative artwork from simple textual descriptions. These tools empowered not only professional artists but also everyday users to experiment with creative outputs, democratizing the art and design process.

In addition to Turing, McCarthy, and Minsky, figures like Demis Hassabis, the co-founder of DeepMind, have advanced reinforcement learning through innovations that predict protein structures with groundbreaking accuracy. Hassabis, who also has a background in neuroscience and game design, emphasized the importance of using AI to tackle grand scientific challenges, bridging the gap between computation and creativity. In recognition of his contributions despite not being a trained chemist, Hassabis was awarded the Nobel Prize in Chemistry in 2024 for his work on AlphaFold and its transformative impact on molecular biology.

Meanwhile, companies such as OpenAI have pushed the boundaries of generative AI with their GPT models, which demonstrated unprecedented capabilities in generating coherent text, crafting poetry, and even mimicking distinct literary styles. These generative models sparked a new era of creative writing tools, enabling journalists, screenwriters, and novelists to collaborate with AI as a "co-author" capable of enhancing their creative workflows.

Sam Altman and Elon Musk have played pivotal roles in shaping the development of artificial intelligence, particularly through their involvement in founding OpenAI in 2015. Their shared vision was to develop AI technologies that would benefit humanity, ensuring that Artificial General Intelligence (AGI) reflected human values and was not monopolized by large corporations or government entities. Under Altman's leadership as CEO, OpenAI became instrumental in developing some of the most influential generative models to date, including the GPT series and DALL-E, which revolutionized natural language processing and generative art, respectively.

However, concerns over the unchecked development of AI and potential misalignment with ethical principles led to a philosophical split between Musk and Altman. Musk voiced strong warnings about the dangers of superintelligent AI, emphasizing the existential threats it could pose to humanity if not properly regulated. His departure from OpenAI in 2018, partly due to conflicts with Tesla's AI initiatives, marked a turning point in their collaboration.

In 2023, Musk launched Grok, a generative AI chatbot developed under his new venture, xAI. Grok was integrated directly with X (formerly Twitter), aligning with Musk's vision of creating an "everything app" that combined social media, communications, and AI-powered assistance. Unlike OpenAI's more measured approach, Grok provided edgier, real-time interactions with fewer content restrictions, reflecting Musk's philosophy of open dialogue and minimal censorship.

Another major player in the AI revolution is NVIDIA, a company renowned for designing high-performance graphics processing units (GPUs) that have become indispensable in the field of artificial intelligence. Originally focused on gaming and graphics, NVIDIA has expanded its influence by creating specialized AI hardware that accelerates machine learning processes. NVIDIA's GPUs and AI hardware have become the backbone of machine learning systems, powering everything from medical diagnostics to autonomous vehicles, as well as enabling complex creative endeavors. NVIDIA's platform Canvas uses AI to convert rough sketches into photorealistic landscapes in real time, making it a revolutionary tool for digital artists and designers. These innovations underscore the role of hardware in supporting increasingly sophisticated AI applications that diminish the distinction between human and machine creativity.

The fusion of deep learning, generative AI, and creative experimentation has made the early twenty-first century a pivotal era not only for scientific advancements but also for the arts and humanities. From AI-generated poetry and music to interactive VR installations powered by neural networks, this period reinforced the notion that creativity, once thought to be an exclusively human domain, could be emulated—and in some ways, redefined—by machines. Generative models such as OpenAI's *GPT* have shown the ability to compose short stories, screenplays, and even persuasive essays, raising questions about AI's role as a "co-author" alongside human creators. Similarly, iterations of *DALL-E* redefined visual storytelling by generating vivid, surreal, or hyperrealistic images from simple textual descriptions. These tools empowered filmmakers, digital artists, and game designers to conceptualize and visualize ideas faster than ever before, significantly expanding the creative process.

AI's integration into the arts has also introduced immersive, cross-sensory experiences. Interactive VR installations powered by neural networks have emerged as a new medium of expression, allowing users to "step into" evolving works of art generated in real time. Google's *Tilt Brush* allows artists to paint in 3D space using VR, opening new creative dimensions and redefining performance and spatial art.

In the film and animation industry, AI tools like NVIDIA's *GANverse3D* have enabled creators to automatically generate 3D models from 2D images, speeding up character and environment design. AI has also influenced fashion and design—*Project Runway*'s AI-powered challenge featured algorithms that could analyze trends and recommend creative combinations of patterns and colors, underscoring the increasing convergence of human intuition and machine learning in aesthetic decisions.

AI's influence extends beyond the arts to other critical industries. In healthcare, systems like IBM Watson Health assist in diagnostics and personalized treatment plans, while medical imaging systems powered by deep learning help detect diseases such as cancer with remarkable precision. In transportation, autonomous systems like Tesla's Full Self-Driving technology showcase the potential for AI to revolutionize mobility. Meanwhile, AI-based recommendation engines have transformed entertainment platforms such as Netflix and Spotify, tailoring content to user preferences and creating personalized experiences.

Neural Networks: The Foundation of AI Creativity

At the heart of AI's capabilities lies neural networks—a computational model inspired by the structure and functioning of the human brain. Neural networks consist of interconnected layers of nodes, or "neurons," that process and analyze data. Each layer in the network performs a specific operation, passing the results to the next, enabling the network to learn and refine its performance over time. While this structure is inspired by the biological brain, it is not an exact replication but rather an abstraction designed to simulate certain aspects of human cognition and learning.

Neural networks learn through a process known as *training*, which involves feeding the system large datasets and allowing it to adjust the "weights" of the connections between nodes. These weights determine the strength of the signal passed between one node and the next. The initial weights are assigned randomly, and the network's early predictions tend to be inaccurate. However, using an algorithm such as *backpropagation*, the system calculates the error in its predictions and adjusts the weights iteratively to minimize that error. This process, much like how the brain strengthens certain synaptic connections through experience, allows the network to improve its accuracy in recognizing patterns.

For example, if a neural network is tasked with identifying images of zebras, it initially makes guesses about which features indicate "zebra-ness." After being corrected for mistakes, it learns that features such as black-and-white stripes, body shape, or mane patterns are more significant than irrelevant details like background scenery. Over time, the network "learns" to generalize from the training data and can identify zebras in new, unseen images.

However, unlike the human brain, neural networks lack the flexibility and complexity to form memories, adapt to ambiguous stimuli, or process emotional and contextual nuances. While the brain can learn from small amounts of data and make connections across different sensory inputs, neural networks require enormous datasets and structured input to function effectively.

Deep neural networks, which form the core of *deep learning*, are advanced neural networks with multiple hidden layers between the input and output nodes. Each layer extracts progressively more abstract features from the data. For example, in image recognition tasks, the first layer may identify edges and contours, the second layer may detect shapes, and later layers may recognize entire objects or scenes.

This layered processing mirrors, to some extent, how the human brain processes sensory information. In the visual cortex, for instance, neurons are organized hierarchically, with early layers detecting simple patterns like edges and later layers recognizing complex shapes, motion, and color. However, a key difference is that neural networks process information sequentially through their layers, whereas the human brain processes information in parallel and integrates multiple types of sensory input simultaneously. Additionally, the brain adapts more efficiently, requiring fewer examples to learn a concept and continuously refining its understanding through experience, context, and reinforcement.

Algorithms and Process Engineers

The performance and creative potential of AI systems depend heavily on the algorithms and processes designed by engineers, data scientists, and artists. Process engineers play a critical role in selecting the architecture of the neural network, curating datasets, and defining the objectives and parameters that guide how the AI generates outputs. The creative decisions made by these engineers shape the "personality" of the AI system, determining how it balances factors like randomness, coherence, and originality in its creations. Ultimately, these systems return us to the fundamental question of who deserves credit as the "artist"—those who program and guide the AI or the machine itself, which executes and manifests the creative process in its final form.

For example, when developing OpenAI's *DALL-E*, process engineers needed to fine-tune the neural network's capacity to interpret natural language prompts and translate them into visually coherent images. They adjusted the system's ability to blend concepts in novel ways—such as generating an image of "an avocado-shaped armchair"—without straying into incomprehensible or overly abstract results. Similarly, in Google's *DeepDream* project, engineers modified the network's settings to exaggerate pattern detection, leading to the generation of surreal, dreamlike images filled with hyperactive fractal patterns and hidden shapes. These results demonstrate that creative outputs from AI are not accidental; they are influenced by the algorithmic "choices" engineers make during training and optimization.

In the realm of music, the development of AI systems like Sony's *Flow Machines* required engineers to design algorithms that balance stylistic adherence with innovation. For example, when *Flow Machines* generated the song *Daddy's Car* in the style of The Beatles, the engineers chose datasets filled with compositions from specific time periods and applied rules to ensure that the music retained certain harmonic structures while still allowing the system to introduce novel elements. In this sense, process engineers acted as curators and conductors, shaping the creative direction of the AI while leaving room for it to "improvise."

In the world of fashion and design, process engineers working on platforms like *The Fabricant* (an AI-driven digital fashion house) use algorithms to combine user-generated prompts with pretrained data on textures, silhouettes, and materials. By adjusting the "randomness" factor of the neural network, they can control whether the outputs are highly conventional or wildly experimental. This illustrates how human creators and engineers collaborate with AI, using algorithmic tuning to find a balance between chaos and structure, much like an artist adjusts their brushstrokes to achieve a specific aesthetic.

The way neural networks "learn" to identify patterns has significant implications for creativity. Just as the brain combines memories, sensory inputs, and learned patterns to generate creative ideas, neural networks can "synthesize" elements from their training data to create new outputs. For instance, in generative AI models such as *DALL-E* or *StyleGAN*, the neural network doesn't merely replicate existing images—it blends features from different inputs to create novel images that have never existed before. This ability to "combine" and "remix" is like how human creativity often involves drawing connections between unrelated ideas.

However, human creativity, as discussed throughout this book, involves more than pattern recognition—it encompasses intuition, emotional resonance, and the ability to bend and break rules in ways neural networks cannot. In the words of Nigerian fine artist Peter Uka, when asked how he creates his paintings, he said, *"I'm pulling from the archive in my head."* This illustrates the deeply human aspect of creativity, where memories, emotions, and lived experiences intertwine to inform artistic expression. Neural networks, to date, operate within the confines of their training data and the constraints set by their human designers. They do not possess intrinsic motivation, self-awareness, or an understanding of aesthetics or narrative meaning. In contrast, the human brain forms dynamic connections across multiple regions, integrating sensory, emotional, and experiential inputs to create meaning and originality that can evoke powerful emotional responses.

Neural Networks and Multimodal Creativity

Recent advancements in neural networks have pushed the boundaries of creative AI further by introducing *multimodal* models that process and combine different types of inputs, such as text, images, and sound. OpenAI's *CLIP* and *GPT-4* are examples of multimodal systems that can "understand" both textual and visual data. These systems reflect, to a degree, the brain's ability to synthesize information from multiple senses to form creative associations. For example, a human may hear a piece of music and visualize a corresponding scene, just as a multimodal AI can generate an image based on a descriptive prompt.

Despite these parallels, neural networks remain a far cry from the holistic, context-driven creativity of the human brain. Neural networks excel at "mimicking" patterns and generating outputs based on probabilistic associations within their data, but they do not possess the lived experience, emotional intelligence, or self-awareness that inform human creativity. Nonetheless, process engineers and data scientists can imbue AI systems with greater flexibility and refinement through algorithmic innovations, reinforcing that the creative power of AI is inherently tied to human decisions and design. Yet, as we embark on this uncharted territory of machine-assisted creativity—something neither wholly human nor entirely artificial—we are left to wonder: what is it within our lexicon of human experience to call this new frontier?

Thus, while neural networks borrow structural inspiration from the brain's interconnected neurons, they function in fundamentally different ways. Engineers and designers play a crucial role in shaping how these networks operate, acting as co-creators who define the system's creative boundaries. This human-AI collaboration has produced remarkable innovations across visual arts, music, and fashion, but it also underscores the complex interplay between algorithmic design and artistic intent.

Generative Adversarial Networks (GANs): A Key Innovation

GANs are a specialized form of neural networks that play a pivotal role in generative AI. Invented by Ian Goodfellow in 2014, GANs consist of two neural networks working in tandem:

1. The Generator: Creates new data based on patterns learned from a training dataset, such as generating images or text.
2. The Discriminator: Evaluates whether the generated data is authentic or artificial by comparing it to the training dataset.

These two networks engage in a competitive process, where the generator attempts to fool the discriminator while the discriminator improves its ability to detect fakes. Over time, the generator becomes increasingly adept at producing data that is indistinguishable from real examples, enabling the creation of highly realistic or imaginative outputs.

AI systems like ChatGPT have revolutionized the creative landscape by generating text, sound, and visual art that replicate styles or produce novel compositions. However, Steven Paley, in *The Art of Invention*, cautions that creativity is tied to intentionality, problem-solving, and the expression of personal vision. AI, lacking consciousness and emotional experience, operates solely on algorithms trained to recognize and mimic patterns. For example:

- An AI-generated painting might replicate Jackson Pollock's drip technique with striking accuracy but lacks the spontaneity or philosophical intent that informed Pollock's work.

- ChatGPT can compose poetic phrases or suggest themes for art but does so by analyzing linguistic patterns rather than experiencing inspiration or emotional resonance.

These distinctions according to Paley underscore a critical limitation: AI can simulate the aesthetic outcomes of creativity but cannot replicate the depth, context, and meaning derived from human experience.

A striking example of AI's application in creative fields that questions these limitations is the case of country musician Randy Travis, who lost his voice due to a debilitating stroke. With the help of GAN technology, his sound-alike voice was reproduced, enabling him to "sing" again. While this application shows AI's ability to preserve and emulate a person's unique vocal identity, it raises profound questions about authenticity. Does a digitally replicated voice evoke the same emotional connection as the original? Can it truly capture the inflections and imperfections that convey human vulnerability and depth?

Supporters of such technology highlight its potential to help the human condition. For artists like Travis, AI offers a way to reconnect with audiences and continue their creative legacy despite physical limitations. It serves as a bridge, preserving artistic expression in the face of adversity. Much like artificial limbs enable individuals to walk or run, restoring mobility and enhancing their quality of life, AI-assisted voice replication empowers artists to regain a form of creative expression they might otherwise have lost. Both technologies provide impressive benefits not just to the individuals who use them but to society, inspiring resilience and demonstrating the possibilities of human ingenuity.

This debate echoes broader concerns about AI-generated images. While AI can mimic aesthetics or techniques with remarkable precision, it often lacks the capacity to evoke the same emotional response. As art critic John Berger suggested in *Ways of Seeing*, art's power lies in its ability to provoke thought and stir emotion, rooted in the context and intention of its creator. AI reproductions, no matter how technically proficient, may struggle to achieve this level of connection.

Ultimately, the use of GAN highlights the dual-edged nature of AI technology. It offers unprecedented possibilities for overcoming human limitations while challenging traditional notions of authenticity and emotional depth.

This tension underscores the ongoing dialogue about AI's role in creativity: whether it can transcend its algorithmic foundations to engage with the human spirit or whether it will remain an extraordinary tool with aesthetic but not emotional capabilities.

Case Study: Portrait of Edmond de Belamy

A landmark example of GAN-generated art is *Portrait of Edmond de Belamy*, prompted by the Paris-based collective Obvious in 2018. The genesis of the portrait lies in a GAN trained on a dataset of 15,000 historical portraits spanning several centuries. The resulting image smudges the lines between human and machine creation, presenting a ghostly, unfinished aesthetic that evokes both familiarity and strangeness. Notably, the portrait does not depict a real person but was algorithmically designed to resemble a historical figure, creating an illusion of authenticity while embodying a figure who never existed.

The portrait made headlines when it sold at Christie's auction for $432,500, far exceeding its estimated value. This sale sparked intense debates about authorship and creativity, with critics questioning whether the credit for the work belonged to the machine or to the human curators behind it. While the GAN-generated the portrait, human involvement was critical at every stage: curating the dataset, fine-tuning the algorithm's parameters, and selecting this image from numerous possibilities.

The collective's decision to leave the portrait unfinished, with milky features and a signature in the form of an algorithm, was a deliberate choice designed to provoke questions about the nature of creativity and the role of AI in art. As David Eagleman observes in *The Runaway Species*, creativity often involves bending, breaking, and blending existing ideas—a process that remains fundamentally guided by human intent, even in AI-generated works.

Portrait of Edmond de Belamy illustrates both the capabilities and limitations of AI in art. While it challenges traditional notions of art and authorship, the work ultimately reflects a collaborative process between human imagination and machine computation, highlighting how technology can augment but not replace the introspective and intentional aspects of human creativity. However, it also raises a critical question: should the output of such processes be considered "art" at all, or does it require a new classification that acknowledges its algorithmic origins? Critics argue that calling AI-generated works "art" risks conflating human creativity, which is driven by emotion and context, with computational mimicry, which operates within predefined parameters. This debate underscores the need to reassess how we define art in an era where machines play an increasingly significant role in creative expression. By reframing such outputs with distinct terminology, we may better capture the unique interplay between human and machine contributions in these creations.

The Next Rembrandt: Reviving a Master's Style

A few years ago, a team of data scientists, art historians, and engineers unveiled *The Next Rembrandt*, an ambitious project that harnessed GANs to create a new painting in the distinctive style of the Dutch master. By analyzing 346 of Rembrandt's known works, the team developed sophisticated algorithms capable of replicating his brushstrokes, color palettes, and compositional techniques. The result was a portrait so convincingly authentic that it could easily be mistaken for an original Rembrandt—an uncanny fusion of technology and artistry that blurred the division between human creativity and machine precision.

The process began with the meticulous digitization of Rembrandt's complete works in high resolution, providing a comprehensive dataset for the AI to analyze. Facial recognition software was employed to study the exact features of his subjects, while deep learning algorithms parsed patterns in lighting, texture, and composition. From this wealth of data, the AI synthesized a "new" Rembrandt portrait, complete with historically accurate attire and facial expressions. To add another layer of authenticity, the final image was rendered using a 3D printer designed to replicate the thickness and texture of Rembrandt's characteristic brushstrokes.

While *The Next Rembrandt* was widely celebrated as a technological marvel, it also ignited intense debate within the art community. Critics questioned whether an AI-generated painting could truly be considered "art" in the traditional sense. Was it merely an impressive imitation, or did it represent a new form of creativity born from the collaboration between humans and machines? These questions, as touched upon earlier, raise even deeper philosophical issues about the nature of art, creativity, and authorship in the AI age.

Beyond philosophical musing, the project also raises critical legal and ethical questions. Who owns the rights to an artwork created by an algorithm? Should credit be given to the team of engineers and historians, the AI itself, or perhaps even Rembrandt's estate? While *The Next Rembrandt* avoided legal complications since the Dutch master's works are in the public domain, allowing the team to freely analyze and replicate his style without copyright infringement, the project foreshadows more complex legal disputes in cases involving modern artists whose works are still protected.

Looking to the future, the implications of *The Next Rembrandt* are far-reaching. The technology used could revolutionize art restoration by reconstructing damaged or incomplete works with unprecedented accuracy. Art historians might leverage similar AI tools to analyze an artist's body of work, uncovering hidden patterns and insights that would otherwise go unnoticed. Museums and galleries could also create immersive exhibitions featuring "new" works by historical artists like Monet or Caravaggio, offering audiences fresh interpretations of their styles and techniques.

However, as promising as these applications may be, they come with concerns. Recreating or extending the works of historical artists risks detaching their art from its original cultural and historical context. Art critic Jonathan Jones, writing in *The Guardian*, condemned *The Next Rembrandt* as a "travesty of surface trickery," asserting that it reduces art to mere technical reproduction, devoid of the profound human understanding and emotional resonance that give it meaning. But is it even fair to invoke Rembrandt in this context? His works were deeply tied to the human experience of his time, shaped by his personal struggles and the socio-political realities of seventeenth-century Europe—elements that no algorithm can genuinely replicate. Furthermore, the use of existing artworks to train AI, particularly without the consent of the original artists or their estates, raises questions about exploitation and the respect owed to artistic legacies.

AI-Da and the Question of Authorship

AI-Da, a humanoid robot equipped with GANs and other AI technologies, represents a disruptive fusion of robotics and artificial intelligence in the arts. Named after Ada Lovelace, often regarded as the first computer programmer, AI-Da was designed to push the boundaries of what machines can achieve in creative expression. Unlike projects solely focused on replicating the styles of historical artists, AI-Da is programmed to create entirely original works. Using her mechanical arm, cameras embedded in her eyes, and advanced algorithms, AI-Da produces drawings, paintings, and even sculptures, showcasing her versatility across mediums.

AI-Da's creative process is guided by her ability to analyze and synthesize various artistic styles and techniques. Her programming allows her to interpret and respond to visual stimuli in real time, enabling her to produce works that are not mere reproductions but unique creations. For instance, she can observe a live subject or an environment and translate these inputs into abstract or representational artworks, blending machine precision with artistic unpredictability. This capability has made AI-Da a focal point of exhibitions worldwide, where her works are displayed alongside those of human artists.

The reception of AI-Da's work has indeed been polarizing, much like *The Next Rembrandt* project. Supporters argue that AI-Da's creations spark critical discussions about the intersection of technology and art, serving as a lens to explore the evolving relationship between humans and machines. Her exhibitions at renowned venues like the Design Museum in London and the Victoria and Albert Museum have drawn significant public interest, presenting her as both an artist and a technological marvel.

Does the rise of AI in the arts lead us toward new horizons of creativity, or does it edge us closer to an unsettling future where human expression is overshadowed by machines? AI-Da, with her ability to generate original works, forces us to confront these questions. Her creations erase the boundaries of artistic practice, offering a provocative glimpse into a world where human and machine creativity intertwine in ways we've never seen before. As technology advances, AI-Da's work becomes both a beacon and a warning—inviting us to explore the philosophical and ethical implications of AI in the arts while cautioning against its unchecked influence.

And if we view AI as an artist independent of its human collaborators, what human qualities might we ascribe to it? Do we see creativity, intention, or emotional depth in its work? Can we attribute to it a sense of purpose or identity? And if so, what rights and responsibilities do we grant it? Shall we treat AI as a "person" subject to our laws, ethics, and social norms, or does it exist within its own universe, free to define its own rules and artistic boundaries?

In moments like this, we might recall the words of philosopher Antonio Gramsci:

The old world is dying,
And the new world struggles to be born;
Now is the time of monsters.

Is AI a harbinger of this monstrous age, or is it the key to unlocking a new realm of artistic potential?

Refik Anadol and the Transformation of Data

Refik Anadol's *Machine Hallucinations* series exemplifies another example of the transformative potential of GANs in creating immersive, data-driven art installations. Anadol, a media artist and pioneer in the integration of artificial intelligence and visual storytelling, uses vast datasets—ranging from architectural archives and satellite imagery to cultural collections—as the foundation for his work. These datasets are fed into GANs, which analyze and reinterpret the information to produce dynamic visuals that resemble abstract dreamscapes or otherworldly virtual environments.

The term *Machine Hallucinations* refers to the way GANs process and transform data, almost mimicking the subconscious mind's ability to interpret and combine memories, impressions, and sensory experiences. By visualizing this process, Anadol's installations provide viewers with a glimpse into the "thought processes" of machines, making the invisible workings of AI tangible and experiential. These visuals often appear as flowing, multi-dimensional forms with shifting colors and patterns that evoke a sense of wonder and contemplation.

A hallmark of Anadol's work is its ability to erase the frontier between physical and digital spaces. For example, his installations often use large-scale projections, LED displays, and spatial audio to envelop audiences in a multisensory environment. The result is a deeply interactive encounter that invites viewers to engage not only visually but also emotionally and intellectually with the artwork. Anadol's use of GANs demonstrates how raw data—often considered sterile and impersonal—can be transformed into something approximating human and emotionally resonant.

One of the most notable pieces in the *Machine Hallucinations* series involved processing over 300 million images of New York City, including architectural blueprints, aerial photography, and street-level visuals. The GANs synthesized this data to create a fluid, dreamlike representation of the city that felt both familiar and surreal. In this way, Anadol's work explores the intersection of memory, perception, and technology, reimagining urban landscapes as living, breathing entities shaped by both human and machine interpretation.

The *Machine Hallucinations* series goes beyond aesthetic appeal to provoke deeper questions about how we perceive and interact with data. By transforming vast amounts of information into immersive images, Anadol invites viewers to reconsider the value and meaning of data in a digital age. His work also sparks conversations about the role of AI in shaping cultural experiences, showcasing how technology can bridge the gap between the analytical and the emotional, the technical and the artistic.

GANs in Popular Culture: Anime Characters and NFTs

GANs have impacted anime culture, transforming both the creation and consumption of anime (animation) characters. Anime, renowned for its vibrant visuals, exaggerated expressions, and intricate designs, has become a global cultural phenomenon, shaping industries such as film, television, and gaming. By leveraging GANs, creators can now generate entirely new anime characters that rival human-made designs in quality and creativity. These AI-generated characters are not only used in creative projects but are also being monetized as NFTs, opening new revenue streams for artists and expanding the frontiers of digital art.

A prominent example of this technology is MakeGirlsMoe, an AI-powered platform that allows users to design customizable anime characters effortlessly. The platform provides tools for adjusting features like hair color, eye shape, and facial expressions, catering to both casual fans and professional artists. With features such as "Random Mode" for spontaneous creation and "Advanced Mode" for detailed customization, MakeGirlsMoe democratizes anime-style character design. Its free access and intuitive interface make it especially appealing to younger audiences and those without traditional artistic skills, enabling broader participation in anime culture.

By simplifying the creative process while maintaining high-quality outputs, platforms like MakeGirlsMoe have become valuable tools for personal projects, storytelling, and artistic experimentation. The impact of such platforms extends beyond individual creativity. They inspire younger generations to explore visual arts and storytelling while fostering a deeper appreciation for anime's distinctive aesthetics. For professional artists, these tools offer opportunities to experiment with new styles and push the boundaries of their creative expression.

The integration of AI into anime culture mirrors a broader trend of blending technology with traditional art forms, expanding both the possibilities for artistic creation and the accessibility of visual media. Anime itself occupies a unique place in global culture. Originating in Japan, it serves as both entertainment and a reflection of Japanese identity and societal values. Through diverse genres that range from science fiction and fantasy to slice-of-life narratives, anime explores universal themes such as friendship, love, resilience, and morality while also addressing societal critiques specific to Japan, including isolation, overwork, and shifting family dynamics.

Globally, anime introduces audiences to Japanese culture through depictions of traditional food, festivals, mythology, customs, and architecture. Iconic series like *Naruto*, *Dragon Ball Z*, and Studio Ghibli films have transcended cultural boundaries to become household names worldwide. Streaming platforms like Crunchyroll and Netflix have further expanded anime's reach by making it accessible to diverse audiences. While anime enjoys widespread global popularity, its influence is particularly profound in Asian cultures. In countries like China, South Korea, Hong Kong, and Taiwan, Japanese animation has significantly shaped local media production and youth culture. For many in Asia, anime serves not just as entertainment but also as a cultural bridge that fosters admiration for Japan's creativity and storytelling traditions.

In contrast, anime's reception in Western cultures has followed a different trajectory. Initially viewed as an exotic or niche art form, it has gradually entered mainstream consciousness through dedicated fandoms, conventions, and collaborations between Japanese and Western studios. This growing acceptance has allowed anime to establish itself as a legitimate component of global pop culture.

The monetization of GAN-generated characters through NFTs further highlights the fusion of AI with blockchain technology in reshaping digital ownership. NFTs provide secure proof of authenticity using blockchain systems while enabling artists to monetize their creations directly. Platforms like OpenSea facilitate marketplaces where collectors can buy or trade these unique assets. Additionally, NFTs often incorporate smart contracts, which are self-executing agreements encoded into the blockchain that automatically enforce terms such as royalty payments or resale conditions whenever an NFT is sold or transferred. This ensures that creators can continue earning revenue from secondary sales without relying on intermediaries or manual processes. This integration exemplifies how AI-driven innovations like MakeGirlsMoe are not only democratizing creativity but also redefining how art is produced, owned, and valued in the digital age—marking a major shift in the commercial landscape of creativity worldwide.

Enhancing Human Creativity: Collaborative Role

Rather than replacing human creativity, AI and especially GANs have emerged as a powerful collaborator—expanding artistic possibilities and challenging traditional notions of originality and authorship. This shift reframes AI as a co-creator, capable of enhancing human vision and pushing creative boundaries. Scholars like University of Pennsylvania professor Ethan Mollick, in *Co-Intelligence*, argue that AI should be embraced as a partner in the artistic process, enabling humans to achieve more than they could alone. In line with Mollick's perspective, the authors also view GAN-based AI as a collaborator in the creative process, one that can inspire, refine, and amplify artistic endeavors while maintaining the human artist's role at the center of meaning and intent.

Mollick emphasizes that the most transformative potential of AI lies in "co-intelligence," where humans and machines work symbiotically to amplify creative outcomes. This collaboration doesn't diminish human agency but rather redefines it, allowing creators to delegate mechanical or time-consuming aspects of their work to AI while retaining control over interpretation, intent, and final decisions. For instance, an artist might use an AI tool to generate a series of variations on a theme, using the outputs as inspiration while imbuing the final revised piece with their personal vision and meaning.

Mollick and Gompertz also highlight the experimental nature of creativity, where failure is a critical part of innovation. AI, with its ability to generate multiple iterations quickly, becomes an invaluable tool for artists, designers, and writers to explore ideas that might otherwise be abandoned due to time or resource constraints. By enabling rapid prototyping and ideation, AI fosters a dynamic environment where creators can experiment freely, embracing the failures and unexpected outcomes that often lead to groundbreaking discoveries.

However, scholars like Mollick caution against over-reliance on AI, stressing that true creativity is rooted in curiosity, intentionality, and the human capacity to challenge norms. While AI excels at "combinational creativity," recombining existing elements in novel ways, it lacks the ability to engage in "transformational creativity"—a paradigm-shifting process that involves redefining the boundaries of artistic and cultural frameworks. The human role in creativity is not just about producing work but also about questioning assumptions, interpreting meaning, and connecting with audiences on an emotional and cultural level.

Ultimately, the integration of AI into the creative process offers both opportunities and challenges. By amplifying human ingenuity while challenging traditional definitions of creativity, AI pushes the boundaries of what is possible in art, design, and storytelling. Moving forward, the key lies in striking a balance: embracing AI as a collaborator that enhances human potential while ensuring that the core of creativity—curiosity, intent, and emotional resonance—remains uniquely human. However, achieving this balance may prove more difficult than anticipated, as AI systems continue to develop at an extraordinary pace, raising the possibility that they may eventually "think" or make decisions independently, without human prompting or intervention. This prospect underscores the urgent need for thoughtful frameworks to guide the ethical and creative use of AI in the years ahead.

Futurists like Jaron Lanier, a computer scientist, philosopher, and one of the pioneers of virtual reality, caution against seeing AI as an autonomous creator.

Lanier emphasizes that AI systems inherently reflect the biases, limitations, and intentions of their human developers and training datasets. He argues that over-reliance on generative technologies risks prioritizing efficiency over depth, leading to homogenized outputs that lack the originality and emotional resonance central to human creativity. Lanier warns of the dangers of "lazy creativity," where artists might bypass the discipline and effort traditionally associated with art-making in favor of quick, machine-generated results, potentially diluting the richness of artistic exploration.

One of Lanier's central critiques is the lack of transparency in how AI systems are trained. Many generative models, such as those used in platforms like MidJourney or ChatGPT, rely on datasets scraped from the internet without proper attribution or consent. This raises ethical questions about exploitation and intellectual property. Legal battles, such as Getty Images' lawsuit against Stability AI for using its copyrighted database without permission, highlight these tensions. Critics also question whether AI-generated art should be clearly identified or watermarked to ensure transparency and prevent the misrepresentation of machine-generated works as human-created.

AI systems trained on large datasets often incorporate works and styles from diverse cultures without understanding or respecting their context or significance. This lack of cultural sensitivity can lead to unintentional appropriation, where traditional motifs or designs are repurposed in ways that commodify or distort their meaning.

To address these concerns, critics like Mary Anne Staniszewski advocate for embedding ethical guidelines into AI training processes. These could include collaboration with cultural experts to curate datasets responsibly, as well as educational efforts to inform users about the origins and meanings of styles invoked by their prompts.

Ethical and Practical Concerns

The rapid adoption of AI in the creative industries also raises questions about over-reliance on technology.

- **Erosion of Traditional Skills**: By automating labor-intensive tasks, AI risks devaluing manual craftsmanship and traditional artistic techniques. Over time, artists may become less inclined to develop foundational skills by learning directly from masters, shifting focus entirely to prompt-based creation.

- **Homogenization of Art**: As AI systems become ubiquitous, the outputs generated may converge stylistically, leading to a loss of diversity and uniqueness in art. Critics fear that an over-reliance on AI could result in a cultural landscape dominated by algorithmically optimized aesthetics.

Transparency and Regulation

Advocates argue that AI-generated works should be accompanied by clear disclosures, identifying them as machine-generated. Watermarking systems could help distinguish AI outputs from human-created art, preserving trust and transparency in creative industries. Moreover, ethical frameworks should address the following:

- **Data Provenance**: AI developers must disclose the sources of their training datasets, ensuring that artists whose works were used are credited or compensated. This transparency would help bridge the gap between technological innovation and the protection of artistic rights.
- **Fair Use and Licensing**: Establishing clear guidelines for how copyrighted works can be incorporated into training datasets would reduce conflicts like those seen in the Getty Images lawsuit.

Continuing New Insights and Examples

The collaborative role of AI is expanding into diverse fields, offering unique insights and possibilities while simultaneously raising complex ethical and philosophical questions.

- **Virtual Sculpting**: Artists like Zach Lieberman use AI to create dynamic digital sculptures that respond to viewer interactions. These "living sculptures" evolve with each engagement, challenging traditional notions of permanence in art.

- **Creative Writing**: Platforms like Sudowrite assist authors in generating storylines, character arcs, and vivid descriptions. These tools act as brainstorming partners, preserving the writer's voice while offering alternative directions or refining prose.
- **Fashion and Design**: AI tools such as CLO 3D allow designers to prototype clothing in real time, offering precise simulations of fabric drape, texture, and movement. This capability reduces material waste and accelerates the design process.

The acceptance of AI as part of the cultural evolution of art will depend on its integration into existing institutions and practices. Art schools may need to adapt curricula to teach students how to collaborate with AI tools effectively, while museums and critics must grapple with how to evaluate and contextualize AI-generated works. Meanwhile, collectors and media critics will play a crucial role in determining whether AI-driven art becomes a staple of the contemporary art market or remains a niche phenomenon.

Creativity Reimagined

Artificial intelligence has undeniably reshaped the creative landscape, offering unprecedented tools for exploration, experimentation, and innovation. Yet its limitations illuminate why human artistry remains irreplaceable. Art is deeply rooted in emotion, intent, and cultural context—qualities that machines cannot replicate. The artist's role extends beyond mere creation; it encompasses interpretation, critique, and the forging of connections with audiences. As Grace Hartigan famously remarked, "The artist must know exactly what the experience is. . . The manipulation of materials in an artwork is a result of this state of mind." This profound connection between creator and creation remains the cornerstone of what we define as art.

While AI-generated works may find acceptance by communities that value innovation and technology, such as digital art collectives, avant-garde galleries, and tech-savvy curators eager to push the boundaries of traditional mediums, they should not be conflated with traditional art forms that are inextricably linked to human experience. Early opinion leaders might emerge from interdisciplinary spaces where art, technology, and philosophy intersect—think of artists who explore generative processes, academic institutions with a focus on media arts, and influential voices in tech-oriented cultural forums. Yet, art is not merely about the final product; it is about the journey of exploration, the intent behind each choice, and the cultural and historical narratives embedded within the work.

Art has always been a dynamic interplay between human imagination and technological innovation, evolving from prehistoric cave paintings to Impressionist landscapes to today's digital canvases. Each technological advancement, from the invention of oil paints to the rise of photography, has expanded the boundaries of artistic possibilities while challenging preconceived notions of what art can be. AI, particularly through GANs, represents the latest chapter in this continuum of innovation, reshaping the creative process and redefining concepts of originality, authenticity, and authorship.

History demonstrates that new tools and technologies do not diminish human creativity but instead amplify it, enabling art to move into uncharted territories. Paint tubes allowed Impressionists to paint outdoors, capturing fleeting moments of light; photography freed artists from the constraints of realism, inspiring abstraction and modernism. Similarly, AI and GANs have the potential to push creativity beyond traditional limits, serving as collaborators that augment human ingenuity rather than replacing it.

However, this partnership demands careful navigation. While AI expands what is possible, it also challenges us to ensure that technology enhances rather than eclipses the emotional depth and cultural richness that define human creativity. This requires ethical frameworks to address issues such as transparency, intellectual property, and cultural sensitivity, as well as a commitment to preserving the human-centered aspects of art—curiosity, intent, and connection.

Art has always been a mirror reflecting how we understand ourselves and our place in the world. The integration of AI and GANs into the creative process invites us to rethink what it means to create, to innovate, and to be human. It offers an opportunity to reimagine creativity not as a solitary endeavor but as a collaborative dialogue between human intuition and machine precision.

As we step further into this transformative era, the challenge lies in balancing innovation with preservation, ensuring that art continues to evolve without losing its essence. In the chapters to follow, we will explore this evolving relationship, probing into what it means to create, to be creative, and to be an artist in an age where artificial intelligence reshapes the foundations of art and creativity. Together, we will examine how this dialogue between humanity and technology redefines not only art but also the very notion of what it means to be a creator.

Works Referenced

Anadol, Refik. *Machine Hallucinations – Sphere*. Exhibition, The Sphere, Las Vegas, 1 Sept. 2023–present.

Berger, John. *Ways of Seeing*. Penguin Books, 1972.

Cohen, Harold. *AARON: The Creative Art Machine*. Computer Program/Art Project, 1973.

DeepMind. *AlphaGo vs Lee Sedol*. Match Series, 2016.

Eagleman, David, and Anthony Brandt. *The Runaway Species: How Human Creativity Remakes the World*. Catapult, 2017.

Feigenbaum, Edward. "Dendral: A Case Study of the First Expert System." *Artificial Intelligence*, vol. 59, no. 1–2, 1993, pp. 233–40.

Getty Images v. Stability AI. Legal Case, 2023.

Goodfellow, Ian, et al. "Generative Adversarial Networks." *Advances in Neural Information Processing Systems*, vol. 27, 2014.

Google. "DeepDream Project." Software Project. Launched July 2015.

Google. *Tilt Brush*." Virtual Reality Software.

Gramsci, Antonio. *Prison Notebooks*. Columbia University Press, 2011.

Hartigan, Grace. *Quote from Artist Statement/Interview*.

Hassabis, Demis, et al. "AlphaGo: Mastering the Ancient Game of Go with Machine Learning." *Nature*, vol. 529, no. 7587, 2016, pp. 484–89.

Hinton, Geoffrey E., et al. "Learning Representations by Back-Propagating Errors." *Nature*, vol. 323, no. 6088, 1986, pp. 533–36.

IBM. *Deep Blue vs Garry Kasparov*. Chess Match, 1997.

Jones, Jonathan. "The Next Rembrandt: A New Way to Mock Art's Human Value." *The Guardian*, 6 Apr. 2016. www.theguardian.com/artanddesign/2016/apr/06/the-next-rembrandt-ai-painting-travesty-artificial-intelligence.

Lanier, Jaron. *You Are Not a Gadget: A Manifesto*. Alfred A. Knopf, 2010.

LeCun, Yann, et al. "Deep Learning." *Nature*, vol. 521, no. 7553, 2015, pp. 436–44.

McCarthy, John. "Programs with Common Sense." *Proceedings of the Teddington Conference on the Mechanization of Thought Processes*, vol. 1, Her Majesty's Stationery Office (HMSO), London, 1959.

McCarthy, John, et al. "Dartmouth College Conference on Artificial Intelligence." *Conference Proceedings*, 1956.

Minsky, Marvin L., and Seymour Papert. *Perceptrons: An Introduction to Computational Geometry.* MIT Press, 1969.

Mollick, Ethan. *Co-Intelligence: Human and Machine Collaboration in Creativity.* [Publication details not provided].

Mollick, Ethan. *Co-Intelligence: How Humans and AI Can Work Together in the Digital Age.* University of Pennsylvania Press.

Obvious Collective. *Portrait of Edmond de Belamy.* Christie's Auction House Sale Catalogue, Oct. 2018.

OpenAI Team. *GPT-4 Technical Report*. OpenAI.com, Mar. 2023.

Paley, Steven M. *The Art of Invention: The Creative Process of Discovery and Design.* Prometheus Books, 2010.

Perpiñán Carreira-Á., Miguel, et al. "Cubist Transformations Using Machine Learning Algorithms." *Journal of Computational Creativity*, vol. 12, no. 3, 2024.

Staniszewski, Mary Anne. *Believing Is Seeing: Creating the Culture of Art.* Penguin Books, 1995.

Turing, Alan M. "Computing Machinery and Intelligence." *Mind*, vol. LIX, no. 236, Oct. 1950, pp. 433–60.

Uka, Peter. "In the Studio With Peter Uka, the Artist Painting From Memory." Interview by Armand Limnander, *W Magazine*, 15 Nov. 2021, www.wmagazine.com/culture/peter-uka-longing-mariane-ibrahim-gallery-interview.

Various Authors. "The Next Rembrandt." Art Project/Technical Documentation.

Weizenbaum, Joseph. "ELIZA—A Computer Program for the Study of Natural Language Communication between Man and Machine." *Communications of the ACM*, vol. 9, no. 1, 1966, pp. 36–45.

Five **Borrowed Brushes**

AI Training, Infringement and Fair Use

Suppose an inquiry something like the following was posted to ChatGPT, Perplexity, Gemini, Claude or any one of the dozens of other AI bots, how might one expect it to respond:

> *THEORETICAL QUESTION: How does AI view the legal and ethical issues of copyright, moral rights, and trademarks when it trains on data sets to create visual art and does AI care about any of these issues?*

From the perspective of AI, the legal and ethical issues surrounding copyright, moral rights, and trademarks are complex considerations that arise primarily from the data it is trained on and how that data is used. However, *AI itself does not possess the self-awareness, intent, or ethical reasoning necessary to engage with these issues independently*—its "perspective" is entirely shaped by the parameters, goals, and values programmed into it by its human developers.

Regarding **copyright**, AI "sees" copyrighted material as *another dataset* for learning patterns rather than something subject to legal protections. However, the use of copyrighted works in training data sets can lead to legal disputes if the resulting outputs are deemed derivative rather than transformative. Copyright laws in many jurisdictions remain unclear about whether training an AI model constitutes infringement or fair use. From AI's perspective, any generated content is a novel synthesis of learned patterns rather than a direct copy, but human courts must interpret whether this synthesis crosses legal boundaries. Ethical considerations include ensuring that artists whose works contribute to training sets are acknowledged or compensated to avoid exploitation of creative labor.

Moral rights, which encompass the right to attribution and the integrity of an artist's work, pose unique challenges for AI-generated content. AI is *indifferent* to concepts like integrity or reputation—it does not recognize an artist's emotional investment or personal narrative tied to their work. However, when an AI-generated image is heavily influenced by a specific artist's style without acknowledgment, this can be perceived as a violation of that artist's moral rights. For example, if an AI-generated painting mirrors the style of a well-known living artist, audiences may falsely attribute the work to that artist or dilute their artistic identity, raising ethical questions about respect and authorship.

Regarding **trademarks**, AI "sees" them not as legally protected symbols or brand identifiers, but as data points within a larger dataset used to train its models. AI does not inherently recognize the legal and ethical boundaries surrounding trademarks or other intellectual property. It processes *without context*, focusing solely on patterns, shapes, and colors. This lack of awareness can lead to legal issues when AI-generated outputs include trademarked elements that might cause consumer confusion, dilute a brand's distinctiveness, or infringe upon the rights of trademark holders. Ethically, the use of trademarked material in training datasets without consent raises concerns about exploitation and the unfair appropriation of brand identity. While AI enables creative possibilities, its "blindness" to the legal and ethical frameworks governing trademarks underscores the importance of human oversight to ensure compliance and fairness in how AI is developed and used.

In summary, copyright, moral rights, and trademarks are not inherent concerns for AI itself but rather constructs shaped by human-designed data structures and algorithmic guidance. AI models operate as sophisticated tools executing programmed instructions, without independent agency or an intrinsic understanding of legal or ethical principles. The challenges surrounding AI's role in creativity and ownership emerge from how these systems are developed and deployed. Addressing these concerns requires human creators and developers to establish frameworks that respect cultural contexts, attribute creative contributions, and safeguard individual privacy, recognizing that accountability rests with the architects of these systems, not the systems themselves.

Authors' Response

Our perceived reactions to the question we theoretically posed stem from our understanding of how AI approaches these issues. Whether entirely accurate or not, these perspectives align with the doomsday warnings discussed by innovators like Reid Hoffman and Greg Beato in their book *Superagency*.

These responses also remind us of the rhetoric often employed by the plastic manufacturers and many other industrial companies. In that narrative, the obligation for addressing environmental damage caused by plastics was largely shifted onto individuals and their local communities, with an emphasis on implementing recycling programs rather than addressing the root cause—namely, the decisions made by chemists, engineers, and corporations during the design and production stages of plastic materials. This strategic framing shifted the burden of environmental cleanup away from the industry that profited from mass production and onto the consumer.

A similar dynamic seems to emerge in the context of AI-generated art and datasets. Developers and companies often position their role as neutral creators of tools, suggesting that it is up to artists, regulators, and users to ensure ethical outcomes. Yet, as with the creation of plastics, the most consequential decisions—such as, what data is used for training, whether consent is obtained, and how outputs are generated—occur upstream, during the design phase of the technology. The system's ethical challenges, much like the waste crisis associated with plastics, are baked into the core of its production process. By focusing primarily on how AI tools are used rather than how they are built, this perspective risks shifting accountability away from the creators and toward end users who may have little control over the underlying structure of the system.

The comparison is striking in several ways. Just as the proliferation of single-use plastics created environmental harm that communities are left to mitigate, AI systems trained on vast, often unregulated datasets can perpetuate cultural erasure, exploit copyrighted materials, and undermine privacy. These are harms that individual users and societies are expected to "clean up" through their responses and adaptations. This includes artists who must fight for attribution, legal scholars who challenge unsettled intellectual property questions, and communities whose cultural heritage may be reduced to aestheticized patterns devoid of context.

However, as in the case of sustainable material science, the AI industry has the power to intervene at the point of origin. Developers can integrate safeguards, such as filtering culturally sensitive content, ensuring transparency in data collection, not infringing upon protected works, and offering opt-in models known as data dignity for creators who wish to contribute their work to training sets. This proactive approach addresses systemic concerns before they arise, rather than placing the onus on the public to resolve the downstream effects of mass adoption.

Ultimately, the lesson from the plastic industry is that downstream solutions whether they take the form of public recycling initiatives or post-hoc regulations are often insufficient if the core design process remains unchanged. The AI industry, like material science, must recognize its role in shaping not only the innovation but also the impacts of its creations. Ethical AI design should focus on integrating accountability at the source, ensuring that technological progress does not come at the cost of cultural, legal, or individual rights. In this way, both fields can move beyond reactive measures toward a model that respects the interconnectedness of creators, communities, and the ecosystems—both digital and environmental—that they inhabit.

Foundations of Copyright Law

Before examining how AI systems can address legal, ethical, and cultural issues "upstream," it is essential to first understand the foundational principles of intellectual property rights, including copyrights, trademarks, and moral rights. Privacy protections and the concept of cultural appropriation will be explored in later chapters, but a strong grasp of intellectual property law sets the stage for these discussions.

Copyright law plays a pivotal role in fostering innovation and protecting intellectual labor. Rooted in the **US Constitution, Article I, Section 8, Clause 8** empowers Congress to "promote the progress of science and useful arts" by securing exclusive rights for authors and other creators for a limited time. This balance between incentivizing creators and ensuring public access to knowledge underpins the legal framework for intellectual property. By granting economic and professional rights to creators, copyright law fosters an environment where creativity can flourish while enriching society.

Creativity is inherently a social construct, shaped by historical and cultural contexts. Artistic expression draws upon collective traditions and experiences, with new works evaluated through the lens of their cultural lineage. This dynamic interplay between tradition and innovation underscores the importance of copyright law in safeguarding the intellectual labor that drives cultural and artistic progress.

The origins of copyright law in the United States trace back to the **Copyright Act of 1790**, modeled after the **British Statute of Anne of 1710**. These early laws emerged in response to Gutenberg's invention of the printing press, which revolutionized the production of books, maps, and charts by enabling mechanical replication. Initially, bookbinders and printers sought protection against unauthorized copying, but authors soon joined the call, demanding a share in the financial benefits their works generated. These laws aimed to grant creators exclusive rights while preventing long-term monopolies on knowledge and creativity, a balance that remains at the heart of copyright law today.

Over the centuries, copyright law has progressed to address emerging technologies and new artistic expressions, from the printing press and sheet music to the phonograph and broadcast television, and later, to the internet and streaming platforms. Despite these transformations, its core purpose remains unchanged: to nurture innovation, reward creative endeavors, and maintain public access to the rich cultural and intellectual heritage that creative works provide.

Copyright law protects a wide range of creative works, including literary, musical, visual, and audiovisual materials, as well as architectural designs and sound recordings. For instance, a best-selling novel, a digital illustration, and a feature-length film are all eligible for copyright protection as long as they meet the criteria of originality and fixation in a tangible form. These protections incentivize creators by granting them exclusive rights to control how their works are used and disseminated.

Additionally, societal responses to technological advancements have led to the creation of new forms of intellectual property protection. For example, Congress enacted the **Semiconductor Chip Protection Act of 1984** to address the unique challenges posed by semiconductor chips, which are used in virtually all electronic, digital and AI machine learning devices. These chips often require tens of millions of dollars and years of research to develop, yet they can be easily copied once created. Recognizing that traditional copyright law did not adequately protect this innovation, Congress crafted a specialized form of intellectual property protection to safeguard the investments and ingenuity behind semiconductor technology.

In the digital age, copyright law faces unique challenges due to the emergence of artificial intelligence technologies. AI systems can analyze and generate content in ways that complicate traditional notions of authorship and originality. This raises critical questions about how to protect creators' rights while encouraging the development of innovative AI applications. Striking this balance is essential to ensuring that copyright law continues to foster both creativity and technological progress.

The primary purpose of copyright law remains to encourage the creation and dissemination of works for the benefit of the public. By granting creators exclusive rights for a limited time, copyright law provides economic incentives for new works to enter the marketplace. This principle is enshrined in the US Constitution and reaffirmed in key Supreme Court cases, such as *Twentieth Century Music Corp. v. Aiken* (422 U.S. 151 (1975)). In this case, the Supreme Court clarified that copyright law not only secures a fair return for creators but also ensures that the public benefits from increased access to artistic and intellectual works. The decision underscored the broader societal impact of copyright law, emphasizing that incentivizing creative efforts ultimately enriches the cultural landscape and supports the public good.

However, some scholars dispute the underlying assumptions behind copyright law, arguing that it can, in some cases, inhibit creativity by creating barriers to collaboration or innovation. As Professor Siva Vaidhyanathan, author of the influential book *Copyrights and Copywrongs: The Rise of Intellectual Property and How it Threatens Creativity*, explains, "Copyright law often assumes a false dichotomy between creativity and access, when in fact, many great works are built on the ability to freely draw upon cultural resources." Vaidhyanathan critiques the dominant narrative of copyright law for overlooking the role of shared cultural heritage and the collaborative nature of creativity. He argues that by imposing restrictive barriers, copyright law can stifle the very innovation it seeks to promote, particularly in cases where transformative or derivative works are essential to artistic and intellectual progress.

Copyright protections extend internationally through agreements like the **Berne Convention for the Protection of Literary and Artistic Works (Berne Convention),** the **World Intellectual Property Organization (WIPO) Copyright Treaty, Madrid Protocol, and Trade-Related Aspects of Intellectual Property Rights (TRIPS**). These treaties establish minimum standards for copyright protection, ensuring that American creators are safeguarded against infringement in foreign markets. The

Berne Convention, for instance, mandates that member countries provide automatic copyright protection for works originating in other member states, eliminating the need for formal registration. Similarly, the **WIPO Copyright Treaty** modernizes these protections to address digital challenges, such as online piracy and the unauthorized distribution of copyrighted works on the internet. **TRIPS** further reinforces these principles by integrating intellectual property rights into global trade frameworks, ensuring that copyright enforcement becomes an integral part of international commerce. Meanwhile, the **Madrid Protocol** simplifies the process of registering trademarks in different countries.

These multi-national agreements collectively provide a safety net for creators, enabling them to seek legal remedies and assert their rights in jurisdictions worldwide, while fostering a collaborative international environment that values and protects intellectual property. By participating in these treaties, the United States not only safeguards the interests of its creators but also strengthens a global framework that promotes creativity and protects cultural and artistic contributions across borders.

Copyright Protection: Exclusive Rights, Criteria, and Limitations

Copyright holders are granted several exclusive rights, including the right to reproduce their work, distribute copies, create derivative works, and publicly display or perform the work. These rights allow creators to control how their works are used and provide legal remedies against unauthorized exploitation. For visual art—whether a two-dimensional drawing, human-generated digital print, or three-dimensional sculpture—copyright provides these same exclusive rights, ensuring creators maintain control over reproductions, adaptations, and public presentations of their works.

Copyright protection is automatic upon the creation of a work when it takes a tangible form. However, registration with the US Copyright Office is required to pursue a federal lawsuit for statutory damages or injunctive relief. Without registration, creators may still rely on common law protections, though their ability to seek damages is more limited.

To qualify for copyright protection, a work must meet four key criteria:

1. Originality: The work must originate from the creator and cannot be a direct copy.
2. Copyrightable Subject Matter: Eligible works include literary creations, musical compositions, pictorial and sculptural works, audiovisual materials, sound recordings, and architectural designs.
3. Fixed in a Tangible Medium: The work must be embodied in a physical or digital form, such as digital photographs or murals.
4. Minimal Degree of Creativity: The work must involve some level of human intellectual effort, even if the threshold is low.

Copyright law also makes a clear distinction between ideas and their expression. Known as the "idea-expression dichotomy," this principle ensures that copyright protection extends only to the original elements of an author's work, not to the underlying ideas, procedures, or systems themselves, which remain free for public use. For instance, **Section 102(b) of the Copyright Act** explicitly states that "in no case does copyright protection for an original work of authorship extend to any idea, procedure, process, system, method of operation, concept, principle, or discovery."

A computer program, as defined in **Section 101 of the Copyright Act**, is a set of statements or instructions used to bring about a certain result and is protected under copyright law as a literary work. This protection, however, does not extend to program logic, systems, methods, layouts, or algorithms, as these are considered ideas rather than the expression of ideas. Yet, source code, which is the human-readable form of a computer program written in languages like Basic, Python, or Java, and its corresponding object code—the machine-readable binary form (0s and 1s)—are both copyrightable. This is because source code and object code are tangible expressions of ideas, meeting the originality and fixation requirements of copyright law.

This distinction between ideas and their expression is critical in ensuring that foundational concepts, like programming logic or algorithms, remain in the public domain, enabling innovation and collaboration. At the same time, it ensures that the creative effort involved in writing and structuring specific code is protected, incentivizing developers and programmers to create without fear of their work being directly copied. This balance fosters both accessibility and protection in technological and creative fields, a cornerstone of intellectual property law. In the AI context, this dichotomy becomes complex when algorithms replicate stylistic elements or artistic "expressions" rather than merely drawing inspiration from ideas, although not easy to follow for lay people.

The Open Source and Open Access movements play a pivotal role in fostering creativity and collaboration, particularly in the context of AI, by removing legal restraints that could otherwise stifle innovation. Open Source software, such as Linux or TensorFlow, thrives on the principle of transparency, allowing developers worldwide to access, modify, and share foundational code. This collaborative approach not only accelerates technological advancements but also democratizes innovation, empowering individuals and organizations, regardless of size or resources, to participate in shaping the future of technology. Similarly, the Open Access movement in academia ensures that research and data remain freely available, enabling scientists and developers to build on each other's work without legal or financial barriers. In the realm of AI, these principles have led to groundbreaking advancements, such as the widespread adoption and enhancement of open AI models like GPT and Stable Diffusion and the Chinese Deepseek R1, which have sparked creative applications in art, literature, and design. However, while these movements encourage unprecedented collaboration, they also continue to raise complex questions about intellectual property in AI-generated outputs.

The exclusive rights granted under the **Copyright Act of 1976**—including reproduction, adaptation, distribution, public performance, and public display— are freely transferable. Copyright holders can license, sell, donate, or bequeath these rights to others. In the case of sound recordings, the copyright also includes the right to public performance via digital audio transmission.

One of the significant challenges of copyright law in the era of AI is defining who qualifies as the "author" of a work created or generated with the assistance of artificial intelligence. Traditional copyright law grants protection to works created by humans, but it remains unclear how to address authorship when an AI system plays a substantial role in the creative process. Questions arise about whether the human programmer, the user who inputs prompts, or the AI system itself should be recognized as the author. Since, at this time, AI cannot hold legal rights, courts have consistently ruled that AI-generated works cannot receive copyright protection unless a human's creative contribution is clearly demonstrated. Without a recognized author, these works often fall outside the bounds of copyright protection unless classified as anonymous or pseudonymous—an unlikely designation in cases involving AI.

It is not far-fetched to view the person who selects or dictates what the AI is to do—whether in selecting training data, refining outputs, or providing iterative instructions—as akin to traditional creative roles. For example, a photographer meticulously working in a darkroom to adjust contrasts, lighting, and composition parallels a digital artist using Photoshop to refine images or a printmaker perfecting tones and textures. Similarly, a process engineer directing an AI system by defining parameters and modifying outputs plays an active creative role, shaping the final product through iterative refinement. This human hand in guiding AI systems may increasingly be recognized as a significant element of authorship, offering a pathway for reconciling the legal and creative complexities of AI-generated works.

Despite the broad protections copyright offers, there are important limitations and exceptions designed to support copyright's fundamental purpose of fostering creativity and public access. These limitations allow certain uses of copyrighted works for socially beneficial purposes, such as education, research, criticism, and parody. Properly crafted exceptions, such as fair use, help maintain a balance between the creator's rights and the public's interest in the free exchange of ideas and cultural expression.

The minimum international standard for copyright protection, as established by the **Berne Convention** and the **TRIPS Agreement**, is the life of the author plus 50 years. However, member countries are free to exceed this standard, and many, including the United States and the European Union, have done so.

Under current US law, for works created by individual authors on or after January 1, 1978, copyright protection begins at the moment of creation and lasts for the life of the author plus 70 years. For anonymous or pseudonymous works, where the author's identity is not disclosed, and for works made for hire, the copyright lasts 95 years from the date of first publication or 120 years from the date of creation—whichever expires first. In the case of joint works, the copyright extends until 70 years after the death of the last surviving author.

The length of copyright protection has changed significantly over time. The original **Copyright Act of 1790** granted protection for 14 years, with the option to renew for an additional 14 years. The **Copyright Act of 1909** extended this to an initial term of 28 years with a 28-year renewal, totaling 56 years. This structure remained until the **Copyright Act of 1976**, which overhauled the system to grant protection for the life of the author plus 50 years. The **Sonny Bono Copyright Term Extension Act of 1998** further extended this period to the life of the author plus 70 years, as mentioned earlier. For corporate "works for hire," the protection was extended to 95 years from publication or 120 years from creation, whichever is shorter.

These extensions have kept many twentieth-century works, such as iconic photographs and paintings, under copyright protection; for example, Dorothea Lange's "Migrant Mother" photograph, Edward Hopper's "Nighthawks," and Jackson Pollock's "No. 5, 1948." Meanwhile, older works—those created before 1928—have entered the public domain. The public domain encompasses creative works whose copyright has expired, been forfeited, or never existed, making them free for public use. Public domain works, such as Shakespeare's plays, the original "Peter Pan" by J.M. Barrie, or nineteenth-century vintage photographs like those by Mathew Brady, can be used, reproduced, or adapted without seeking permission or paying royalties, enabling wide-ranging cultural and creative reuses.

In contrast, copyrighted works, such as a contemporary lithograph by Philadelphia printmaker Alan Edmunds or a Cape Cod scene by photographer Joel Meyerowitz, require authorization for certain uses. This distinction is vital in the age of AI, where algorithms scrape vast amounts of data to train models. When AI systems access public domain material, they do so freely; however, when they use copyrighted works, such as Annie Leibovitz's photographs or original digital art like *Crossroads* by digital artist Beeple (Mike Winkelmann), they risk infringing exclusive rights unless the use qualifies as "fair use" or permission is granted.

Copyright infringement occurs when someone exercises the exclusive rights of a copyright holder without permission. These rights include reproducing the work, preparing derivative works, and publicly displaying or distributing the work. However, the fair use doctrine under 17 USC. § 107 provides a defense if the unauthorized use meets certain criteria:

- **Purpose and Character**: Whether the use is transformative or primarily commercial. A transformative work adds something new, with a different purpose or message, rather than merely superseding the original.

- **Nature of the Work**: The level of creativity and originality in the original work. Factual works are more likely to qualify for fair use compared to highly creative works.
- **Amount and Substantiality**: The quantity and significance of the portion used. Using a small, non-central part of a work may weigh in favor of fair use, but if the "heart" of the work is used, this factor may weigh against fair use.
- **Effect on the Market**: Whether the use adversely impacts the potential market for or value of the original work. If the new work usurps the market for the original, it is less likely to be considered fair use.

Fair Use and the Warhol v. Goldsmith Decision

The US Supreme Court's 2023 decision in *Andy Warhol Foundation for the Visual Arts, Inc. v. Goldsmith* (598 U.S. 508 (2023)) represents a defining moment in copyright law, particularly in how courts assess transformative use under the fair use doctrine. The dispute arose from Andy Warhol's Prince Series, which was based on Lynn Goldsmith's 1981 photograph of the musician Prince. Goldsmith had licensed the photograph to *Vanity Fair* for a one-time use as an artist reference. Unbeknownst to Goldsmith, Warhol created sixteen silkscreens and drawings using her black-and-white photograph as the foundation for his creation. The legal conflict escalated in 2016 when the Andy Warhol Foundation (AWF) licensed *Orange Prince*, one of Warhol's works, to *Condé Nast* for a commemorative magazine cover following Prince's death. Goldsmith claimed that this secondary use infringed her copyright, while AWF argued that Warhol's alterations were transformative and therefore protected by fair use.

In a 7–2 ruling authored by Justice Sonia Sotomayor, the Court sided with Goldsmith, concluding that *Orange Prince* did not qualify as fair use. The majority emphasized that the "purpose and character of the use" under the first fair use factor was critical to the analysis. Both Goldsmith's photograph and Warhol's silkscreen were licensed for a similar purpose: to depict Prince in a magazine feature. Because the works shared the same commercial function, the Court found that Warhol's artistic changes in style and medium were insufficient to render the work transformative. Sotomayor noted that for a work to be transformative, it must serve a new and fundamentally different purpose or convey new meaning beyond the original's intent. The Court distinguished this case from *Campbell v. Acuff-Rose Music* (510 U.S. 569 (1994)), where two Live Crew's parody of "Oh, Pretty Woman" was deemed transformative because it ridiculed the original song rather than merely recontextualizing it, thereby, qualifying as parody as a free speech exception to infringement.

In contrast, Justice Elena Kagan, joined by Chief Justice John Roberts, issued a strong dissent, warning that the majority's decision could stifle artistic creativity. Kagan argued that Warhol's silkscreens did add new meaning, reinterpreting Goldsmith's photograph to comment on celebrity culture and the commodification of fame. She highlighted Warhol's bold use of color and stark contrast, which transformed Prince from a vulnerable musician, as captured by Goldsmith, into a pop icon. Kagan contended that focusing narrowly on the commercial licensing of *Orange Prince* ignored the broader cultural significance of Warhol's work. She cautioned that restricting such reinterpretations could have a chilling effect on artists who draw inspiration from existing works, potentially impoverishing the creative landscape.

The Warhol decision underscores a pivotal shift in the legal interpretation of fair use, emphasizing that stylistic changes alone are insufficient to meet the transformative use standard if the new work serves a similar commercial purpose—such as advertising or digital media illustrations—as the original. This has far-reaching implications for generative AI tools like Stable Diffusion, which creates content using datasets such as those collected by LAION from Common Crawl's web scraping efforts, including data from websites like Wikipedia, news outlets, blogs, social media websites like Reddit, and other publicly accessible sources, sometimes without proper licensing. Unlike AI language models that produce text, diffusion models specialize in visual outcomes by inventing images from scratch based on word prompts provided. Overall, the ruling suggests that AI-generated outputs that closely resemble existing works, particularly those used commercially, may face increased scrutiny and potential infringement claims.

When materials such as photographs or other copyrighted works are used without permission—whether intentionally or by accident—they are not directly copied into the AI system. Instead, these materials are used to train the AI machine or bot by creating a system of "weights" that represent patterns, features, and associations learned from the dataset. For example, an AI model might analyze thousands of images to understand the composition, style, and attributes of a particular artistic medium, encoding this information into mathematical representations. These weights allow the AI to generate new outputs that may emulate certain styles or characteristics but are not identical reproductions of the training data.

This process, while innovative, raises ethical and legal concerns about whether such use constitutes an infringement, especially when the outputs are used commercially or resemble copyrighted works. Critics argue that even though the data itself is not replicated, the underlying creative essence is effectively "borrowed," creating a gray area in copyright law. Courts, as highlighted by the *Warhol* ruling, may increasingly scrutinize whether such uses are transformative enough to qualify as fair use, especially in cases where commercial interests are involved as opposed to using an AI-generated image or meme for personal use. This interpretation underscores the need for clearer legal frameworks to address the unique challenges posed by AI in the creative industries.

By narrowing the scope of what qualifies as transformative, the *Warhol* decision complicates the landscape for artists and developers working with generative AI technologies. For example, an AI-generated image that mimics the style of a famous painting for use in a marketing campaign could now require a license, where previously it might have been argued as transformative. This creates potential legal risks for digital creators relying on AI to reinterpret existing works.

The decision also highlights the challenges of intent in fair use analysis when applied to AI. Generative AI systems do not "intend" to replicate specific works but rely on copyrighted datasets to generate new content. This reliance raises questions about whether AI-generated creations can be considered independent works or derivative ones. A digital artist using DALL-E to create a derivative work inspired by a copyrighted photograph may unintentionally infringe, even if the output has stylistic differences.

On the other hand, the *Warhol* case reinforces the importance of permissions and licensing when reinterpreting existing works. This shift may encourage the development of licensing models tailored to generative AI tools, where creators of source materials are compensated for their contributions. Such frameworks could help balance the competing interests of protecting intellectual property and enabling creative expression in the digital age.

Ultimately, the *Warhol* ruling underscores the delicate balance courts must strike between safeguarding creators' rights, AI developers and fostering artistic innovation for the public good. It also serves as a reminder that copyright law must continue to progress to address the unique challenges posed by new technologies like AI.

Lawsuits and Global Legal Developments

The rapid advancement of artificial intelligence (AI) technologies has sparked numerous legal disputes, including high-profile cases such as *Andersen v. Stability AI* (No. 3:23-cv-00201 (N.D. Cal. 2024)) and *Getty Images v. Stability* AI (No. 1:23-cv-01339 (D. Del. 2024)). These lawsuits address fundamental concerns about the unauthorized use of copyrighted materials to train generative AI models. The outcomes of these cases could establish critical legal precedents for licensing requirements, the interpretation of fair use, and the broader implications for intellectual property rights in the AI era. These disputes are shaping the legal and economic framework surrounding AI development, underscoring the urgent need for clearer guidelines on ownership, licensing, and the use of copyrighted content in AI training datasets.

In *Andersen v. Stability AI*, artists Sarah Andersen, Kelly McKernan, and Karla Ortiz filed a lawsuit against Stability AI, alleging that their copyrighted works were unlawfully used to train the AI model Stable Diffusion. This model, according to the plaintiffs, enables the production of outputs that mimic their unique artistic styles. In late 2024, US District Judge William Orrick allowed key copyright infringement claims to move forward, particularly focusing on the unauthorized reproduction of their works. However, the court dismissed claims of unjust enrichment, emphasizing that remedies must align specifically with copyright law. This case is pivotal because a ruling in favor of the plaintiffs could set a precedent requiring mandatory licensing agreements for copyrighted materials used in AI training datasets. Such a decision could fundamentally alter the economic and operational dynamics of generative AI technologies.

Similarly, in *Getty Images v. Stability AI*, the global stock image provider accused Stability AI of using millions of its copyrighted photographs, including images with embedded watermarks, without authorization to train its AI models. Getty contended that this unauthorized use undermined its licensing business by enabling AI-generated alternatives to licensed images, potentially eroding its revenue streams. While the case is still pending, it underscores the commercial ramifications of AI training in industries heavily reliant on intellectual property.

In a notable European case involving the intersection of copyright law and the use of photographs, a French court ruled in favor of a photographer who successfully sued an auction house for using thumbnail-like images of his paintings without consent. The photographer had taken high-quality images of artworks for use in an auction catalog, but the auction house subsequently used these images to promote the sale of the artworks online. The photographer argued that this unauthorized use violated his copyright under French and EU copyright law, which protects original photographic works as intellectual creations.

The court found that the auction house's use of the photographs constituted a breach of the photographer's exclusive rights, particularly the right to control reproduction and public display. While the auction house claimed that its use of thumbnail images was incidental and necessary for promoting the sale of the artworks, the court rejected this argument. It emphasized that even small or low-resolution reproductions could infringe copyright if used without proper authorization. The ruling was based on EU copyright principles, including those established in cases like *Painer (C-145/10)*, which affirmed that photographers retain exclusive rights over their creative decisions, such as framing, lighting, and composition. This decision underscores the importance of obtaining explicit permission from copyright holders when using their works for commercial purposes, even in contexts like auctions or online sales. It also highlights how European courts balance copyright protections with commercial practices, ensuring respect for creators' intellectual property rights.

Another landmark case is *Authors Guild v. OpenAI Inc.* (No. 1:23-cv-08292 (S.D.N.Y., 2024)), where prominent New York Times best-selling authors such as George R.R. Martin and John Grisham joined forces with the Authors Guild to sue OpenAI for allegedly using their copyrighted books without permission to train large language models like ChatGPT. The plaintiffs argue that OpenAI's use of their works constitutes direct copyright infringement and undermines their ability to license or monetize their creations effectively. This case also raises questions about whether machine learning models transform copyrighted materials sufficiently to qualify under fair use provisions

In a related vein, *Thaler v. Perlmutter* (687 F. Supp. 3d 140 (D.D.C., 2023)) addressed whether works generated entirely by artificial intelligence can qualify for copyright protection under US law. Stephen Thaler sought to register a visual artwork created by his "Creativity Machine" as a copyrightable work but was denied by the US Copyright Office on the grounds that human authorship is a prerequisite for copyright eligibility under current law. The US District Court for the District of Columbia upheld this decision, reinforcing that copyright protections are limited to works created by humans.

In 2022, the US Copyright Office revoked the copyright registration for the graphic novel *Zarya of the Dawn* by Kris Kashtanova after it was revealed that the work had been created using the AI-generative tool MidJourney. Initially registered as a copyrighted work, the registration was canceled upon scrutiny of the AI-generated visuals. However, a year later, the Copyright Office issued a new copyright registration for the graphic novel, covering Kashtanova's text and their creative selection, coordination, and arrangement of the text alongside the AI-generated visual elements. While Kashtanova is recognized as the creator of the graphic novel, copyright protection applies exclusively to the human-authored portions of the work, excluding the visual elements generated by MidJourney's text-to-image tool.

Additionally, music companies have brought significant cases against generative AI developers accused of using unlicensed sound recordings to train their models. In *RIAA v. Suno Inc.* (No. 1:24-cv-11611 (D.D.C., 2024)), major record labels such as Sony Music and Warner Records alleged that Suno's music generation tools infringed on their copyrights by copying and exploiting sound recordings without authorization during training processes.

The global nature of copyright disputes surrounding artificial intelligence (AI) highlights the varying approaches taken by jurisdictions to balance innovation and intellectual property rights. In Europe, copyright law is heavily influenced by the **Berne Convention**, which mandates automatic protection for original works without requiring formal registration. However, recent legal and regulatory developments reflect a growing effort to address the complexities introduced by generative AI.

For instance, the **European Union's Digital Single Market Directive (Directive 2019/790/EU**) reinforces copyright holders' rights by allowing them to opt out of text and data mining exceptions. This is critical for creators seeking to prevent unauthorized use of their works in AI training. A landmark case in Germany, Hamburg Regional Court, 2024, involved a photographer suing an AI company for using his images without consent to train its models. The court ruled that such unauthorized use constitutes copyright infringement under German law, emphasizing the necessity of obtaining explicit permission from rights holders. This decision underscores the importance of licensing agreements for copyrighted materials used in AI training across the European Union.

Meanwhile, courts in the Czech Republic have explored whether AI-generated works can receive copyright protection. A ruling suggested that if a human provides detailed and creative instructions to an AI system, the resulting output could qualify as a work of authorship under EU copyright law.

This interpretation aligns with broader European jurisprudence, such as the Court of Justice of the European Union's (CJEU) decision in *Infopaq International A/S v. Danske Dagblades Forening* (C-5/08), which established that copyright requires "the author's own intellectual creation." These cases highlight the significance of human involvement and originality in determining copyright eligibility for AI-assisted creations.

In Asia, China has taken significant steps in addressing AI and copyright issues. In a groundbreaking ruling by the Beijing Internet Court in November 2023, an AI-generated image was recognized as copyrightable because it demonstrated sufficient human input during its creation process. However, a subsequent case in February 2024 before the Guangzhou Internet Court found a generative AI service provider liable for copyright infringement when its outputs closely resembled copyrighted characters from Japan's "Ultraman" series. These rulings illustrate China's willingness to recognize copyrightability for certain AI-generated works while holding developers accountable for unauthorized use of copyrighted material (*Beijing Internet Court, 2023; Guangzhou Internet Court, 2024*).

India has also entered this arena with *ANI Media v. OpenAI*, 2025, where the news agency alleged that OpenAI used its copyrighted news content without permission to train ChatGPT. ANI claimed this use not only violated its copyrights but also spread misinformation by attributing fabricated news stories to ANI. OpenAI defended its actions under the fair use doctrine but blocked ANI's domain following legal notice, signaling an effort toward compliance.

In Canada, *CanLII v. Caseway AI* (Supreme Court of British Columbia, 2024) represents another pivotal case where CanLII alleged that Caseway AI infringed on its copyright by using its legal database without authorization to train its models. The case raises questions about whether bulk data scraping for machine learning purposes constitutes fair dealing under Canadian copyright law

Similarly, Canadian news outlets have filed lawsuits against OpenAI for allegedly using their articles without authorization to train GPT models. Australia is also grappling with these issues as it considers updating its laws to address generative AI's use of copyrighted materials. While no major lawsuits have been filed yet, policymakers are debating whether Australia's narrower "fair dealing" exceptions can adequately address these challenges.

Finally, in England, *Getty Images (US) Inc v. Stability AI Ltd* (High Court of Justice (UK), 2024). has become one of the most prominent cases addressing generative AI and copyright law in the UK context. Getty alleges that Stability AI collected its library of images, amounting to millions of copyrighted works, and used them without permission to train Stable Diffusion's generative model. The claim includes allegations of both copyright infringement and database rights violations under UK law, as well as trademark infringement and passing off due to watermarked images being included in training datasets without authorization. Stability AI has denied liability but failed in an early attempt at summary judgment dismissal, allowing key issues to proceed toward trial soon.

The United States Copyright Office (USCO) has also launched an initiative to explore the broader implications of AI on copyright law, recognizing the transformative potential and challenges posed by generative AI technologies. This initiative examines key issues such as licensing requirements, the use of copyrighted materials in training datasets, and the creation of digital replicas that mimic the styles or likenesses of original works.

Through public listening sessions, USCO seeks to engage stakeholders, including artists, developers, industry leaders, and legal experts, to better understand the multifaceted impact of AI on copyright. Policy reports generated from these sessions aim to address complex legal and ethical questions, such as determining authorship, establishing fair use boundaries, and ensuring equitable compensation for creators in the age of AI. By proactively addressing these challenges, USCO is working to ensure that copyright law remains robust and adaptable.

These legal disputes and policy developments highlight the need for clearer legal frameworks to balance technological innovation with the protection of intellectual property. As courts and policymakers grapple with issues such as fair use, licensing, and liability in the context of rapidly evolving AI technologies, the stakes remain high for creative industries such as visual art, photography, and music. Unauthorized replication of style or content through AI-generated outputs could undermine creators' livelihoods and reshape entire industries. Both the United States and the EU face the challenge of adapting traditional copyright principles to address the realities of AI while fostering an environment that encourages both creativity and technological progress, while protecting the rights of the authors or creators.

Moral Rights

Following the exploration of copyright law and its relationship with AI, it is important to examine moral rights, a highly European concept that holds a unique place within the framework of intellectual property law. Rooted in the French concept of *droit moral*, moral rights emerged as part of a broader effort to protect the personal and reputational interests of creators, beyond the economic rights typically associated with copyright. These rights prioritize the connection between an author and their work, recognizing that creative works often represent deeply personal expressions of identity and creativity.

Moral rights have their origins in nineteenth-century France, where they were developed to ensure that authors retained a degree of control over how their works were used, even after transferring their economic rights. This concept later spread throughout Europe and was codified in the **Berne Convention**, first adopted in 1886. **Article 6bis** formalized the recognition of moral rights, granting authors the right to claim authorship of their works (the right of attribution) and to object to any distortion, mutilation, or modification of their works that would harm their honor or reputation (the right of integrity).

Moral rights typically include:
Right of Attribution: Ensures the creator is credited for their work.

Right of Integrity: Protects the work from alterations or uses that could damage the creator's reputation.

Right of Disclosure: Allows creators to decide when and how their work is made public.

Right of Withdrawal: Enables creators to remove their work from public view in certain circumstances.

Moral rights, particularly the right of integrity, have been a focal point in disputes over the digital colorization of black-and-white films, such as *The Wizard of Oz* or *The Last Picture Show* by large media and entertainment companies that acquired the film rights for broadcasting purposes. These examples highlight the stark differences between European and US approaches to moral rights and their implications for creative works. In Europe, moral rights are deeply embedded in copyright law, granting creators enduring protections over their works' artistic integrity.

A landmark case illustrating the European perspective is *Turner Entertainment Co. v. Huston*, where John Huston's heirs sued Turner Entertainment for colorizing his black-and-white film *The Asphalt Jungle*. The French court ruled that the colorization violated Huston's moral right of integrity, as it distorted the original artistic vision of the film. The court emphasized that moral rights are inalienable and persist even after the creator's death, awarding Huston's heirs 600,000 Francs in damages and barring the broadcast of the colorized version in France (*Turner Entertainment Co. v. Huston*, Cour de Cassation, May 28, 1991).

Similarly, in *Zinnemann v. TeleMontecarlo* (Court of Rome, November 2005), film director Fred Zinnemann successfully challenged an Italian broadcaster for repeatedly airing a colorized version of his 1944 film *The Seventh Cross* without his consent. The Italian court ruled that the unauthorized alteration breached Zinnemann's moral right of integrity under Italian copyright law, reinforcing that such changes could harm the creator's reputation and artistic vision.

These cases stand in stark contrast to US law, where directors and creators face significant challenges in asserting moral rights over their works. For instance, while Congress debated the issue of colorization during hearings in the late 1980s, no comprehensive moral rights protections were enacted for filmmakers or audiovisual works.

The work-made-for-hire doctrine under US copyright law further complicates matters by designating producers as the "authors" of films in many cases, leaving directors with limited recourse to challenge alterations like colorization. Instead, US courts have occasionally relied on alternative legal frameworks, such as trademark law or contractual agreements, to address concerns about artistic integrity.

The **Berne Convention's** recognition of moral rights has led to their widespread adoption in Europe and other signatory countries. However, the implementation of moral rights varies significantly by jurisdiction. In Europe, moral rights are often perpetual, inalienable, and separate from economic rights, granting creators enduring protections. This means that even after the creator's death, moral rights are typically passed to heirs or other representatives who can enforce them.

In contrast, moral rights are far more limited under US copyright law. The **Visual Artists Rights Act (VARA**) of 1990 provides moral rights protection for certain works of visual art, including paintings, drawings, limited-edition numbered prints, sculptures, and still photographic images produced for exhibition. **VARA** grants authors the right to attribution and integrity but applies only to works that meet specific criteria, and its protections terminate with the death of the creator. Unlike in Europe, moral rights in the United States are not perpetual and do not extend to heirs in the same way.

A striking example of moral rights violations involves the attempted fragmentation of Pablo Picasso's artwork. Advertisements in a national publication once promoted the sale of a Picasso lithograph that had been cut into two-inch squares, with each square being sold individually. In Europe, this act would likely constitute a violation of Picasso's moral rights under the right of integrity, as it distorts and mutilates the original artwork, harming its artistic and cultural value. His heirs could enforce these rights even after his death. In contrast, such an act would not necessarily violate moral rights under US law, where protections are more limited.

Moral rights in Europe and in the USA when it applies are independent of the physical ownership of a work of art or the copyright associated with it. For example, owning the physical painting of a painting, say, by Lee Krasner, wife of Jackson Pollock, does not grant the owner the right to reproduce it or create derivative works, as those rights are tied to the copyright. Meanwhile, because Krasner is deceased her limited moral rights expired upon her death.

Conversely, in Europe, an artist retains their moral rights to the work, such as the right of attribution and integrity, even if they no longer own the copyright or the physical artwork itself. For instance, the buyer of a reproduction print or giclée may own the physical item, but they cannot claim authorship or alter the work without potentially violating the artist's moral rights. The Picasso lithograph example demonstrates this distinction: while a collector might physically own the lithograph, mutilating it by dividing it into smaller pieces would violate the moral rights of Picasso or his heirs in Europe.

AI and Moral Rights

The rise of AI raises new questions about moral rights, particularly in cases where AI-generated content mimics the style or identity of human creators. For instance, if an AI system generates an image in the style of a well-known European living artist like Wolfgang Tillmans (a renowned photographer and conceptual artist known for his innovative approach to photography, incorporating elements of collage, abstraction, and digital manipulation) without their authorization, does this violate their moral rights under the right of integrity? Does it matter whether AI is prompted to create in that style or if AI randomly generates a similar image to Tillmans? Similarly, AI tools that generate deepfakes or digital replicas could implicate the right of attribution if the original creator is not credited.

Another illustrative example is the potential use of AI to create unauthorized sequels or adaptations of a famous author's work whether a film or literary publication. While copyright law may address economic rights, moral rights could provide an additional avenue for creators or their heirs to challenge such uses on the grounds of misrepresentation or damage to the author's reputation.

In jurisdictions like France or Germany, moral rights could substantially impact how AI-generated content is regulated, ensuring that creators retain control over their identity and reputation. However, the limited scope of moral rights under US law highlights the limited protection afforded to those working in the creative industries under current US legislation.

Trademarks in the United States and the EU

Having explored the extensive implications of artificial intelligence (AI) on copyright law and sparse application on moral rights, it is important to recognize that while copyright often dominates discussions on intellectual property protection in the AI era, trademarks also play a crucial role in the ongoing development of machine learning and AI technologies. A trademark is a legally recognized symbol, word, phrase, design, or combination thereof that identifies and distinguishes the source of goods or services from those of others. Trademarks protect brand identity and ensure that consumers can reliably identify the origin of a product or service, preventing confusion in the marketplace and safeguarding the reputation of businesses.

In the United States, trademarks are governed by the **Lanham Act** (1946), which outlines protections against trademark infringement, dilution, and unfair competition. The European Union similarly provides robust trademark protections through **the EU Trademark Regulation (EUTMR)**, offering a harmonized system for registering trademarks across member states and shielding them from unauthorized use that could lead to consumer confusion or damage a brand's reputation. Both the United States and the EU grant trademark protection for 10 years with opportunities to renew continuously every 10 years thereafter.

Trademark infringement occurs when an unauthorized party uses a mark in a manner likely to cause confusion about the origin of goods or services. For example, if a company were to develop an AI-generated logo closely resembling Adidas' three-stripe design for its sportswear, it could face legal challenges for infringing upon Adidas' trademark. Remedies for trademark holders under both US and EU law include injunctions to halt unauthorized use, monetary damages, and the removal of infringing products from the market.

In the context of AI and machine learning, trademarks face novel challenges and opportunities. For instance, generative AI tools that create brand logos or product designs may inadvertently produce outputs that closely resemble existing trademarks, raising the risk of unintentional infringement. Additionally, AI-powered virtual assistants and search engines play a growing role in consumer decision-making, making it essential for trademarks to remain easily recognizable and distinct in digital environments. As AI technologies continue to integrate into marketing, e-commerce, and brand development, the role of trademarks in protecting brand identity and preventing confusion will become increasingly significant, warranting continued legal and policy attention.

The practical importance of these issues is underscored by research conducted by Jennifer Haase and Paul Hanel, whose study, "GPT-4 Outperforms Most Humans in Creative Ideation Tasks," demonstrated that the latest GPT-4 model exceeded the performance of over 90 percent of humans tested in generating creative ideas. Tasks such as developing brand names or proposing new product colors—areas traditionally associated with human innovation and directly tied to trademark law—highlight the remarkable capabilities of generative AI. In some cases, a basic generative pretrained transformer (GPT) might even outperform human brand managers in speed and efficiency, raising concerns about the potential displacement of traditional roles in creative industries.

Karl Ulrich of The Wharton School at the University of Pennsylvania suggests that while AI excels in generating ideas, its creativity can be limited without deliberate and strategic human prompting. Their findings indicate that AI tends to produce repetitive or similar ideas without careful guidance, emphasizing the continued importance of human intervention in refining and directing AI-generated outputs. And as earlier chapter material discussed, humans are the only species that throws themselves at reimagining new brands, product names, logos, and symbols with vitality and persistence. The software of creativity comes preinstalled on the human hard drive, ready to bend, break, and blend—especially when working collaboratively with other creative types and now, as Professor Mollick and other experts suggest, using AI as a co-collaborator in the process.

AI and Trademark Use in Virtual Environments

The rise of artificial intelligence (AI) and its integration into virtual environments, such as video games, virtual reality (VR), and NFTs, has led to significant legal challenges regarding trademark use. For instance, a landmark decision in the United States, *Hermès International v. Rothschild* (No. 1:22-cv-00384-JSR (S.D.N.Y., 2023)), involved Hermès suing digital artist Mason Rothschild for creating "MetaBirkins" NFTs—digital renditions of the Hermès Birkin bag.

Hermès argued that Rothschild's use of its trademarked name and iconic product design created consumer confusion and misappropriated the brand's goodwill. The court ruled in favor of Hermès, affirming that trademark protections extend to virtual goods as they do to physical ones. This decision underscored the importance of protecting brand identity in digital marketplaces while raising questions about artistic freedom in the NFT space.

Similarly, in *Nike v. StockX*, Nike filed a lawsuit against StockX for using images of its sneakers in NFT offerings. Nike alleged that StockX's NFTs, which included recognizable shoe designs and branding, were unauthorized and created consumer confusion. StockX defended its NFTs as "receipts" for physical shoes sold through its platform, arguing that they did not function as standalone digital goods. This case highlighted the complexities of trademark law in the digital realm, particularly regarding whether NFTs referencing physical goods require trademark licenses (*Nike v. StockX*, No. 1:22-cv-00983 (S.D.N.Y., 2023)).

In Europe, similar disputes have arisen as courts adapt to the challenges posed by virtual environments. In *Juventus v. Blockeras* (Tribunale di Roma, decision of July 20, 2022, ref. 32,072/2022), Juventus Football Club sued Blockeras S.r.L for minting NFT player cards featuring the club's trademarks without authorization. The Court of Rome ruled that this constituted trademark infringement and unfair competition, emphasizing that even if trademarks are not registered specifically for NFTs, their use in this context still requires permission from rights holders. The court also noted that well-known marks like Juventus' enjoy broader protection across various categories of goods and services

A related UK case, *Manchester United v. Sega* (High Court of Justice (UK), 2023) involved the soccer (football in European parlance) franchise Manchester United suing Sega and Sports Interactive for using its trademarked name and logo in the "Football Manager" video game without permission. The football club argued that incorporating its intellectual property into a commercial product without a license constituted infringement. Sega countered that the use was incidental and necessary for creating an accurate simulation experience. While this case remains unresolved, it highlights the tension between building realistic virtual environments and adhering to intellectual property.

The European Union has also taken proactive steps to address these issues through regulatory measures such as the **Digital Single Market Directive** and guidance from the European Union Intellectual Property Office (EUIPO). The EUIPO's guidelines classify virtual goods like NFTs under Class nine of the Nice Classification for "downloadable digital files authenticated by non-fungible tokens," ensuring that trademarks extend to digital assets when properly registered. Additionally, the European Parliament's October 2024 resolution confirmed that EU intellectual property law applies fully to virtual worlds like the metaverse, reinforcing that what is illegal offline as an infringement is equally illegal online.

Globally, China and Canada have also begun to tackle the challenges of trademarks in virtual environments. In China, courts have addressed disputes involving AI-generated content and virtual goods. A notable trend in China is the judicial recognition of the need to regulate digital replicas and ensure that AI-generated content does not undermine the rights of trademark holders. Chinese courts have emphasized the protection of well-known marks, even in digital contexts, as part of their broader goal of fostering fair competition and innovation.

Meanwhile, Canada is experiencing early cases exploring trademark use in metaverse applications. Canadian intellectual property law has started to grapple with the implications of virtual storefronts and AI-generated branding, with policymakers increasingly advocating for updates to address the rapidly developing digital marketplace. These cases highlight how nations outside the United States and Europe are also adapting to the rapid expansion of AI and virtual environments.

Reimagining Copyright, Trademark, and Moral Rights in the Digital Age: A Collaborative Path Forward

The advent of generative and diffusion AI models has revolutionized creative industries, offering unprecedented opportunities while simultaneously challenging the foundations of copyright, trademark, and moral rights law. These technologies frequently erase the lines between human and machine creativity, raising complex questions about authorship, ownership, and the scope of intellectual property protections. To address these challenges and harness the potential of AI responsibly, a reimagining of intellectual property frameworks is essential.

Generative AI disrupts the traditional notion that copyrightable works must be created by humans. Current laws in jurisdictions like the United

States require meaningful human contribution for copyright protection, as reaffirmed in cases such as *Thaler v. Perlmutter*, where a court ruled that works generated entirely by AI lack copyright eligibility. However, this approach may no longer suffice in an era where AI systems can produce outputs that rival human creativity. A potential solution could involve creating a new category of intellectual property rights specifically for AI-generated works, with ownership assigned to developers, users, or even shared between them based on their contributions.

Globally, there is significant variation in how these issues are addressed. For example, Japan has adopted a broad interpretation of fair use for AI training data to encourage innovation, while the European Union is considering more restrictive regulations requiring creators to "opt-in" for their works to be included in training datasets. These differing approaches highlight the need for international harmonization to avoid regulatory fragmentation and foster cross-border collaboration.

Copyright law must strike a delicate balance between protecting creators' rights and fostering innovation. One area ripe for reform is the duration of copyright protection. Current terms—life of the author plus 70 years in many jurisdictions—may be excessive in an age where AI can rapidly generate new works. Shortening these terms could accelerate the transition of works into the public domain, fueling creativity by providing raw material for reinterpretation and innovation.

The application of the fair use doctrine also requires reevaluation, especially considering the explosive *Warhol* decision by the US Supreme Court. Courts have historically applied fair use to transformative uses that add new meaning or purpose to original works. However, as seen in cases like *Authors Guild v. Google*, this standard becomes murky when applied to AI training datasets that repurpose copyrighted material on a massive scale. The *Warhol* decision further complicates this analysis by emphasizing that even transformative works may not qualify as fair use if they serve a similar commercial purpose as the original. This case has major implications for AI-generated images used commercially, particularly when the original source material was also created for commercial purposes. Under this framework, such uses could more readily constitute copyright violations, highlighting the need to reexamine how fair use applies to generative AI outputs. A conditional fair use framework could be introduced, requiring developers to demonstrate that their use of copyrighted works does not harm market value or excessively replicate original content. This approach would incentivize transparency and ethical data use while preserving creators' rights.

Trademark law faces unique challenges in virtual environments and digital marketplaces where AI-generated content can inadvertently infringe on established marks. Cases like *Hermès v. Rothschild* and *Nike v. StockX* illustrate how unauthorized digital replicas can dilute brand identity and mislead consumers. To adapt to these realities, trademark law could incorporate mandatory labeling requirements for AI-generated goods and services to ensure transparency and prevent consumer confusion. AI also presents opportunities for trademark enforcement. Tools powered by machine learning can monitor online platforms for infringement more efficiently than traditional methods, enabling brand owners to respond quickly to unauthorized uses. However, these tools must be deployed responsibly to avoid overreach or misuse.

Moral rights, particularly the right of integrity and attribution, are increasingly relevant in an era where AI can distort or misrepresent an artist's original work. European jurisdictions provide robust moral rights protections that persist even after a creator's death, as seen in cases like *Turner Entertainment Co. v. Huston*, where a French court ruled against colorizing a black-and-white film without the director's consent. In contrast, US law under the VARA offers limited protections that do not extend to many forms of creative expression. To address these disparities, moral rights could be expanded globally to cover emerging technologies like generative AI. For instance, creators whose works inform training datasets should have a right to attribution, ensuring their contributions are recognized even if their economic rights are not directly implicated.

The path forward lies not only in legal reform but also in fostering collaboration between creators, developers, and policymakers. Licensing frameworks tailored to generative AI can ensure fair compensation for creators while enabling developers to access high-quality training data ethically. Transparency measures—such as requiring documentation of training datasets or labeling AI-generated outputs—can further build trust among stakeholders. Moreover, public-private partnerships could play a pivotal role in shaping ethical guidelines for AI development. Initiatives like the Flemish museum's use of AI to create a "new" Rembrandt painting, based on extensive analysis of the artist's style and techniques, demonstrate how human-AI collaboration can yield innovative results.

As generative AI reshapes creative industries, it presents both challenges and opportunities for intellectual property law. By reimagining copyright, trademark, and moral rights frameworks to accommodate this transformative technology, we can ensure that creators' rights are protected while fostering an environment that encourages innovation. This moment calls for bold thinking and international cooperation to address the complexities introduced by generative AI. By prioritizing ethical practices, transparency, and collaboration among stakeholders, we can build a sustainable model where human ingenuity and machine intelligence coexist harmoniously redefining creativity for generations to come.

Works Referenced

Andersen v. Stability AI. No. 3:23-cv-00201. United States District Court for the Northern District of California, 2024.

Andy Warhol Foundation for the Visual Arts, Inc. v. Goldsmith. 598 U.S. 508. Supreme Court of the United States, 2023.

ANI Media v. OpenAI. Supreme Court of India, 2025.

Authors Guild v. OpenAI Inc. No. 1:23-cv-08292. United States District Court for the Southern District of New York, 2024.

Berne Convention for the Protection of Literary and Artistic Works. Adopted 1886, revised 1971.

Campbell v. Acuff-Rose Music. 510 U.S. 569. Supreme Court of the United States, 1994.

CanLII v. Caseway AI. Supreme Court of British Columbia, 2024.

Copyright Act of 1790. United States Congress.

Copyright Act of 1909. United States Congress.

Copyright Act of 1976. Pub. L. No. 94–553, 90 Stat. 2541.

Digital Single Market Directive. Directive 2019/790/EU. European Parliament and Council of the European Union, 2019.

Du Sautoy, Marcus. *The Creativity Code: How AI Is Learning to Write, Paint and Think*. Harvard University Press, 2019.

EU Trademark Regulation (EUTMR). European Union.

Getty Images v. Stability AI. No. 1:23-cv-01339. United States District Court for the District of Delaware, 2024.

Getty Images (US) Inc. v. Stability AI Ltd. High Court of Justice, United Kingdom, 2024.

Haase, Jennifer, and Paul Hanel. "GPT-4 Outperforms Most Humans in Creative Ideation Tasks." 2024.

Hermès International v. Rothschild. No. 1:22-cv-00384-JSR. United States District Court for the Southern District of New York, 2023.

Infopaq International A/S v. Danske Dagblades Forening. C-5/08. Court of Justice of the European Union, 2009.

Juventus v. Blockeras. Decision of July 20, 2022, ref. 32072/2022. Tribunale di Roma, 2022.

Lanham Act (Trademark Act of 1946). Pub. L. No. 79–489, 60 Stat. 427.

Madrid Protocol. World Intellectual Property Organization.

Manchester United v. Sega. High Court of Justice, United Kingdom, 2023.

Nike v. StockX. No. 1:22-cv-00983. United States District Court for the Southern District of New York, 2023.

OpenAI Team. "GPT-4 Technical Report." OpenAI.com, Mar. 2023.

Painer v. Danske Dagblades Forening. CJEU Case C-145/10, European Court of Justice. Dec. 1, 2011.

RIAA v. Suno Inc. No. 1:24-cv-11611. United States District Court for the District of Columbia, 2024.

Semiconductor Chip Protection Act. United States Congress, 1984.

Sonny Bono Copyright Term Extension Act. United States Congress, 1998.

Thaler v. Perlmutter. 687 F. Supp. 3d 140. United States District Court for the District of Columbia, 2023.

Trade-Related Aspects of Intellectual Property Rights (TRIPS). World Trade Organization.

Turner Entertainment Co. v. Huston. Cour de Cassation, France, May 28, 1991.

Twentieth Century Music Corp. v. Aiken. 422 U.S. 151. Supreme Court of the United States, 1975.

Ulrich, Karl. *Research on AI Creativity and Innovation*. The Wharton School, University of Pennsylvania, 2024.

Vaidhyanathan, Siva. *Copyrights and Copywrongs: The Rise of Intellectual Property and How It Threatens Creativity*. New York University Press, 2001.

Visual Artists Rights Act (VARA). Pub. L. No. 101–650, Title VI, §602(a), Dec. 1, 1990

WIPO Copyright Treaty. World Intellectual Property Organization.

Zarya of the Dawn by Kris Kashtanova Copyright Decision (US). US Copyright Office Ruling, Revised Jan. 2024.

Zinnemann v. TeleMontecarlo. Court of Rome, November 2005.

Six Cultural (Mis)appropriation in the Age of AI

The intersection of cultural appropriation and artificial intelligence represents one of the most complex challenges facing the art world today. As Dr. Sarah Richardson, Professor of Digital Ethics at MIT, observes, "We are witnessing an unprecedented transformation in how cultural elements can be appropriated, replicated, and commodified through AI systems. The scale and speed of this transformation demand immediate attention and thoughtful response." Cultural appropriation has long been a critical concern in the arts, but AI technology has fundamentally altered both its scope and impact. This chapter examines how traditional understandings of cultural appropriation must change to address these new challenges posed by AI in the fine arts while examining potential pathways toward ethical innovation and cultural preservation.

Auguste Rodin's assertion that "the artist must create a spark before he can make a fire, and before art is born, the artist must be ready to be consumed by the fire of his own creation" underscores the deeply personal, passionate, and transformative process of artistic creation. Art is an act of self-sacrifice, steeped in cultural memory and individual emotion. Yet, this vision contrasts sharply with how AI systems now engage with art—particularly through their appropriation of cultural artifacts. By extracting patterns from datasets often built on uncredited or misappropriated works, AI generates art devoid of the emotional depth and cultural connection that define human creativity. This mechanized replication trivializes sacred symbols, perpetuates stereotypes, and undermines the sovereignty of marginalized communities. Rodin's vision of art as an intimate act of creation highlights the ethical concerns surrounding AI's commodification of cultural expressions, reducing historic human stories to algorithmic outputs lacking authenticity or respect.

The Mechanics of Appropriation in AI Art

The mechanics of appropriation in AI art lie in how these systems process, analyze, and generate creative outputs by leveraging vast datasets. These datasets often include culturally significant works—traditional paintings, sculptures, motifs, and designs—sourced from digital archives, museums, and even personal uploads. AI art generators, powered by algorithms like GANs and Diffusion Models, analyze these datasets to learn patterns, textures, colors, and styles. Once trained, these systems can synthesize new images that often borrow heavily from existing artistic traditions, presenting them as novel creations.

Generative AI, such as GANs, typically involves two neural networks: a generator that creates new data (in this case, images) and a discriminator that tries to distinguish between real data (the training set) and the generated data. The two networks are trained against each other, with the generator improving its ability to create realistic images and the discriminator improving its ability to spot fakes. The result is an AI capable of generating novel images that often mimic the styles and patterns found in its training data, including culturally significant designs.

Diffusion Models, on the other hand, work by progressively adding noise (deliberate introduction of randomness into data during the model's training and generation processes) to an image until it becomes pure static. The model is then trained to reverse this process, learning to remove the noise step-by-step and reconstruct the original image. By training on a dataset of images, including culturally significant works, the diffusion model learns to generate new images by "diffusing" noise and recreating patterns and styles present in the training data. This process can lead to the generation of images that appropriate cultural motifs without understanding their context or meaning.

This process has historical parallels with artistic practices like collage or pop art, where artists such as Jasper Johns and Robert Rauschenberg recontextualized existing cultural elements to create new works. Johns famously incorporated everyday objects like flags, targets, and numbers into his paintings, transforming mundane symbols into layered works of art that invited viewers to question their cultural and personal significance.

Rauschenberg took this approach further with his "combine paintings," blending non-traditional materials and found objects such as newspapers, fabric, taxidermied animals, and even a quilt and a pillow in his iconic work *Bed*. These artists elevated ordinary items into fine art, challenging the boundaries of artistic media and interpretation. However, AI fundamentally differs in its approach and scale. Traditional artists engage with cultural materials through intent and understanding, often acknowledging the origins of their source material and, in some cases, forming collaborations or dialogues with the cultures they borrow from. In contrast, AI systems operate without cultural awareness or ethical considerations. These algorithms treat inputs as raw data, devoid of the historical, spiritual, or emotional significance embedded in the original works.

For instance, an AI system trained on Indigenous patterns might generate visually striking designs that mimic these cultural motifs. While the output may appear innovative to an uninformed audience, it strips the patterns of their cultural context and sacred meanings. Many of these symbols are deeply tied to specific ceremonies, histories, or spiritual beliefs within Indigenous communities. By commodifying such elements without consent or acknowledgment, AI risks perpetuating cultural erasure and exploitation.

For example, AI-generated patterns inspired by Indigenous or African textile designs have been used in the fashion industry to create clothing and accessories sold on platforms like Instagram and Etsy, often marketed as "unique" or "tribal-inspired" without any involvement or benefit to the original cultures. These designs are further popularized when worn by celebrity influencers on TikTok, where trends can rapidly amplify their visibility while distancing the works from their cultural origins. This issue becomes even more problematic when AI blends elements from multiple cultures into a single output—creating hybrid designs that may be visually appealing but misrepresent or distort their original meanings.

The scale of AI operations exacerbates these issues. A human artist might appropriate elements from a single culture for a specific project, but AI systems can replicate and distribute thousands of such works globally within seconds. Platforms like MidJourney, for example, allow users to generate art based on text prompts describing traditional aesthetics or cultural themes. For instance, a user could input a prompt like "Japanese ukiyo-e-inspired waves" or "Nigerian tribal patterns," resulting in a flood of outputs that imitate these styles without understanding their significance. Some of these AI-generated designs have been commercialized as wall art or clothing prints on marketplaces like Redbubble or Society6, further disconnecting the work from its cultural origins.

Additionally, AI systems have been used to create replicas of historical art styles, such as ancient Greek pottery designs or Aztec carvings, which are then incorporated into home décor or digital assets in gaming platforms. This often occurs without regard for the cultural contexts or the rights of the communities to whom these traditions belong. For example, AI-generated Mayan glyph-inspired fonts have appeared in digital projects marketed on creative platforms like Envato.

This rapid production raises ethical concerns about cultural exploitation and threatens to devalue original works by flooding markets with inauthentic imitations. With thousands of such AI-generated pieces saturating platforms like Pinterest and Canva, the original artistry is overshadowed, and audiences are left with a distorted understanding of these cultural aesthetics.

AI systems often replicate Indian cultural motifs in ways that reflect a "Western gaze," homogenizing diverse traditions into oversimplified or exoticized visuals. Research shows that text-to-image generators frequently portray Indian subcultures inaccurately, with traditional clothing styles poorly represented, draped incorrectly, or paired with ornaments and patterns from unrelated regions. These depictions reduce the complexity of Indian culture into generic or stereotypical representations, reinforcing biases and diminishing the richness of its heritage.

Similarly, Indigenous iconography, often treated as public domain due to its age, is frequently appropriated by AI systems for commercial purposes without any acknowledgment of its sacred or cultural significance. Because these symbols fall outside the scope of copyright or trademark protection, their use does not violate intellectual property laws, allowing companies and individuals to monetize them without legal repercussions. However, this lack of legal protection often leads to their commodification, stripping these symbols of their spiritual and historical meanings. For instance, sacred Navajo patterns or Maori designs may be reproduced by AI tools and then sold as prints, home décor, or fashion items on e-commerce platforms like Etsy and Zazzle.

Furthermore, this unregulated use of public domain materials by AI amplifies cultural erasure. By prioritizing visual appeal over authenticity, these systems risk trivializing the cultural heritage they draw from, reducing deeply meaningful traditions into decorative or commercial assets. For communities that rely on these cultural expressions to assert their identity and history, such appropriation undermines their efforts to protect and preserve their heritage, contributing to ongoing cultural exploitation.

The ethical implications of these practices are disturbing. By "remixing" cultural artifacts at unprecedented speed and scale, AI deepens existing inequalities in artistic representation and commodifies sacred symbols for profit. Unlike human artists who can engage in dialogue with the cultures they draw from—or face accountability for their actions—AI systems bypass these ethical responsibilities entirely. This raises urgent questions about authorship, consent, and the preservation of cultural heritage in an era dominated by algorithmic creativity. It also creates a situation where the original creators are not only not benefiting from the use of their cultural heritage, but they are also being actively harmed by the misrepresentation and dilution of its meaning.

The Evolution of Cultural Appropriation

Cultural appropriation in the arts has historically reflected power imbalances, where dominant cultures adopt, modify, and profit from the cultural expressions of marginalized communities without proper understanding or acknowledgment. As Professor James Chen of the University of California, Berkeley, explains, this process is "a complex interplay of power dynamics," often perpetuating inequities and erasing the cultural significance of the appropriated elements.

One of the most prominent and well-discussed examples is the colonial legacy embodied by institutions like the British Museum. The museum's possession of the Parthenon Marbles—removed by Lord Elgin from Athens under questionable circumstances during Greece's Ottoman occupation—illustrates how powerful entities have historically justified cultural appropriation under the guise of preservation.

Despite Greece's ongoing demands for their return, the British Museum continues to argue that they are better preserved and more accessible in London, perpetuating a colonial mindset that strips artifacts from their cultural context and silences the voices of their rightful owners. As historian Dr. Shashi Bhat notes, "The Parthenon Marbles symbolize a broader issue—the enduring power imbalance that allows institutions to dictate the narrative of cultural heritage while marginalizing those who created it."

This dynamic extends beyond ancient artifacts to more contemporary forms of cultural appropriation in art and commerce. For example, Native American symbols such as dreamcatchers, headdresses, and tribal patterns have been widely co-opted by fashion brands and mass-market industries without consultation or benefit to Indigenous communities. These symbols often hold deep spiritual or ceremonial significance, yet they are commodified as decorative motifs or trendy accessories. Native American artist John Thompson has spoken out against this practice, stating: "Our sacred symbols and traditional designs are routinely copied and commercialized without any understanding of their spiritual significance or connection to our communities."

A striking example is the widespread use of feathered headdresses in music festivals and fashion campaigns—items traditionally reserved for leaders or warriors who have earned them through acts of honor within their communities. Such commercialization not only misrepresents Indigenous cultures but also undermines efforts to preserve their traditions.

The appropriation of African art in early twentieth-century modernism offers another illustrative example. Artists like Henri Matisse famously incorporated African masks and sculptures into their works, using these elements to shape movements such as Cubism and Fauvism. While these artists acknowledged the visual power of African art, they often failed to recognize its cultural and spiritual significance. Art historian Susan Vogel observes that "the modernist appropriation of African art stripped these objects of their cultural essence, reducing them to exotic curiosities that served Western artistic ambitions."

Similarly, Italian artist Amedeo Modigliani's elongated portraits drew heavily on African masks but presented them through a lens that prioritized European aesthetic innovation over cultural respect. These practices not only erased the original context but also reinforced colonial narratives by framing non-Western art as raw material for Western creativity.

The Japonisme movement in late nineteenth-century Europe further illustrates how dominant cultures have historically appropriated marginalized ones. Western artists such as Claude Monet, Mary Cassatt, and Edgar Degas were inspired by Japanese prints, ceramics, and textiles during a period when Japan was forcibly opened to trade with Western powers. While these artists admired Japanese aesthetics, they often disregarded the cultural philosophies underpinning these works.

For instance, Mary Cassatt's *The Bath* adopts stylistic elements from Japanese portraiture but strips them of their original meaning, transforming them into decorative features for Western audiences. Cultural theorist Ruth Benedict has noted that this fascination with Japanese art was frequently accompanied by "a complete disregard for the cultural and philosophical principles underpinning these creations."

More recently, examples like Mexican Ayuujk designs highlight how contemporary industries continue to exploit Indigenous cultures for profit. Ayuujk refers to the intricate and vibrant textile traditions of the Mixe people of Oaxaca, Mexico, who are renowned for their exceptional weaving and embroidery techniques. Their textiles are characterized by intricate geometric patterns, vibrant natural dyes, and the use of traditional backstrap looms. The most iconic example is the huipil, a traditional blouse worn by Mixe women. Each huipil is unique, reflecting the weaver's identity, community, and cultural heritage, with its geometric patterns often symbolizing natural elements, deities, or mythological figures that convey deep cultural stories and beliefs.

Despite their cultural and artistic significance, Mixe Ayuujk designs have been appropriated without consent or acknowledgment. One glaring example is the case of French designer Isabel Marant, who plagiarized traditional Ayuujk blouses—collective creations that represent ancestral wisdom—and sold them at exorbitant prices under her luxury brand. This act not only commodified sacred designs but also stripped them of their cultural context, reducing centuries of Mixe heritage to a marketable product for Western consumption. Mixe community leaders decried this act as a blatant theft of their cultural identity, calling for greater recognition of their artistic traditions and legal protections to prevent future exploitation.

Similarly, non-Indigenous artist Amanda PL faced backlash for copying the distinctive Woodland style pioneered by Anishinaabe artist Norval Morrisseau. Her unauthorized use of the style, rooted in Anishinaabe spiritual and cultural traditions, demonstrated a lack of understanding or respect for the sacred significance of the motifs she reproduced. This incident, like the appropriation of Ayuujk designs, underscores how marginalized communities remain vulnerable to exploitation in both fine art and commercial markets.

These cases exemplify how cultural appropriation consistently reflects systemic power imbalances that favor dominant cultures while undermining marginalized ones. By taking elements from these communities without acknowledgment or respect, such practices dilute the richness of original cultural expressions while reinforcing inequities rooted in colonialism. As Native American artist and activist Wendy Red Star observed, "Our stories, symbols, and traditions are not just decorative. They carry the essence of who we are. To steal them is to deny our existence."

The introduction of artificial intelligence into artistic creation has transformed traditional patterns of cultural appropriation in profound ways. Dr. Maya Patel, leading researcher at the AI Ethics Institute, explains: "AI systems don't just copy cultural elements—they can analyze, deconstruct, and recombine them at an unprecedented scale, creating thousands of derivative works in seconds. This technological capability raises entirely new questions about cultural ownership and authenticity."

The MidJourney Indigenous Art controversy of 2023 vividly illustrates the challenges posed by AI's ability to replicate culturally significant art styles. When MidJourney, a popular AI-powered art generator, began creating images in the style of various Indigenous traditions—including motifs from the Navajo, Hopi, and Maori cultures—it sparked international debate about digital colonialism, a term that critiques how advanced technologies are used by dominant groups to exploit the knowledge, art, and heritage of marginalized communities.

One of the key criticisms stemmed from the way MidJourney's algorithms processed publicly available Indigenous art. The AI's training dataset likely included countless images uploaded online, often without permission or proper attribution. By analyzing these works, the AI learned to reproduce the intricate patterns, colors, and symbols integral to Indigenous art forms, often combining elements from multiple traditions into hybridized outputs. These AI-generated images were then widely distributed, appearing on platforms like Etsy, Instagram, and commercial print-on-demand services, where they were marketed as "Indigenous-inspired art" or sold as home décor and fashion accessories. This not only devalued the original works but also diverted potential revenue from Indigenous artists, many of whom rely on these art forms for their livelihoods.

The MidJourney controversy highlighted the stark inadequacies of existing intellectual property (IP) laws in protecting Indigenous art from the unique challenges posed by AI technologies. Current IP frameworks are designed to safeguard individual creators or corporate entities but fail to address the communal and intergenerational nature of cultural heritage. This legal gap has left Indigenous art—particularly ancient or collectively created designs—vulnerable to appropriation and exploitation. As IP attorney Daniel Alvarez, an expert in Cultural IP law, explains: "The law was designed to protect individual creators and corporations, not entire cultures. This puts Indigenous groups at a significant disadvantage when their heritage is appropriated by advanced technologies."

A clear example of this failure is the **Indian Arts and Crafts Act of 1990**, a US law intended to prevent the misrepresentation of Native American arts and crafts. While the act prohibits non-Indigenous individuals or entities from falsely marketing products as Native-made, it does not extend to the digital domain or AI technologies. The law is focused on fraudulent claims rather than the use or reproduction of cultural designs in new contexts. Thus, AI systems like MidJourney, which replicate Indigenous art styles without falsely claiming to be Indigenous-made, fall outside the scope of this legislation. The result is a legal loophole that allows AI-generated works to flood the market, commodifying sacred and culturally significant designs without any consent, acknowledgment, or benefit to the originating communities.

The Case for Cultural Intellectual Property (Cultural IP) Law

To address these challenges, Alvarez and other experts advocate for the creation of a new legal framework—Cultural IP Law—that recognizes the unique ownership rights of Indigenous and marginalized communities. Unlike traditional IP laws, which focus on individual authorship, Cultural IP law would protect the collective ownership of cultural expressions. For example, the intricate patterns of Mixe Ayuujk textiles or Navajo weavings would be legally recognized as the communal property of the Mixe and Navajo peoples, ensuring that these communities have control over how their cultural heritage is used, particularly in AI applications.

Cultural IP law would operate on several foundational principles. First, it would recognize communal ownership, affirming that cultural heritage belongs to the community as a whole rather than any single individual. Second, it would include mandatory consent mechanisms, requiring AI developers and commercial entities to obtain explicit permission from cultural communities before using their art or symbols in training datasets or products. Third, the law would mandate benefit-sharing agreements, ensuring that communities receive compensation or royalties when their cultural heritage is commercialized. Finally, cultural significance thresholds would protect sacred or ceremonial objects from replication or misuse, preventing their decontextualization and commodification.

The call for Cultural IP law is not without precedent. Scholars and organizations have long advocated for better protections of Indigenous heritage. For example, Professor Erica-Irene Daes, former Chair of the United Nations Working Group on Indigenous Populations, has argued that "Indigenous peoples have the right to maintain, control, protect, and develop their cultural heritage, including traditional knowledge and cultural expressions." Her contributions to the UN Declaration on the Rights of Indigenous Peoples (UNDRIP) provide a foundation for reimagining international IP laws to include collective cultural protections. Similarly, legal scholar Deborah Root, in her book *Cannibal Culture: Art, Appropriation, and the Commodification of Difference*, highlights how the commodification of Indigenous art reduces dynamic cultural expressions to static marketable goods, exacerbating systemic inequities.

Creating a robust Cultural IP framework would require a multi-pronged approach:

1. National Legislation: Countries could enact domestic laws to protect the cultural heritage of Indigenous groups. For instance, expanding the Indian Arts and Crafts Act to address AI technologies and digital platforms could provide a blueprint for national action.
2. International Agreements: Building on treaties like the UNESCO Convention on the Protection and Promotion of the Diversity of Cultural Expressions, a global treaty could establish shared standards for protecting cultural IP. This would ensure consistency across borders, addressing the global nature of AI-generated art.
3. Industry Standards: Technology companies could adopt voluntary ethical guidelines that prioritize consent and benefit-sharing when

using cultural materials. Companies like OpenAI and MidJourney could implement opt-in systems, allowing communities to decide whether their cultural heritage can be included in AI training datasets.

4. Cultural Registries: Governments or international bodies could create cultural registries where communities document their heritage. These registries would provide a clear reference for determining ownership, ensuring that consent is obtained before cultural elements are commercialized.

The development of Cultural IP law offers a pathway to address the systemic inequities exposed by controversies like MidJourney. Without such protections, Indigenous communities face ongoing risks of exploitation, their cultural expressions reduced to aesthetic commodities. As Maria Running Wolf eloquently stated, "Our cultural expressions are not relics for others to use as they please. They are living parts of our identity and our history. Protecting them isn't just about preserving the past—it's about safeguarding our future." By prioritizing collaboration, consent, and respect for cultural heritage, a new framework for Cultural IP law could ensure that technological innovation is aligned with ethical responsibility, fostering a future of mutual respect rather than exploitation.

Ethically, the Midjourney controversy brought attention to the lack of consent and benefit-sharing in AI art generation. Indigenous communities were not consulted before their art was fed into the AI training datasets, nor did they receive any compensation for the commercial use of these works. This practice has been widely criticized as a continuation of colonial extraction, where resources—including cultural expressions—are taken from marginalized groups without their input or benefit.

Culturally, the controversy sparked fears about the erosion of Indigenous identities. Many Indigenous art forms are deeply tied to rituals, spiritual beliefs, and community practices. By divorcing these designs from their cultural contexts, AI-generated art risks stripping them of their original meanings. For example, Navajo patterns created for ceremonial use were reproduced by the AI in ways that could be considered disrespectful or inappropriate if misused, such as being printed on casual clothing or home décor.

The Japanese Woodblock Print controversy provides a compelling example of how AI's use of cultural heritage can spark significant debate. Several AI art platforms, including MidJourney and DALL-E, began generating images in the style of traditional ukiyo-e prints, a revered Japanese art form that dates to the Edo period. Ukiyo-e prints are characterized by their intricate designs, vibrant colors, and layered woodblock printing techniques, which often depict landscapes, kabuki actors, or scenes from everyday life. These works are not just visually striking; they carry deep cultural, historical, and spiritual significance, embodying centuries of artistic mastery and Japanese cultural identity.

The controversy arose when these AI-generated ukiyo-e-style images began to flood online marketplaces like Etsy and Redbubble, often labeled as "Japanese-inspired art." Critics argued that these platforms profited from culturally significant designs while undermining the value of authentic ukiyo-e prints. Takashi Yamamoto, a master printmaker, voiced his concerns: "These systems cannot understand the spiritual and cultural significance embedded in our techniques. Each traditional print carries centuries of cultural knowledge that cannot be reduced to mere visual patterns." His statement underscores the gap between the cultural depth of traditional ukiyo-e and the superficial mimicry of AI-generated versions.

A key issue in this controversy was the lack of consent and acknowledgment. AI platforms trained their algorithms on publicly available images of ukiyo-e prints without consulting Japanese artists, historians, or cultural institutions. This practice sparked accusations of digital colonialism, as these platforms appropriated a cornerstone of Japanese heritage for commercial purposes without contributing to its preservation or benefiting the communities tied to it. Furthermore, the AI-generated prints often lacked the nuanced craftsmanship and symbolic depth of traditional ukiyo-e, reducing a centuries-old art form to a generic aesthetic.

The controversy also raised legal questions about intellectual property. Many ukiyo-e prints are in the public domain due to their age, which meant that AI platforms were not legally required to seek permission to use them as training data. However, critics argued that the ethical considerations of cultural appropriation go beyond the limitations of copyright law. The lack of safeguards for communal cultural heritage allowed companies to profit without accountability, setting a troubling precedent for the exploitation of other art forms.

Public backlash prompted some AI platforms to respond. MidJourney, for instance, announced updates to its dataset curation process, pledging to include more ethical considerations when incorporating culturally significant works. However, these measures were widely criticized as reactive rather than proactive, with little transparency about how cultural heritage would be protected moving forward. Advocacy groups in Japan called for stricter regulations to prevent the unauthorized use of cultural materials, emphasizing the importance of respecting traditional art forms in an age of AI-driven innovation.

The outcome of the controversy remains unresolved, but it has reignited discussions about the need for global standards to protect cultural heritage in the digital era. The case highlighted the tension between technological advancement and cultural preservation, with many calling for a more ethical approach that prioritizes consent, collaboration, and the acknowledgment of cultural significance. As Yamamoto warned, "If we allow technology to strip away the meaning of our traditions, we risk losing the soul of our culture." His words echo the broader challenge of balancing innovation with respect for the cultural legacies that enrich human creativity.

Economic Impact and Market Disruption

The economic implications of AI-driven cultural appropriation extend far beyond individual artists, reshaping entire markets and threatening the livelihoods of traditional creators. Economic analyst Maria García notes, "We're seeing a fundamental restructuring of the traditional art market, where AI-generated 'traditional' art can be produced at virtually no cost, directly competing with authentic cultural artifacts and traditional artists."

This disruption is particularly pronounced in markets tied to Indigenous art, where authenticity and cultural significance are intrinsic to the value of the works. For instance, the Aboriginal Art Market Study of 2024 revealed that AI-generated "Aboriginal-style" artwork captured 15 percent of the digital art market in this category, leading to a staggering 30 percent decrease in income for traditional Aboriginal artists. This decline has significant consequences for Indigenous communities, as art sales often fund essential cultural practices and community programs.

Aboriginal artist David Yirrkala highlights this impact: "Our art is not just about patterns and colors—it tells the stories of our Dreamtime, our connection to country. AI-generated imitations strip away this meaning while undermining our ability to maintain our cultural practices." The financial losses extend beyond Indigenous markets. A recent report from researchers at Washington University and New York University found that freelancers in digital art experienced a sharp decline in employment opportunities due to the proliferation of AI-generated content on platforms like Upwork and Fiverr. Many reported reduced incomes as clients opted for cheaper AI alternatives rather than commissioning human artists.

Similarly, digital marketplaces such as Adobe Stock and Shutterstock have been flooded with AI-generated images mimicking Indigenous designs, often priced significantly lower than authentic works. For example, one contributor on Adobe Stock offered over 8,000 digital designs resembling Aboriginal art for approximately $88 each—none of which benefited Indigenous communities. An AI-generated image resembling a Navajo rug design might be offered for a few dollars, while an authentic Navajo rug woven by a skilled artisan could cost hundreds or thousands of dollars. This price disparity creates unfair competition, making it difficult for traditional artists to compete in the digital marketplace. This "race to the bottom" in pricing devalues the skill and cultural knowledge embedded in authentic artwork.

The broader art market has also faced challenges due to market saturation caused by AI-generated art. The ease and speed with which AI can produce visually appealing works have led to an oversupply that devalues original human-made art. Buyers increasingly struggle to distinguish between authentic pieces and AI imitations, further eroding trust in the market. This phenomenon mirrors economist George Akerlof's "lemons problem," where uncertainty about authenticity lowers buyers' willingness to pay for genuine works. As a result, traditional artists often find it difficult to sell their creations at fair prices, leading to further economic precarity.

Specific examples illustrate the scale of this disruption. In Australia, a Productivity Commission report revealed that 75 percent of products featuring Indigenous-style elements were crafted by non-Indigenous individuals, with 60 percent of these listings generated by creators using AI tools. This trend undermines efforts to protect Indigenous Cultural and Intellectual Property (ICIP) and deprives communities of revenue streams tied to their heritage.

Amy Allerton, a Gumbaynggirr and Bundjalung artist, expressed concern over how AI-generated "fake" Indigenous art combines styles from various nations without understanding or respecting their unique cultural contexts. She noted that such practices not only misrepresent Indigenous cultures but also harm their economic well-being.

Moreover, the commodification enabled by AI threatens to dilute the value of artistic labor itself. Traditional artists invest years in developing unique styles and techniques that reflect their personal experiences and cultural heritage. However, AI systems can replicate these styles within seconds based on scraped data from online sources—often without credit or compensation to the original creators. This dynamic has led some artists to withdraw their work from online platforms entirely out of fear that it will be appropriated by AI systems.

The rise of generative AI in the art market underscores a troubling economic trend: while companies developing these tools raise billions from venture capitalists, many artists face financial instability or are forced out of their professions altogether.

New Economic Models

The rise of AI in the arts has necessitated the development of alternative economic models to ensure fair compensation and empowerment for artists and cultural communities. These models aim to address the economic disruption caused by AI-generated art and foster equitable relationships between creators and users of cultural heritage. By integrating ethical practices and innovative mechanisms, these models provide pathways for preserving cultural integrity while enabling sustainable economic participation.

Community licensing frameworks offer structured mechanisms for cultural groups to retain control over their artistic expressions while enabling ethical commercial use. These frameworks ensure that creators are compensated fairly and that their cultural heritage is respected. A prominent example is the work of the Aboriginal Artists Agency (AAA) in Australia, which has implemented licensing agreements that allow Indigenous artists to authorize specific uses of their works, such as reproduction on textiles, merchandise, or other products. These agreements include provisions for royalties, attribution, and cultural consultation, ensuring that the artists and their communities benefit economically and socially.

One notable case involves the licensing of Aboriginal dot paintings for fashion collaborations. These agreements often include clauses that require consultation with community elders to ensure cultural appropriateness, reflecting a holistic approach to cultural preservation. Such frameworks could be adapted for the AI era by requiring developers to seek explicit permission before incorporating culturally significant works into training datasets. For example, AI systems could operate under licensing agreements that mandate benefit-sharing with Indigenous communities, similar to existing frameworks in environmental resource management like the Nagoya Protocol.

Artist cooperatives provide a collaborative platform where creators can pool resources, share knowledge, and collectively market their work, especially in regions or communities with limited access to traditional markets. These cooperatives empower marginalized artists by reducing overhead costs and ensuring equitable profit distribution. An excellent example of this model is Stocksy United, a photographer-owned cooperative that prioritizes artistic integrity and ensures that profits are shared among its members. Similarly, the Meerkat Media Collective blends creative residencies with collective decision-making, offering members access to shared equipment and networking opportunities.

In the context of AI, such cooperatives could evolve into centralized hubs where artists collectively negotiate licensing terms for their works. For instance, a cooperative for digital artists could collectively license their works to AI developers under unified terms, ensuring that no individual artist is left vulnerable to exploitation by large tech companies. These cooperatives could also provide legal support, helping artists navigate the complexities of AI-related licensing agreements and intellectual property laws.

Hybrid marketplaces serve as a vital bridge between traditional art forms and modern digital platforms, offering new revenue streams for artists and cultural communities while ensuring cultural preservation and authenticity. Platforms like Saatchi Art and Artfinder have already proven the viability of this model by enabling artists to sell both physical works and digital reproductions to a global audience. Expanding this concept to include culturally significant art forms could open new opportunities for underrepresented communities. For example, a hybrid marketplace could feature Mixe Ayuujk textiles, Zulu beadwork, or Maori carvings, alongside authenticated digital replicas secured with blockchain technology. Blockchain-based systems could verify the provenance of each item, ensuring buyers are confident in the authenticity of their purchase while allowing artists and their communities to benefit from transparent royalty structures.

These marketplaces could also be designed to function as educational hubs, providing buyers with rich background information about the cultural and historical significance of each piece. For example, a buyer of a Navajo weaving might gain access to videos or written content detailing the spiritual and ceremonial role of the patterns and the traditional techniques used in its creation. Similarly, a marketplace selling Aboriginal dot paintings could offer insights into the Dreamtime stories that inspire the designs, fostering deeper respect and appreciation for the heritage represented.

In addition to selling finished products, hybrid marketplaces could integrate immersive digital experiences to further connect buyers with the cultures they are supporting. For instance, buyers could attend virtual workshops led by Indigenous artisans or participate in live-streamed events where cultural experts explain the significance of certain motifs or methods. These interactive features would not only enrich the purchasing experience but also create new income streams for artists by monetizing their cultural knowledge and expertise.

Furthermore, marketplaces could adopt subscription-based models that offer exclusive access to new collections, limited-edition digital artworks, or curated experiences tied to specific cultural traditions. For example, a subscription could provide members with early access to a line of handwoven Andean textiles, along with a digital library containing stories about the region's weaving traditions and the challenges faced by local artisans.

A particularly innovative expansion of hybrid marketplaces could involve collaborations with the gaming and VR industries. Digital replicas of traditional art forms could be sold as virtual assets for use in VR environments or as skins in video games. For instance, a VR platform could partner with Indigenous communities to offer culturally inspired clothing or environments within the virtual world, with a portion of proceeds directly supporting the artists and their communities.

Fair Trade Certification for AI Art

Fair Trade certification in cultural arts offers a transformative model for addressing the exploitation of cultural heritage in the age of AI. Inspired by existing Fair Trade principles in commodities like coffee and creative industries like music, this framework seeks to ensure ethical practices, fair compensation, and cultural preservation. Just as Fair Trade coffee protects small-scale farmers from exploitation by guaranteeing fair wages and sustainable practices, a Fair Trade AI certification would require developers to obtain explicit consent from cultural communities before using their artistic works in training datasets. Moreover, it would ensure recurring royalties and attribution for communities whose cultural expressions influence AI-generated outputs. This approach provides a mechanism to counter the unchecked commodification of cultural heritage, ensuring that it is treated not as a free resource but as a living tradition deserving recognition and respect.

The model builds on successful precedents from the music industry, where initiatives like LANDR's Fair Trade AI and the Fair Trade Music campaign have empowered creators by ensuring transparency and equitable revenue distribution. LANDR, an AI-driven music mastering platform, introduced a Fair Trade AI model to help musicians retain control over their intellectual property while benefiting financially from AI-assisted tools. Similarly, the Fair Trade Music campaign in Seattle negotiated agreements between local musicians and venues to guarantee fair wages and better working conditions. These efforts demonstrate that Fair Trade principles can level the playing field in creative industries by addressing systemic power imbalances and ensuring creators receive their fair share of the economic benefits generated by their work.

Applying this framework to cultural arts in the AI era presents unique challenges, such as determining how to fairly compensate contributors when AI systems learn from thousands of works or how to attribute influence when AI outputs blend multiple cultural traditions. Potential solutions include transparent documentation of datasets to track cultural influences, royalty pools to distribute earnings fairly among contributors, and attribution standards to ensure communities receive recognition. These measures not only protect the economic interests of creators but also preserve the visibility and integrity of cultural heritage.

Beyond financial compensation, Fair Trade AI certification could include mechanisms to support cultural preservation and community development. For instance, companies could allocate a portion of their profits to fund traditional art workshops, cultural education programs, or initiatives to document endangered cultural practices. Such efforts would ensure that communities benefit directly from the commercialization of their heritage while empowering future generations to sustain their traditions.

By combining lessons from Fair Trade coffee's focus on labor rights with the music industry's emphasis on intellectual property and revenue transparency, Fair Trade certification in cultural arts offers a scalable framework for ethical AI practices. It appeals to socially conscious consumers who value equitable innovation and cultural preservation. As AI continues to reshape the creative landscape, this model ensures that technological progress respects and uplifts the cultural legacies that inspire it, fostering a future of collaboration, fairness, and sustainability.

These new economic models provide innovative ways to integrate ethical practices into the evolving relationship between AI, art, and cultural heritage. By emphasizing community control, collective action, and transparency, these frameworks address the challenges posed by AI-generated art while fostering sustainable opportunities for artists and cultural communities. Whether through licensing agreements, cooperatives, hybrid marketplaces, or fair-trade certifications, these models represent a promising step toward a more equitable and respectful future for the global arts ecosystem.

Technical Solutions and Cultural Protection

Emerging technologies offer promising solutions for protecting cultural heritage in the AI era, addressing the challenges of unauthorized use, misrepresentation, and exploitation of cultural expressions. Dr. Robert Chang, Chief Technology Officer at Cultural Heritage AI, highlights the potential of advanced recognition algorithms: "We're developing sophisticated recognition systems that can identify and protect specific cultural elements, styles, and sacred symbols. These systems can help prevent unauthorized use of protected cultural elements in AI training and generation." Such tools could play a critical role in safeguarding culturally significant designs by flagging their use in AI datasets or outputs, ensuring that they are not misappropriated without proper consent.

One of the most innovative developments is the blockchain-based Cultural Heritage Protection System (CHPS), launched in collaboration with several Indigenous communities. Blockchain technology's decentralized and immutable nature ensures that data about cultural artifacts and traditions cannot be altered or erased. CHPS allows communities to register their traditional art forms on a secure ledger, giving them control over how these works are used in the digital realm. As community leader Samuel White Eagle explains: "For the first time, we have a technical framework that recognizes our right to control how our cultural heritage is used in the digital realm." This system not only preserves authenticity but also empowers communities by providing a transparent mechanism for tracking usage and enforcing permissions.

Blockchain technology is emerging as a powerful tool for cultural protection due to its ability to create unalterable records, ensure provenance, and facilitate benefit-sharing. For example, blockchain-based platforms like HeriLedger and TemDAO have been designed to protect cultural heritage by linking digital records to physical artifacts or intangible traditions. These systems enable communities to establish ownership over their cultural assets while providing a transparent framework for managing their use. In practice, blockchain can document every transaction involving an artifact or design—whether it's being licensed for commercial use or included in an AI training dataset—ensuring accountability at every stage.

One notable success is the use of blockchain to protect Maori taonga (treasures) in New Zealand. By registering traditional designs and symbols on a blockchain ledger, Maori communities have been able to prevent unauthorized commercial use while also creating new revenue streams through licensing agreements. Similarly, in Mexico, Ayuujk artists have begun using blockchain to authenticate their traditional textiles, ensuring that buyers can verify the origins of their purchases and support ethical trade practices.

AI-Powered Recognition Systems

AI itself can also be leveraged to protect cultural heritage through recognition systems capable of identifying specific patterns, motifs, or styles associated with different cultures. These systems could act as gatekeepers during the development of AI models by flagging culturally sensitive materials before they are included in training datasets. For instance, an AI-powered recognition tool could detect when sacred Navajo patterns or Aboriginal dot paintings are being used without authorization and alert developers or regulators. Such systems are already being explored in other domains. For example, UNESCO has partnered with AI researchers to develop algorithms that identify and catalog endangered languages based on speech patterns and text samples. A similar approach could be applied to visual art forms, enabling communities to document their cultural expressions comprehensively while protecting them from unauthorized use.

Digitization and Virtual Preservation

Digital technologies such as 3D modeling and augmented reality are also playing a key role in preserving cultural heritage while minimizing physical interaction with delicate artifacts. For example, 3D modeling has been used to digitally replicate ancient San rock art in South Africa, protecting the originals from damage while making them accessible for educational purposes. Similarly, AR applications allow users to explore virtual reconstructions of heritage sites or view traditional dances performed by avatars in immersive environments like the metaverse. These technologies not only preserve physical artifacts but also provide a platform for showcasing intangible cultural heritage such as rituals, music, and oral histories. For instance, VR platforms have been used to recreate traditional ceremonies from Indigenous communities in Canada, ensuring that these practices are documented and accessible for future generations.

To prevent unauthorized use of cultural heritage in AI systems, advanced technical solutions are being developed that prioritize protection, transparency, and accountability. Content filtering systems powered by machine learning algorithms can identify and block unauthorized use of culturally sensitive materials during both training and generation phases. For example:

- Protected Element Identification: Algorithms trained on datasets of sacred symbols or traditional patterns can flag these elements when they appear in unauthorized contexts.
- Style-Based Filtering: Systems can detect when an output mimics specific artistic styles associated with particular cultures.
- Sacred Imagery Detection: Tools can identify sacred objects or motifs (e.g., Maori ta moko) to prevent their replication without consent.

- Provenance Tracking: By embedding metadata into digital files, these systems can trace the origin of artworks used in AI models.

Such technologies are already being explored in content moderation systems like those used by DeviantArt and Adobe Stock. However, they must be tailored specifically for cultural heritage protection to address its unique challenges.

Blockchain technology offers a decentralized solution for tracking the use of cultural assets in AI systems. Key developments include:

- Smart Contracts for Cultural IP: Smart contracts automatically enforce licensing terms when an artwork is used commercially.
- Automated Royalty Distribution: Blockchain systems can distribute royalties directly to artists or communities based on usage data.
- Transparent Usage Tracking: Blockchain ledgers provide an immutable record of how cultural assets are used across different platforms.
- Decentralized Governance: Communities can collectively manage their cultural assets through blockchain-based voting mechanisms.

For example, Indigenous communities in New Zealand have begun using blockchain to authenticate Maori designs and track their use in global markets. This ensures that any commercial benefit flows back to the community while preserving cultural integrity.

Protecting training data from misuse is critical for safeguarding cultural heritage in AI development. Proposed measures include:

- Cultural Watermarking Protocols: Digital watermarks embedded into artworks signal their protected status.
- Metadata Preservation Systems: Metadata attached to digital files ensures that information about an artwork's origin and usage rights remains intact during distribution.
- Opt-Out Registries: Artists or communities can register their works on opt-out lists that prevent inclusion in AI training datasets without explicit consent.
- Usage Limitation Controls: Tools like Fairly Trained's certification system verify that datasets comply with ethical standards before being used for training.

While these technical solutions hold great promise, they also come with challenges that must be addressed to ensure their effectiveness and ethical implementation. For example:

- Cultural Sensitivity: Recognition algorithms must be developed in consultation with cultural experts to avoid misclassification or oversimplification of complex traditions.
- Access Inequality: Many Indigenous communities face barriers such as limited internet access or technological infrastructure, which could hinder their ability to adopt blockchain or AI-based systems.
- Data Sovereignty: Ensuring that communities retain ownership over their digital records is critical; this requires robust governance frameworks aligned with Indigenous values.
- Cost: Developing and maintaining these technologies can be expensive; funding models such as benefit-sharing agreements or government grants may be necessary.

Despite these challenges, the integration of advanced technologies into cultural preservation efforts represents a significant step forward. By combining tools like blockchain for provenance tracking with AI-powered recognition systems and immersive digital environments, we can create a more equitable framework for protecting cultural heritage in the digital age. As Dr Chang notes: "Technology is not just part of the problem — it's also part of the solution."

Community Voices and Resistance

The response of cultural communities to AI-driven appropriation has been both creative and determined, as they seek to reclaim control over their heritage and assert their rights in the digital age. The Indigenous Digital Rights Coalition, formed in 2024, represents a groundbreaking collaboration between traditional artists, Indigenous leaders, and technology experts. This coalition aims to address the challenges posed by AI systems that exploit cultural expressions without consent or benefit-sharing.

Coalition leader Maria Blackfeather emphasizes their approach: "We're not against technology—we're for responsible innovation that respects our cultural rights and supports our communities' ability to maintain our traditions." Their initiatives include advocating for ethical AI development, creating educational resources on data sovereignty, and lobbying for legal reforms to protect Indigenous cultural heritage from exploitation.

In Japan, traditional artisans have adopted a proactive strategy through the Digital Crafts Preservation Initiative, which focuses on documenting the intricate techniques and knowledge embedded in their art forms. Master craftsman Kenji Tanaka explains: "We are working to document the subtle aspects of our traditional techniques that cannot be captured by AI systems. This isn't just about preserving visual styles—it's about maintaining the living knowledge embedded in our artistic traditions."

For example, Japanese papermakers have collaborated with researchers to digitize their craft processes while ensuring that these records remain under community control. The initiative also includes workshops and online platforms where younger generations can learn these techniques, bridging the gap between tradition and modernity.

Efforts to resist AI appropriation extend beyond documentation and advocacy. In Latin America, UNESCO's recent report on Indigenous People-Centered Artificial Intelligence highlights pilot projects aimed at empowering Indigenous communities to manage their own cultural data. One such project in Mexico uses AI to catalog and identify variations in Indigenous garments from the Altos de Chiapas region, helping communities detect plagiarism and assert ownership over their designs.

These tools not only protect cultural expressions but also enable communities to participate actively in the digital economy. Additionally, grassroots movements have emerged to confront the economic and cultural impacts of AI-generated art. In Australia, Aboriginal artists have organized campaigns to raise awareness about the harm caused by unauthorized reproductions of their art. These efforts include public exhibitions showcasing authentic works alongside AI-generated imitations to educate consumers about the differences in quality, meaning, and cultural significance. Similarly, organizations like Cultural Survival have launched global campaigns advocating for stronger protections against intellectual theft of Indigenous motifs and techniques.

Urban initiatives also play a role in defending digital rights. The Cities Coalition for Digital Rights, a global network of cities committed to promoting equitable digital environments, has begun integrating cultural protections into its policies. By leveraging municipal governance, coalition members are developing frameworks that require companies operating within their jurisdictions to adhere to ethical standards when using culturally significant data.

For example, cities like Barcelona and Amsterdam are piloting programs that mandate transparency and consent mechanisms for AI systems trained on local cultural assets. These diverse strategies demonstrate how communities worldwide are resisting the commodification of their heritage by AI technologies. Whether through coalitions like the Indigenous Digital Rights Coalition or initiatives such as Japan's Digital Crafts Preservation Initiative, these efforts underscore a shared commitment to preserving cultural integrity while engaging with modern technology.

Policy Development and Legal Frameworks

The legal landscape surrounding AI and cultural appropriation continues to evolve. Legal scholar Dr. Elizabeth Chen notes: "We're seeing a shift from traditional intellectual property frameworks toward more nuanced approaches that recognize communal ownership of cultural heritage." The UNESCO Cultural AI Guidelines of 2024 represent a significant step forward, establishing international standards for the protection of cultural heritage in AI development.

The **Australian Aboriginal Cultural Heritage Protection Act of 2024** provides a practical model for national legislation. The act requires AI companies to obtain explicit permission from Aboriginal communities before incorporating their artistic traditions into training data or generation systems. Aboriginal elder Sarah Djambawa reflects: "This law recognizes our right to control our cultural heritage in the digital realm, just as we have always controlled it in the physical world."

Education plays a pivotal role in addressing the challenges of AI-driven cultural appropriation, fostering awareness, and equipping individuals with the tools to navigate the ethical complexities of AI technologies. Dr. Jennifer Wong, Director of the Digital Ethics Education Initiative, emphasizes: "We need to develop comprehensive educational programs that help both AI developers and users understand the cultural implications of their work. Technical expertise must be paired with cultural literacy." This dual focus on technical and ethical education is essential for creating a generation of AI practitioners who are not only skilled but also culturally sensitive.

The Success Academy for AI Ethics, established by a consortium of cultural institutions and tech companies, exemplifies this approach. The academy integrates ethics into technical training, aiming to instill a deep understanding of cultural sensitivity in future AI developers. Program director Dr. Michael Standing Bear describes their mission: "We're training the next generation of AI developers to understand that cultural sensitivity isn't an obstacle to innovation—it's a pathway to more ethical and sustainable technological development." By embedding ethical considerations into the curriculum, the academy ensures that students learn to recognize and mitigate the risks of cultural misappropriation in AI systems.

Programs like the Success Academy are part of a broader movement to integrate cultural literacy into AI education. This approach builds on frameworks such as Culturally Relevant Pedagogy (CRP), which emphasizes academic success, cultural competence, and critical consciousness. CRP has been adapted for STEM education through initiatives like MIT's Inclusive AI Literacy & Learning program, which prepares students to become ethical designers and users of AI technologies. By incorporating students' cultural backgrounds into learning activities, these programs foster inclusivity while addressing issues like algorithmic bias and cultural misrepresentation. For example, CRP principles have been applied in classrooms where students analyze how AI systems perpetuate stereotypes or misrepresent marginalized cultures. In one case study, students used AI tools to examine biases in facial recognition algorithms, uncovering how these systems disproportionately misclassify individuals from non-Western cultures. Such projects not only teach technical skills but also encourage critical thinking about the societal impacts of AI.

Educational initiatives are also leveraging technology to make lessons on AI ethics more engaging and impactful. For instance:

- Project-Based Learning: Programs like MIT's Inclusive AI Literacy encourage students to create authentic learning artifacts, such as designing culturally sensitive algorithms or developing tools to detect bias in datasets. This hands-on approach ensures that students not only understand theoretical concepts but also apply them in meaningful ways.

- Cultural Sensitivity Simulations: VR platforms are being used to simulate scenarios where students must navigate ethical dilemmas involving cultural heritage and AI. These immersive experiences help learners understand the real-world implications of their decisions.
- AI-Assisted Teaching Tools: Adaptive learning platforms are being developed to personalize instruction based on students' cultural contexts. For example, an AI-powered biology lesson might use analogies drawn from Indigenous knowledge systems to explain ecological concepts, making the material more relatable and engaging.

Despite these advancements, there are significant challenges to integrating cultural literacy into AI education. One major barrier is the lack of diversity among educators and curriculum developers in STEM fields. To address this issue, institutions like Queen Mary University have adopted bottom-up approaches that involve diverse stakeholders—students, educators, and community leaders—in curriculum design. Another challenge is ensuring that educational materials remain up to date with rapidly evolving technologies. Programs like Harvard's Ethics of AI course tackle this by combining theoretical instruction with real-world case studies, enabling participants to stay informed about emerging issues such as generative AI's impact on cultural narratives.

To scale these efforts globally, organizations like UNESCO are working on frameworks that standardize ethical guidelines for teaching AI across diverse cultural contexts. These frameworks emphasize the importance of tailoring education to local needs while fostering cross-cultural understanding. For example:

- The UNESCO Competency Framework for Teachers includes modules on data sovereignty and cultural preservation, equipping educators with the knowledge needed to address issues like cultural appropriation.
- The CATE-AI Framework (Culturally Adaptive Thinking in Education for AI) focuses on contextualizing AI education for learners from different ethnic, gender, and age-based backgrounds.

As Dr. Standing Bear notes, "Education is our most powerful tool for shaping how technology interacts with culture." By integrating ethics and cultural literacy into AI education at all levels—from K-12 classrooms to professional training programs—we can ensure that future generations are equipped to develop technologies that respect and celebrate cultural diversity rather than exploit it. These efforts represent a crucial step toward creating an inclusive digital future where innovation aligns with equity and respect for all cultures.

The challenge of cultural appropriation in the AI era compels us to rethink how we protect and preserve cultural heritage in a rapidly expanding digital landscape. Artificial intelligence, with its capacity to replicate and reimagine cultural expressions at an unprecedented scale, presents both risks and opportunities. While it has the potential to democratize creativity and expand artistic possibilities, it also threatens to commodify sacred symbols, misrepresent cultural traditions, and undermine the livelihoods of traditional artists.

To address these challenges, a multifaceted approach is essential—one that integrates ethical, legal, technical, economic, and educational solutions. Legal reforms, such as the proposed Cultural IP framework, offer a pathway to recognizing communal ownership of cultural heritage, mandating consent mechanisms, and ensuring benefit-sharing agreements with marginalized communities. These protections are critical for safeguarding traditions from exploitation while fostering equitable partnerships between cultural communities and the global technology industry.

On the technical front, emerging tools like AI-powered recognition systems and blockchain-based CHPS demonstrate how technology itself can be part of the solution. By enabling communities to register their cultural assets, track their use, and enforce permissions, these innovations empower Indigenous and marginalized groups to reclaim control over their heritage in the digital realm.

At the same time, advancements in AI ethics—such as algorithms designed to detect and prevent unauthorized use of culturally significant materials—highlight how responsible innovation can align with cultural preservation. Economic considerations are equally vital. The rise of AI-generated art has disrupted traditional markets, often devaluing authentic works by flooding them with imitations. Studies like the Aboriginal Art Market Study reveal significant income losses for traditional artists due to AI-generated replicas.

To mitigate these impacts, fair economic models must be developed—ones that include royalties for communities whose cultural expressions are used commercially and mechanisms to ensure that traditional artists can compete in an increasingly digitized art market.

Education plays a foundational role in shaping a future where technology uplifts rather than exploits culture. Initiatives like the Success Academy for AI Ethics exemplify how comprehensive educational programs can pair technical expertise with cultural literacy. By training AI developers to understand the ethical implications of their work and fostering critical awareness among users, these programs lay the groundwork for a more informed and responsible approach to AI development.

Finally, community-led resistance efforts underscore the importance of centering cultural voices in this conversation. From the Indigenous Digital Rights Coalition's advocacy for data sovereignty to Japan's Digital Crafts Preservation Initiative documenting living knowledge embedded in traditional techniques, these movements highlight how communities are actively reclaiming their narratives.

Their work serves as a reminder that solutions must be co-created with those most affected by AI-driven appropriation. Success in addressing these challenges will require ongoing collaboration between technology developers, traditional artists, cultural communities, policymakers, educators, and consumers.

By combining new legal protections, technical innovations, fair economic practices, robust education programs, and community empowerment, we can envision a future where technological innovation supports rather than undermines cultural heritage and artistic traditions. This is not just about preserving the past. It is about building a more equitable future where diverse cultures are celebrated as living sources of creativity and meaning in an increasingly interconnected world.

Works Referenced

Aboriginal Artists Agency. "Licensing Agreements for Aboriginal Dot Paintings in Fashion Collaborations." *Aboriginal Artists Agency*, 2024, pp. 1–2.

"Aboriginal Art Market Study of 2024." *Cultural Economics Journal*, vol. 20, no. 1, 2024, pp. 79–141.

Allerton, Amy. "The Economic Impact of AI-Generated Indigenous Art." *Gumbaynggirr and Bundjalung Artists Collective*, 2024, pp. 1–2.

Alvarez, Daniel. "Cultural Intellectual Property Law: Protecting Indigenous Heritage in the Digital Age." *Journal of Cultural IP Law*, vol. 12, no. 3, 2024, pp. 15–27, 76–7, 123–9.

Alvarez, Daniel. "Cultural IP Law and Indigenous Rights." *Journal of Intellectual Property and Cultural Heritage*, vol. 12, no. 3, 2023, pp. 210–25.

Benedict, Ruth. *Patterns of Culture*. Houghton Mifflin, 1934.

Benedict, Ruth. "Cultural Philosophies in Japanese Art." Quoted in *The Japonisme Movement: Western Fascination with Japanese Aesthetics*, edited by Yuko Kikuchi, ArtHouse Press, 2024, pp. 15–22.

Bhat, Shashi. "The Enduring Legacy of Colonialism in Cultural Institutions." *Museum Studies Quarterly*, vol. 28, no. 1, 2022, pp. 55–70.

Bhat, Shashi. "The Parthenon Marbles and the Narrative of Cultural Heritage." *Historical Studies Quarterly*, vol. 18, no. 2, 2024, pp. 112–35.

Blackfeather, Maria. "Reclaiming Digital Sovereignty: The Indigenous Digital Rights Coalition." *Indigenous Perspectives on AI Ethics*, 2024, pp. 32–45.

Chang, Robert. "Blockchain Technology for Cultural Heritage Protection." *Cultural Heritage AI Journal*, vol. 5, no. 1, 2024, pp. 18–33.

Chen, James. *Cultural Appropriation and Power Dynamics in the Arts*. University of California Press, 2024.

Chen, James. "Power Dynamics in Cultural Appropriation." *Sociological Review*, vol. 45, no. 4, 2021, pp. 380–95.

Daes, Erica-Irene. "Indigenous Peoples and Their Cultural Heritage." *United Nations Working Group on Indigenous Populations Report*, UN Doc. E/CN.4/Sub.2/1993/28, 1993, pp. 1–57.

Djambawa, Sarah. "Aboriginal Cultural Heritage Protection Act of 2024: A Community Perspective." *Australian Journal of Indigenous Policy*, vol. 10, no. 1, 2024, pp. 20–37.

García, Maria. "Economic Disruption in the Art Market Due to AI." *Global Economic Trends Report*, vol. 7, no. 3, 2024, pp. 111–35.

García, Maria. "Economic Impacts of AI-Driven Cultural Appropriation." *Journal of Cultural Economics*, vol. 35, no. 2, 2024, pp. 112–28.

"Indian Arts and Crafts Act of 1990." *Public Law 101–512*, 1990.

MidJourney Controversy Report. "Digital Colonialism and AI Appropriation of Indigenous Art." *AI Ethics Review*, vol. 9, no. 2, 2023, pp. 72–94.

Patel, Maya. "AI and Cultural Ownership: Ethical Challenges in Algorithmic Creativity." *AI Ethics Institute Publications*, vol. 6, no. 2, 2024, pp. 41–68.

Patel, Maya. "AI and the Evolution of Cultural Appropriation." *AI Ethics Review*, vol. 7, no. 1, 2023, pp. 15–30.

Red Star, Wendy. "Preserving Indigenous Stories through Artistic Integrity." *Cultural Survival Quarterly*, vol. 48, no. 1, 2024, pp. 20–9.

Richardson, Sarah. "Cultural Appropriation and Artificial Intelligence: Ethical Challenges in the Arts." *Digital Ethics Quarterly*, vol. 15, no. 1, MIT Press, 2023, pp. 105–28.

Richardson, Sarah. "Digital Ethics and the Transformation of Cultural Appropriation." *MIT Digital Ethics Journal*, vol. 15, no. 1, 2023, pp. 22–38.

Rodin, Auguste. *Art: The Principles of Art*. Translated by John Greig, John Murray, 1912.

Running Wolf, Maria. "Protecting Cultural Expressions for Future Generations." *UNESCO Cultural Preservation Report*, vol. 11, no. 3, 2024, pp. 108–30.

Standing Bear, Michael. "Ethics in AI Development: Training the Next Generation." *Success Academy for AI Ethics Publications*, vol. 3, no. 2, 2024, pp. 51–73.

Tanaka, Kenji. "Documenting Traditional Japanese Craft Techniques for Digital Preservation." *Digital Crafts Preservation Initiative Report*, vol. 8, no. 1, Japan Cultural Agency Press, 2024, pp. 14–42.

Thompson, John. "The Commercialization of Native American Symbols." *Indigenous Voices in Art*, vol. 11, no. 3, 2021, pp. 150–65.

Thompson, John. "The Sacred Significance of Native American Symbols in Art." *Native American Art Today*, vol. 12, no. 1, Indigenous Arts Press, 2024, pp. 17–38.

United Nations General Assembly. "United Nations Declaration on the Rights of Indigenous Peoples (UNDRIP)." Resolution 61/295, September 13, 2007, UN Doc. A/RES/61/295, pp. 1–18.

Vogel, Susan. *Africa and the Art of Appropriation*. Thames & Hudson, 1991.

Vogel, Susan. "Modernist Appropriation of African Art and Its Implications." *Art History Review Journal*, vol. 22, no. 2, Yale University Press, 2024, pp. 70–92.

Yamamoto, Takashi. "The Spiritual Depth of Ukiyo-e Prints Versus AI Mimicry." *Japanese Art Perspectives Quarterly*, vol. 14, no. 3, Tokyo University Press, 2024, pp. 44–61.

Yirrkala, David. "The Impact of AI on Aboriginal Art Markets." *Aboriginal Cultural Review*, vol. 18, no. 4, 2024, pp. 320–35.

Seven Faces in the Machine

Artistic Innovation or Invasion

On November 15, 2024, Elon Musk's X, formerly known as Twitter, unveiled its newest terms and conditions of service:

"By submitting, posting or displaying Content on or through the Services, you grant us a worldwide, nonexclusive, royalty-free license to make your Content available to the rest of the world," which includes the right to analyze any of that Content "including, for example, for use with and training of our machine learning and artificial intelligence models, whether generative or another type."

At first glance, this may seem like a routine adjustment to the fine print of social media governance. However, beneath the surface lies an astonishing legal and ethical dilemma about privacy, publicity rights, and the commodification of human creativity and identity. Every photo, video, or text post shared on X is now, potentially, fuel for the development of AI models—models that may generate deepfakes, synthetic faces, or even creative outputs that mimic the original work of the users themselves.

The implications are pronounced, particularly in the context of:

1. **Privacy:** How does this license affect users' expectations of privacy when their personal images, including photos of their faces, are analyzed by AI systems? Do users truly understand the extent of this data usage?
2. **Publicity Rights:** For public figures and ordinary individuals alike, does such a license infringe on the right to control how one's likeness is used, especially when commercial AI products could eventually profit from these datasets?
3. **Creativity:** What happens when user-generated content, originally created with artistic or personal intent, becomes an integral part of AI systems capable of generating art, music, or text? Does this extinguish the line between human creativity and machine-generated works?

4. **Ownership and Consent:** Can the broad, all-encompassing language of platform terms of service truly substitute for informed consent, particularly when the scope of AI applications is so vast and evolving?
5. **Reputation and False Light:** What safeguards exist to prevent AI-generated content from misrepresenting individuals, whether by associating their likeness or data with inappropriate, misleading, or defamatory contexts? The risk of placing someone in a false light or causing reputational harm becomes particularly acute when AI systems generate outputs that mimic human expression or behavior, potentially distorting public perception of the individuals involved.

For artists and creators, the consequences are especially concerning, as platforms like X claim the right to incorporate their work into AI models, diluting originality and creative ownership while eroding the ability to consent or maintain control over how their work is used. This shift not only has the potential to diminish the value of human creativity but also reinforces a broader trend of commodifying personal identity and intellectual property for the benefit of corporate AI systems. As this chapter transitions to a detailed exploration of privacy, these concerns set the stage for understanding how such policies implicate fundamental rights, challenge existing legal frameworks, and demand urgent attention to safeguard human dignity, creativity, and ownership in an AI-dominated world.

The modern legal concept of privacy owes its roots to the seminal 1890 *Harvard Law Review* article by Samuel D. Warren and Louis D. Brandeis, titled *The Right to Privacy*. The authors famously described privacy as "the right to be let alone" and emphasized the need to protect individuals from the invasive effects of technological advancements like photography and the mass media. This article marked the first formal articulation of privacy as a legal right and laid the groundwork for its recognition as a central element of personal autonomy in the modern world.

Privacy in the United States: A Constitutional Absence

Unlike many fundamental rights explicitly enshrined in the **US Constitution,** the right to privacy is not directly mentioned in the document. Instead, it has been inferred by courts over time through interpretations of various constitutional provisions. The US Supreme Court has recognized privacy as a vital concept inherent in individual liberty, reading it into the "penumbras" and "emanations" of the Bill of Rights. This judicial interpretation has evolved over decades to provide a legal framework for privacy, even in the absence of explicit constitutional language.

The absence of explicit language in the US Constitution has made privacy a complex and often contested legal principle in the United States. However, landmark Supreme Court decisions have expanded its scope over time, framing it as an essential component of individual freedom.

Over the years, the Supreme Court has played a pivotal role in defining and expanding the concept of privacy, particularly as technology evolves. In *Katz v. United States* (1967), the Court expanded privacy protections to include technology by ruling that the Fourth Amendment protects individuals from warrantless wiretaps on public payphones. This case introduced the concept of a "reasonable expectation of privacy," a standard that remains central to privacy law today. In *Carpenter v. United States* (2018), the Court addressed digital privacy, ruling that the government's warrantless collection of cell phone location data violated the Fourth Amendment, emphasizing the need to adapt privacy protections to modern technological realities.

More recently, cases such as *NetChoice LLC v. Paxton* (pending decision, 2024) and *NetChoice LLC v. Bonta* (2024) have raised questions about government regulation of social media platforms, content moderation policies, and user privacy in the context of free speech. These cases explore the balance between state consumer privacy protections and **First Amendment** concerns. Similarly, in *TikTok Inc. v. Garland* (2025), the Court upheld a federal law banning TikTok in the United States on national security grounds, while also addressing broader privacy concerns about data collection by foreign-owned apps.

In addition to federal interpretations, numerous states have enacted their own privacy laws, often granting broader protection than those recognized at the federal level. State constitutions and statutes address privacy in areas ranging from personal data protection to employee surveillance and consumer rights. These laws aim to protect against the misuse of personal data in the face of rapid advancements in digital technology and artificial intelligence (AI).

State Privacy Protections

Many states have stepped up to protect personal data, addressing the growing risks posed by modern technology and AI systems, especially in how personal information—including facial recognition data—is used. California, for instance, leads with the **California Consumer Privacy Act (CCPA)** and its successor, the **California Privacy Rights Act (CPRA)**. These laws give residents the right to know what personal data companies collect, access it, request its deletion, and opt out of its sale. Importantly, they also require businesses to disclose their use of AI for profiling and assessing potential risks. This is crucial because data such as names, email addresses, geolocation, browsing history, and facial images are often collected by social media platforms and other companies. AI systems can use this data to create targeted ads, predict behaviors, or generate personalized content. Without safeguards, this data can also be exploited—users may unknowingly grant broad permissions under terms of service they don't fully read, enabling misuse like deepfakes, unauthorized impressions, or invasive profiling.

New York similarly prioritizes protecting personal data, particularly around images, likenesses, and biometric identifiers. Under **Civil Rights Law Sections 50 and 51**, it's illegal to use someone's name or image for commercial purposes without their explicit consent. The pending **New York Biometric Privacy Act** builds on these protections, addressing sensitive data like facial recognition, fingerprints, and voice patterns. Without these safeguards, data from social media profiles could be repurposed for AI-generated avatars, emotion detection tools, or even virtual influencers—all potentially done without the individual's knowledge or permission. This raises concerns about whether users truly give informed consent when they agree to sweeping terms of service, especially when their data could be used in ways that misrepresent them or harm their reputation.

Illinois stands out for its **Biometric Information Privacy Act (BIPA)**, one of the strictest laws protecting biometric data in the country. It requires companies to obtain informed consent before collecting or storing biometric information, such as facial recognition scans or fingerprints. High-profile cases, like Facebook's $650 million settlement over unauthorized facial recognition tagging, highlight the importance of this legislation. Without such protection, businesses might use facial recognition data collected from platforms like social media to create digital profiles, sell insights to third parties, or even enable identity theft. BIPA sets a standard for ensuring people's data isn't used without their understanding or approval.

Virginia and Colorado have taken steps inspired by the **European Union's GDPR.** Their laws, like the **Virginia Consumer Data Protection Act (VCDPA)** and **Colorado Privacy Act (CPA),** grant residents the right to access, correct, delete, and opt out of the use of their personal data. These laws also require businesses to minimize data collection and assess risks from AI-driven decision-making. AI platforms often use purchasing habits or behavioral data to predict trends, but this can unintentionally lead to outcomes like reinforcing biases or excluding individuals unfairly. Transparency in these processes is critical to preventing misuse.

Lastly, states like Texas and Washington have focused on specific risks tied to facial recognition. Texas, for example, requires companies to notify and obtain consent before collecting biometric data, while Washington has implemented laws aimed at ensuring accountability and transparency. These protections are particularly important as facial recognition data, often scraped from social media, could otherwise be used to create AI-generated content or profiles that misrepresent individuals or use their likeness without permission. Without such safeguards, users could lose control over how their personal data is used and risk having their identities exploited in ways they never intended.

Privacy in Europe: A Fundamental Human Right

In Europe, privacy is recognized as a fundamental human right, deeply embedded in its legal and cultural framework. This perspective differs significantly from that of the United States, where privacy is often treated as a patchwork of laws rather than an explicit constitutional guarantee. The **European Convention on Human Rights (ECHR)** enshrines privacy in **Article 8**, which declares: *"Everyone has the right to respect for his private and family life, his home and his correspondence."* This recognition as a core human right has shaped not only Europe's legal systems but also its societal values, fostering a collective commitment to protecting personal autonomy and dignity.

Building on this foundation, the European Union (EU) introduced the **GDPR** in 2018, which stands as one of the most comprehensive privacy frameworks globally. **GDPR** imposes strict rules on how personal data is collected, processed, and stored, granting individuals significant control over their information. Key rights include the ability to access personal data, request its deletion (the "right to be forgotten"), and object to its use for certain purposes, such as targeted advertising. What sets **GDPR** apart is its extraterritorial application—companies worldwide must comply if they handle data belonging to EU citizens, ensuring a global impact on privacy practices.

The European Court of Justice (ECJ) has also played a vital role in advancing privacy rights. A landmark case in 2014, *Google Spain SL v. Agencia Española de Protección de Datos*, established the "right to be forgotten," requiring search engines like Google to remove links to outdated or irrelevant personal information when requested. This decision underscored the importance of balancing public access to information with an individual's right to control their digital footprint.

When viewed through the lens of arts and creativity, these privacy protections take on unique significance. For artists, writers, and other creatives, **GDPR** and related regulations ensure their personal data whether tied to their identity, artistic process, or collaboration is safeguarded. In the digital age, where AI systems can mine personal data to generate art, music, or other creative works, European privacy laws act as a critical buffer. They give creators the ability to object to their data being used in ways that may misrepresent their vision, distort their artistic identity, or exploit their intellectual property without consent.

For example, an artist's social media profile might contain images, sketches, or personal reflections that an AI system could use to train algorithms capable of generating art in a similar style. Without robust privacy protection, these works could be reproduced or commercialized without acknowledgment or compensation to the original creator. Similarly, the "right to be forgotten" empowers artists to remove outdated or harmful content tied to their names, enabling them to curate how their digital presence influences public perception of their work.

By treating privacy as a fundamental human right, Europe sets a precedent for how personal autonomy can intersect with creativity in the digital realm. These protections not only guard against the misuse of personal data but also foster an environment where artists and creatives can thrive without fear that their identities, processes, or works will be unfairly exploited or misrepresented.

Right of Publicity

The right of publicity safeguards individuals from the unauthorized commercial exploitation of their name, image, or likeness, ensuring that they retain control over how their identity is used for profit. The right of publicity and privacy law, while distinct, are closely related and often overlap in their application, particularly when addressing issues arising from deepfake technology. Rooted in the concept of protecting personal and economic interests, the doctrine emerged in the mid-twentieth century as courts recognized the value of an individual's persona in commercial contexts.

One of the earliest cases, *Haelan Laboratories v. Topps Chewing Gum Co.* (1953), established the right of publicity by ruling that individuals had a transferable property right to control the commercial use of their likenesses. Similarly, in *Carson v. Here's Johnny Portable Toilets, Inc.* (1983), the court affirmed that using the phrase "Here's Johnny"—a reference to Johnny Carson's famous introduction—violated his publicity rights, emphasizing that the right extends beyond direct use of a person's name or image to include aspects of their persona closely associated with their identity.

The *Midler v. Ford Motor Co.* (1988) case remains particularly relevant in today's technological era. Bette Midler successfully sued Ford for hiring a singer to imitate her distinctive voice in a commercial, with the court recognizing that her voice was an integral part of her identity. This decision set a precedent for protecting against identity misappropriation even when the likeness is not directly used, underscoring the importance of consent in commercial applications. With today's advancements in generative AI (GAI), such as deepfake technology, the *Midler* case takes on new significance. GAI tools can now replicate not only voices but also faces and entire personas, raising concerns about unauthorized deepfake endorsements or performances that exploit a person's identity without their permission.

In the realm of art and creativity, the doctrine of transformative use, established in cases like *Comedy III Productions v. Saderup* (2001), adds complexity to the enforcement of publicity rights. Courts have ruled that works adding major creative elements that transform the likeness into something new and expressive may qualify for First Amendment protection. However, with AI-generated content, distinguishing between transformative art and exploitative commercial use becomes increasingly difficult. For instance, a deepfake video that mimics a celebrity's voice and appearance in a fictional performance might shade the line between transformative expression and unauthorized commercial exploitation.

However, when artist *Chris Ume* created a deepfake mimicking Scarlett Johansson's voice, it sparked global outrage. Johansson, who has previously spoken out against the misuse of her image in deepfake pornography, expressed deep concern over how such technology invades her personal space and identity and misleads audiences. Her reaction underscored the emotional and reputational harm caused by unauthorized uses of her likeness, even when the intent might be artistic or expressive.

Deep Fakes

Invasion of privacy concerns or violations of publicity rights are heightened in the context of deepfakes, particularly when they are used in harmful or exploitative ways, such as in revenge porn or satirical content. Deepfakes are created using advanced artificial intelligence systems, such as GANs or diffusive AI models, which generate highly realistic digital manipulations by superimposing or synthesizing an individual's face, voice, or likeness onto another person's body or within fabricated scenarios. These manipulations often involve the unauthorized use of an individual's likeness, placing them in false or compromising scenarios that can cause significant emotional and reputational harm.

University of California Berkley professor Hany Farid points out that: "The capacity to generate deepfakes is proceeding much faster than the ability to detect them. . . We are outgunned." GANs are a primary method used to create deepfakes. As described in earlier chapters, GANs consist of two neural networks—the generator and the discriminator. The generator creates synthetic images or videos, while the discriminator evaluates their realism. Through iterative processes, the generator improves until it produces highly convincing outputs indistinguishable from real media.

Another method is diffusive AI models, such as Stable Diffusion or DALL-E, which train on large datasets to generate or modify high-quality visuals, often starting from random noise and iteratively refining the output to match the input prompt or training data. Additionally, tools for voice cloning, like Descript or Resemble AI, use large datasets to clone voices, enabling realistic simulation of speech patterns and tones. For video synthesis and face-swapping, applications like DeepFaceLab, FaceApp, and Zao are commonly used to manipulate video footage by swapping faces or generating entirely new clips.

Common examples of deepfakes include celebrities such as Taylor Swift, whose likeness is often used to place her in scenarios or performances she never participated in, and Tom Cruise, who has been depicted in humorous or outlandish deepfake videos, often intended as parody or satire. Other examples include Elon Musk, with fake clips showing him endorsing products or delivering fabricated speeches, and Barack Obama, who has been the subject of realistic fake videos in which he appears to make statements he never actually made. These examples illustrate how deepfakes can manipulate public perception and exploit individuals for various purposes.

While these uses clearly infringe upon privacy rights and may violate publicity rights, particularly when an individual's image or likeness is exploited for commercial gain without consent, they also raise complex legal questions. Under the **First Amendment**, courts may grapple with whether such deepfakes qualify as protected speech, especially if they are presented as parody or satire. This tension between privacy, publicity, and free speech underscores the growing need for clear legal standards and ethical boundaries to address the misuse of deepfake technology.

The Risks of AI Applications

The risks associated with AI applications become even more concerning when these tools generate derivative works from private or sensitive images, such as family photos or personal selfies. This danger is exacerbated by advances in generative AI tools like DeepFaceLab, Artbreeder, and Runway ML, which rely heavily on massive datasets to create hyperrealistic outputs. These tools are often trained on data sourced from the internet, including content shared on social media platforms, without the explicit consent or awareness of users.

For instance, a family photo uploaded to X (formerly Twitter) could be unknowingly incorporated into a dataset used to train AI models, enabling the generation of synthetic images that closely resemble the original subjects. Similarly, selfies posted on platforms like TikTok or Instagram may inadvertently contribute to the development of facial recognition algorithms or the creation of deepfakes that misappropriate users' likenesses for unintended purposes.

These practices raise significant ethical and legal concerns, especially when users are unaware of or unable to control how their images are being utilized. Even when users agree to the terms of service (TOS) of a platform, the vague and permissive language often obscures the true extent of data exploitation, leaving individuals vulnerable to misuse.

One such example arose during the tenure of one of the authors serving as a Fulbright-Nehru Specialist teaching intellectual property and publicity rights to law students at a leading law school outside New Delhi. A particularly striking case came to light when a student enrolled in the course shared her personal experience: her image had been lifted without her knowledge from an Indian social media platform and used in billboard advertisements to endorse a product she was entirely unaware of and had not consented to. The misuse of her image not only caused her significant emotional distress but also raised broader concerns about the lack of legal recourse in such cases. Complicating the matter further was the fact that her father was a prominent judge, which added layers of public and familial scrutiny to an already sensitive situation. This example underscores the real-world implications of vague TOS agreements and unregulated data use, highlighting the urgent need for stronger legal frameworks and greater transparency to protect individuals from such violations.

In addition to these concerns, a company co-founded by Dr. Rana el Kaliouby and Dr. Rosalind Picard, computer scientists who conducted leading edge research in emotion recognition and analysis at the MIT Media Lab, formed Affectiva, a technology company later acquired by Smart Eye. They developed Emotion AI, software capable of analyzing human facial expressions, gestures, and body posture to understand emotions and reactions. The technology is sophisticated enough to identify and interpret complex emotional states, with applications ranging from consumer research to healthcare and education. Notably, in the arts and creative fields, Emotion AI holds transformative potential. It can be used to gauge audience reactions to films, music, or theater productions in real-time, providing creators with actionable insights into how their work resonates emotionally. Additionally, it can enhance interactive media and immersive experiences, enabling artists and designers to create adaptive content that responds dynamically to the audience's emotional cues. By integrating this technology, the arts can explore new dimensions of emotional engagement, condensing the division between creators and consumers in powerful, innovative ways.

How Social Media Platforms Collect Facial Images and Private Data

Social media platforms serve as a primary source for AI systems to gather facial images and link them with private data. This data collection often occurs through multiple mechanisms. First, platforms like Instagram, TikTok, and Facebook (Meta) amass vast amounts of visual data from user-uploaded content. Second, tools such as Facebook's now-retired "Tag Suggestions" used facial recognition to identify individuals in photos, linking facial images with specific identities. Third, platforms track behavioral data, combining facial images with personal information such as location, preferences, and activity patterns to construct detailed user profiles. Lastly, companies like Clearview AI engage in third-party scraping, extracting publicly available images from social media platforms without user consent, to compile massive databases for use in law enforcement or commercial applications.

Recent developments underscore the ongoing concerns and evolving policies surrounding the use of user data for AI training by platforms like Meta and TikTok. Meta's terms of service now explicitly allow the company to use publicly shared content from Facebook, Instagram, and other platforms it owns to train AI models, including generative systems like Llama. This includes public posts, photos, videos, and comments but excludes private messages and content from private accounts unless users interact with Meta's AI tools.

In the United States, users cannot opt out of this data usage, while in the EU and UK, stricter privacy regulations allow users to file objection forms to opt out. In 2025, Meta introduced a memory feature for its AI assistant designed to recall personalized details, such as user interests and preferences, using data from Facebook, WhatsApp, Threads, and Instagram. Although users can delete specific memories, there is no option to entirely opt out of this feature.

Additionally, Meta has reintroduced facial recognition tools for purposes like scam prevention and account recovery. These tools are optional, with assurances that facial recognition data will not be used for other purposes and will be deleted after use.

Similarly, TikTok's terms of service explicitly state that user-uploaded content, such as photos and videos, can be analyzed for improving its algorithms and machine learning models. This includes the use of such data for AI training, TikTok does not provide any opt-out mechanism for this practice. In line with its focus on transparency, TikTok requires creators to label content that has been significantly altered or generated by AI, adhering to its community guidelines. However, the platform continues to face scrutiny over its expansive data usage policies and lack of user control.

Snapchat and YouTube are also major players in the ongoing debate surrounding data usage for AI training and platform improvements. Snapchat explicitly reserves the right to use public content shared by its users for purposes such as marketing, AI training, and the development of its AR features. This includes leveraging the massive amounts of publicly shared Snaps and Stories to enhance the accuracy and capabilities of its AR tools, which are integral to the platform's user experience. For example, Snapchat's AI-driven AR lenses are refined using real-world data to make them more dynamic and engaging, enabling the platform to maintain its competitive edge. However, Snapchat's terms of service provide limited transparency on whether users can opt out of these practices, raising concerns about how much control users have over their data and how it is repurposed.

Similarly, YouTube plays a central role in refining its algorithms and promoting its services using user-uploaded content. Under its terms of service, YouTube reserves the right to analyze uploaded videos to improve its recommendation algorithms, which are critical to personalizing user experiences and driving engagement. Additionally, YouTube explicitly states that it may repurpose user-generated content for promotional and marketing purposes. For example, popular videos or creators' content may appear in advertisements or campaigns promoting the platform without direct compensation to the creators, unless otherwise outlined in separate agreements such as YouTube's Partner Program. While users retain ownership of their content, YouTube's broad licensing terms allow the platform to use and monetize this content in ways that may not always be clear to creators.

These practices by Snapchat and YouTube illustrate the growing trend among major social media platforms to leverage user-generated content for technological advancements and business growth. By using public content to train AI models, refine algorithms, and enhance platform features, these companies are pushing the boundaries of innovation while simultaneously raising important questions about user privacy and data control. The lack of comprehensive opt-out options or clear limitations in their terms of service reflects a broader industry trend, where users often sacrifice control over their data in exchange for access to free services. Together with Meta and TikTok, Snapchat and YouTube highlight the urgent need for clearer communication, enforceable privacy protection, and increased transparency to ensure a fair balance between innovation and user rights.

Recent controversies have highlighted the broader implications of these practices. For instance, LinkedIn faced a class-action lawsuit for allegedly using private messages from premium subscribers to train AI models without obtaining explicit consent. Public backlash led LinkedIn to revise its privacy policy, but the incident emphasized the risks of unclear data usage policies. Similarly, Meta's rollout of its AI assistant's memory feature sparked concerns over the lack of a full opt-out option, drawing attention to the increasing integration of AI into user experiences.

Artists, content creators, and other professionals can take proactive steps to protect themselves and their work on platforms like Meta and other social media companies. First, they should regularly audit their accounts to ensure posts, especially older ones, are private and not inadvertently shared publicly. Utilizing tools like Block Party or similar automation programs can help efficiently delete or manage Instagram posts to minimize exposure. Keeping accounts private adds an additional layer of protection, limiting access to personal and professional content to only trusted followers. They should also avoid logging into third-party apps or websites through Facebook or other social media accounts, as this can allow those apps to collect and sell non-public information. Instead, they should create standalone logins for external services to prevent unauthorized data-sharing.

Another essential step is to review and customize privacy settings on social media platforms. For instance, when permissible turning off features like facial recognition, restricting data-sharing permissions, and controlling who can tag or mention you can significantly reduce the risk of misuse. Artists should also watermark their original work, making it more difficult for others to appropriate it without attribution. In addition, using copyright protections, registering key works, and leveraging takedown tools provided by platforms can help ensure personal and property rights are enforced. Finally, staying informed about the platform's terms of service and updates is crucial, as these policies dictate how user data and content may be used, particularly in AI training or commercial applications. By combining these practices, artists, content creators, and professionals can better safeguard their work and personal information in an increasingly data-driven world.

Bias in AI Models and Its Broader Implications

An additional concern with AI applications is their potential to perpetuate or amplify societal biases. Many generative AI models, including tools like DeepFaceLab or Runway ML, have been criticized for disproportionately favoring white male subjects while producing lower-quality results for women and people of color. This bias stems from the datasets used to train these models, which are often unbalanced and overrepresent white male faces. Consequently, outputs from these tools may lack accuracy or realism for underrepresented groups, further marginalizing these communities in the digital space. For example, facial recognition systems have been shown to misidentify people of color at significantly higher rates than white individuals, leading to potential misuse in surveillance or law enforcement. Similarly, AI-generated images may reinforce stereotypes or exclude diverse representations, limiting the inclusivity of AI-driven creative and commercial applications.

Ethical and Legal Implications

The unauthorized or opaque use of personal images for AI applications raises several critical issues. First, it represents a significant invasion of privacy, as using images without explicit consent violates users' expectations regarding how their data should be handled. Second, it infringes upon publicity rights, as individuals lose control over how their likeness is used, particularly in commercial contexts. This misappropriation of likenesses can lead to emotional, reputational, and financial harm. Third, platforms often fail to provide transparency, leaving users unable to make informed decisions about their privacy or how their data is processed. Finally, the vague language in TOS agreements creates legal ambiguities, particularly when privacy rights, publicity rights, and free speech protections clash.

The growing use of AI applications like deepfakes and facial recognition highlights the urgent need for clearer legal frameworks, ethical guidelines, and stricter enforcement of privacy and data protection laws. As these technologies evolve, it is essential to empower users with greater control over their personal data and the ability to opt out of invasive practices. At the same time, addressing biases in AI systems is critical to ensuring that these tools are fair and inclusive, rather than reinforcing existing societal inequalities.

Defamation

The tort of defamation arises when false statements cause harm to someone's reputation. Defamation law distinguishes between public figures and private individuals by imposing different standards of proof. For private individuals, defamation claims can be established on a negligence standard—requiring the plaintiff to prove that the defendant failed to exercise reasonable care in verifying the truth of the statement. For public figures, including public officials or limited-purpose public figures, a higher burden applies. The plaintiff must demonstrate "actual malice," meaning the false statement was made with knowledge of its falsity or with reckless disregard for the truth. This standard was established by the US Supreme Court in *New York Times Co. v. Sullivan* (376 U.S. 254 (1964)) and aims to protect free speech, particularly in matters involving public debate.

In the context of AI-generated content, such as deepfakes, the issue of defamation becomes increasingly complex. Deepfakes can falsely portray individuals in ways that harm their reputation, whether through fabricated videos, altered images, or other generative AI outputs. If a private individual is harmed by a deepfake, they may pursue a claim based on negligence. However, if a public figure is targeted—particularly in the realm of news reporting or commentary—they must prove actual malice. Determining actual malice in AI-related cases can be challenging, as intent must be inferred from circumstances such as the creator's awareness of the deepfake's falsity, the purpose behind its creation, and whether reasonable steps were taken to verify its accuracy.

A key question in these cases is accountability: who should bear responsibility for defamatory deepfakes? Potential defendants include the creator of the deepfake, platforms hosting the content, the person who prompted the request, and possibly the developers of the AI tools used to create it. For example, if a deepfake was created using publicly available AI software and subsequently shared on a social media platform, liability might extend to the individual who created the content, the platform for distributing it, or even the AI tool developer, depending on the degree of knowledge or negligence involved. Courts would also consider whether the harm arose from private acts—such as revenge or pranking—or matters of public concern.

However, suing internet platforms for harmful content, including defamatory deepfakes, is extraordinarily difficult due to the broad protection afforded by **Section 230** of the **Communications Decency Act (CDA)**. **Section 230**, enacted in 1996, provides online platforms with a powerful liability shield, effectively insulating them from civil suits related to most user-generated content. This legal protection has been pivotal in enabling platforms to flourish as conduits for content, but it has also made it nearly impossible to hold them accountable when harmful content circulates on their systems.

To understand the implications of **Section 230**, it is helpful to examine how it applies in practice. Online platforms, such as social media networks (e.g., Facebook, Twitter), review sites (e.g., Yelp), and video-sharing platforms (e.g., YouTube), serve as intermediaries for user-generated content. When content uploaded by a user defames another person or causes harm, **Section 230(c)(1)** expressly prevents the platform from being treated as the "publisher" or "speaker" of the content, even if the platform deliberately encouraged or facilitated the posting of that material. For instance, if someone posts a defamatory review on Yelp, the injured party cannot sue Yelp for publishing the review; **Section 230** protects the platform from liability. This immunity extends even to platforms that profit from or curate such content, so long as the content originates from a third-party user.

Moreover, **Section 230(c)(2)** provides additional protection for platforms that take proactive measures to filter or remove harmful content. It ensures that platforms cannot be sued for their good-faith efforts to screen out offensive material, including obscenity, harassment, or violent threats. Without this provision, platforms might hesitate to moderate content, fearing that such actions could expose them to liability. For example, if Facebook removes harmful deepfakes or other offensive material in good faith, it cannot be held liable for doing so under **Section 230**. This incentivizes platforms to engage in some level of self-regulation, though the law stops short of requiring any specific action.

While **Section 230** was designed to encourage innovation and free expression by protecting platforms from an overwhelming burden of liability, it also creates significant challenges in addressing the harms caused by user-generated content, including defamatory deepfakes. Because creators of harmful deepfakes are often difficult to identify or deter, platforms remain the most visible and efficient targets for mitigating harm. However, **Section 230** largely shields them from individualized accountability. This immunity applies even in cases where platforms play a key role in distributing harmful content, leaving victims of defamation or other harm with little recourse.

Critics of **Section 230** argue that this liability shield is outdated and insufficiently responsive to the realities of modern platforms, which have evolved into highly influential entities capable of curating and amplifying content at scale. While moral suasion, market dynamics, and political pressure encourage platforms to adopt content moderation policies, there are no significant legal consequences for failing to do so. As a result, **Section 230** makes it exceedingly difficult—if not impossible—for victims to seek redress against platforms that serve as conduits for harmful and defamatory content. As Justice Clarence Thomas noted in his statement regarding *Malwarebytes, Inc. v. Enigma Software Group USA, LLC*, "Extending § 230 immunity beyond the natural reading of the text can have serious consequences," suggesting that Congress should reconsider its scope to address the far-reaching immunity it grants to platforms for activities unimaginable when the law was enacted in 1996.

Examples of deepfake defamation underscore the significant challenges victims face in protecting their reputation and pursuing legal remedies. In one widely publicized case, Indian actor Anil Kapoor took legal action against the unauthorized creation and distribution of AI-generated deepfake images and videos that misrepresented him in defamatory contexts, including unapproved product endorsements. Kapoor's case highlights how celebrities, whose public personas are integral to their livelihoods, can be especially vulnerable to reputational harm caused by deepfakes. By successfully securing a court injunction to remove the content and hold the creators accountable, Kapoor set a precedent for leveraging legal tools to combat this growing issue.

Similar cases abound, including the use of deepfake technology to superimpose individuals' faces onto explicit or compromising images, often without their knowledge or consent. For example, in a notorious incident involving an online platform, deepfake pornographic videos featuring well-known actresses were widely circulated, causing significant emotional distress and reputational harm to the victims. While platforms hosting such content were shielded by **Section 230** from direct liability, victims sought legal remedies by targeting the creators and distributors of the deepfakes. These cases often involve claims of defamation, invasion of privacy, and intentional infliction of emotional distress, but the anonymous nature of many deepfake creators makes enforcement and redress difficult.

In another high-profile case, a journalist was targeted with deepfake content that depicted her in fabricated, compromising situations, leading to widespread harassment and professional harm. The journalist filed a suit against individuals believed to be responsible for creating and sharing the content, citing reputational damage and emotional trauma. Although the perpetrators were difficult to identify, the case drew attention to the limitations of current legal frameworks in addressing deepfake defamation and the lack of accountability for platforms that host such content.

Platforms themselves have occasionally faced lawsuits aimed at forcing greater accountability. For example, in *Doe v. MySpace*, a case unrelated to deepfakes but illustrative of broader issues, the platform was sued for failing to prevent harmful user-generated content that facilitated harassment. Although the lawsuit was ultimately dismissed due to **Section 230** protections, it reflects the frustrations victims face when attempting to hold platforms accountable for harmful content distributed on their systems. Similarly, lawsuits targeting Reddit, Twitter, and Pornhub for hosting nonconsensual deepfake content have highlighted the persistent gap in liability for platforms, even as these companies profit from user engagement with such materials.

In one of the rare cases where a platform took direct action, YouTube removed numerous deepfake videos at the request of individuals and organizations, acknowledging the harm caused by such content. However, these removals were voluntary and not prompted by legal requirements, showcasing the limitations of relying on platform discretion rather than enforceable laws. Critics argue that platforms often fail to act decisively unless public outrage or legal threats compel them to do so.

These examples reveal the pressing need for updated legal frameworks that address the harm caused by deepfake defamation. They also emphasize the challenges of balancing **Section 230** protections with the necessity of holding platforms accountable for their role in enabling the creation and dissemination of harmful content. Without clearer mechanisms for redress and liability, victims of deepfakes are left with limited options, even as the prevalence of this technology continues to grow.

Parody

The artistic process raises unique concerns when AI tools are used to create content that parodies or criticizes public figures, blurring the line between protected speech and actionable harm. Parody has long been protected under the First Amendment as a form of artistic and political expression, even when it mocks or satirizes public figures in ways that may be offensive. For example, the Supreme Court case *Hustler Magazine, Inc. v. Falwell* (485 U.S. 46 (1988)) famously upheld the right to parody public figures, ruling in favor of a satirical ad that depicted Jerry Falwell in a false and offensive light. The Court found that, as a public figure, Falwell had to tolerate such speech unless he could prove actual malice or that the content was presented as factual rather than satirical. This case highlights how the First Amendment prioritizes robust public discourse, including satire and parody.

However, the complexity grows when AI technology is involved, as it enables the creation of highly realistic deepfake videos or images that may not be immediately distinguishable as satire. For instance, an AI-generated video falsely depicting a politician making inflammatory statements could be argued as satirical in intent, but it may cross the line if viewers reasonably believe the content to be true. Unlike traditional forms of parody, which often employ exaggerated or comedic elements to signal their satirical nature, deepfakes can mimic the precise mannerisms, voice, and appearance of the subject with unsettling realism. This realism increases the risk of misinterpretation and potential harm, particularly when the subject of the deepfake does not view the content as parody.

For example, an AI-generated deepfake video might portray a celebrity endorsing a controversial political position or engaging in inappropriate behavior as a form of parody or commentary. While the creators of such content might argue that their work is protected satire, the individual depicted may feel that the video crosses into defamation, invasion of privacy, or emotional distress. A high-profile example of such complexity occurred when comedian Jordan Peele created a deepfake of Barack Obama to raise awareness about the dangers of AI-generated misinformation. While the video was clearly labeled as a demonstration, its hyperrealistic nature highlighted the risks of viewers mistaking similar content for genuine statements or actions, particularly in less controlled contexts.

Similarly, deepfakes targeting actors like Tom Cruise—who has been the subject of several widely circulated AI-generated videos—illustrate the precarious balance between parody and exploitation. In some cases, these videos mimic Cruise performing exaggerated stunts or delivering humorous monologues, often framed as lighthearted entertainment. However, even when comedic in tone, such deepfakes can raise concerns about consent, as the subject may not have agreed to their likeness being used in this manner. If the content damages their reputation or is monetized without their permission, questions about the limits of parody and the rights of individuals over their image arise.

The tension between artistic expression and personal harm becomes particularly fraught in politically charged contexts. Consider the use of AI to create deepfake videos depicting public officials in damaging or scandalous situations under the guise of satire. While the creators might claim **First Amendment** protection, the potential for real-world consequences, such as public outrage, electoral harm, or reputational damage, complicates the analysis. Courts may need to examine whether the content was intended as parody and whether it was reasonably identifiable as such, while also considering the subject's right to protect their reputation from demonstrably false portrayals.

Adding to the complexity is the global reach of deepfake technology, which allows such content to spread rapidly across social media platforms, often devoid of context. In some cases, deepfake parodies could violate terms of service on platforms like YouTube or TikTok, but these policies vary and are not legally enforceable standards. Moreover, what may be considered acceptable satire in the United States under the First Amendment could be deemed defamatory or harmful in jurisdictions with stricter limits on free expression, further complicating efforts to establish a clear boundary between parody and defamation in the age of AI.

As courts begin to address these challenges, they may need to refine the application of **First Amendment** principles to deepfake technology. Traditional parody relies on overt signals, such as exaggeration or comedic tone, to alert viewers to its satirical nature. Deepfakes, by contrast, often lack these markers, making it difficult for audiences to distinguish satire from reality. This ambiguity poses a unique challenge in balancing the societal value of parody as a tool for critique and commentary with the rights of individuals to be free from harm caused by false representations. As AI continues to shape the landscape of artistic and political expression, the line between protected parody and harmful defamation will likely become a focal point of legal and ethical debate.

The Next Steps

The rapid rise of generative AI has introduced far-reaching hurdles to the privacy and publicity rights of artists, as well as to the broader landscape of creativity. AI's transformative power is accompanied by a range of ethical, legal, and societal implications that must be carefully considered

Generative AI models, as described earlier, rely on vast datasets, often compiled through data scraping from the internet. These datasets frequently include personal information and creative works collected without explicit consent, raising serious concerns about privacy violations. Artists and creators may unknowingly find their works used to train AI systems, leading to questions about ownership, ethical data use, and consent.

The terms of service for major platforms like Meta amplify these challenges. Under Meta's updated terms, users who submit, post, or display content grant the company a "worldwide, nonexclusive, royalty-free license" to make their content available globally. This license explicitly allows Meta to analyze and use uploaded content for purposes such as training its machine learning and AI models, including generative AI.

This provision raises alarm for artists and content creators, who may find their intellectual property co-opted for purposes they neither authorized nor benefit from financially or creatively. Such terms highlight the growing power imbalance between creators and tech platforms, where artists effectively relinquish control over their work simply by participating in the digital ecosystem.

Moreover, AI-powered facial recognition and biometric analysis introduce new privacy risks, tracking movements, recognizing identities, and manipulating appearances in ways that infringe on individuals' privacy. Deepfakes, for example, can misrepresent someone's identity in convincing but fabricated ways, leading to misuse in personal defamation, fraud, and misinformation.

The pervasive use of AI in surveillance, data collection, and automated analysis undermines individuals' ability to control their personal information, and artists, in particular, face unique challenges as their private lives and creative identities are commodified in a digital landscape increasingly dominated by AI.

AI technologies also enable the unauthorized commercial exploitation of an individual's likeness. Lifelike images, videos, and audio can mimic real people, including public figures and celebrities, and be used without their consent or compensation.

For artists, AI models trained on their works can replicate their distinctive styles, blending and recombining elements to create derivative outputs. This not only diminishes the commercial value of an artist's unique creations but also erodes their ability to maintain their artistic identity and legacy. Many artists have discovered their works used as training data without their permission, raising concerns about plagiarism, compensation, and the ethics of using intellectual property without consent. Meta's terms of service serve as a case in point, as artists whose works are posted on Meta platforms risk having their creations absorbed into AI models, further extinguishing the lines between innovation and exploitation.

The increasing prevalence of AI-generated content challenges traditional notions of creativity, originality, and authorship. As AI systems become more capable of producing high-quality art, music, literature, and other creative forms, the distinction between human and machine creativity grows increasingly ambiguous.

The opacity of AI systems complicates our understanding of how AI-generated works are produced. Without transparency, it becomes difficult to determine whether these outputs are genuinely original or heavily derivative of existing human-created works. These issues highlight the urgent need for updated ethical guidelines and legal frameworks that balance technological innovation with the preservation of human creativity, ensuring that artists retain control over their works while benefiting from advancements in AI.

Addressing these challenges requires a multifaceted approach. Stronger legislation is essential to protect individuals' privacy rights, particularly in regulating data collection, sharing, and use for AI training. As described in an earlier chapter, reforming copyright law to redefine concepts of authorship and ownership, establish fair use parameters, and ensure equitable compensation for creators whose works contribute to AI training is critical.

Ethical guidelines must prioritize human rights, privacy, and creativity, fostering responsible innovation while empowering artists to retain control over their work. Mechanisms allowing artists to opt out, enforce transparent data use policies, and secure fair compensation models are essential. For instance, the sweeping language in Meta's terms of service could be counterbalanced by legal requirements that mandate transparency, compensation, and the ability to opt out of content use for AI training.

European Union data protection laws, such as the **GDPR,** offer a valuable model for safeguarding artists' rights. **GDPR** emphasizes individual control over personal data and imposes strict requirements on data collection, consent, and transparency. For creative works, adopting similar principles could empower artists to protect their intellectual property, ensure fair use, and maintain agency over their contributions.

Moreover, **GDPR's** recognition of biometric data as a "special category" requiring explicit consent, combined with the proposed EU AI Act categorizing biometric systems as "high-risk," demonstrates a proactive approach to addressing privacy and accountability in AI technologies. However, enforcement remains a challenge, as seen in legal critiques of Elon Musk's X (formerly Twitter), which uses user-generated content to train its Grok AI model without explicit consent. These examples underscore the need for clear opt-in mechanisms, labeling requirements for AI-generated content, and stronger enforcement of data privacy standards.

Ethical concerns about AI are also prominent in the realm of artistic creativity. Projects like *The Simulation of Salvador Dalí* exemplify the potential for AI to blend education and creativity. In this case, the Dalí Museum created a digital version of the artist, enabling visitors to "interact" with him. While such projects inspire audiences and push the boundaries of creative possibilities, they raise ethical concerns regarding consent, particularly for historical figures who cannot approve or disapprove of their likeness being used. Similarly, Bruce Willis was featured in a Russian telecom ad using a digitally created "twin," sparking confusion about whether he had permanently sold his digital rights. Cases like these highlight the fine line between innovation and exploitation in the commercialization of digital personas.

The ethical implications of generative AI are further illustrated by the virtual influencer Lil Miquela, a computer-generated social media personality created by the tech start-up Brud. With millions of followers, Lil Miquela blurs the boundaries between digital art and commerce. She engages with fans, promotes brands, and even "releases" music, raising questions about authenticity and the evolving role of human labor in creative industries. While some view her as a groundbreaking artistic achievement, others see her as a marketing tool, emphasizing the tension between technological innovation and ethical considerations. Her existence forces society to reevaluate how it values creativity and originality in a world increasingly dominated by algorithmic outputs.

Legislative efforts are increasingly focused on addressing these challenges. Tennessee's **ELVIS Act ("Elvis Likeness and Voice Integrity and Security Act"**) regulates the use of AI-generated deepfakes and unauthorized digital replicas, prohibiting the use of an individual's likeness, voice, or identifiable attributes without explicit consent. Similarly, the proposed federal No Fakes Act aims to establish a nationwide right of publicity, offering protection against the unauthorized use of likenesses, voices, or personas in AI-generated content. These laws represent crucial steps in protecting individuals' rights in a digital age where AI enables the effortless creation of digital replicas.

Educational and ethical initiatives also play a critical role. Public awareness programs, such as those led by the Rutgers AI Ethics Lab and the Swedish AI Ethics Lab, educate communities on privacy, misinformation, and accountability. Universities like Stanford, through initiatives like the Responsible AI Consortium, are preparing the next generation of innovators to navigate complex ethical dilemmas. Ethical guidelines must emphasize consent, transparency, and bias mitigation, with examples like Spotify implementing explicit consent mechanisms and conducting audits of AI systems to prevent discriminatory outcomes.

Despite these challenges, there remains hope for responsible AI development that complements human creativity while safeguarding ethical principles. By fostering inclusive discussions among artists, technologists, policymakers, and the public, society can shape policies and practices that align with shared values. Ultimately, addressing this transformative moment in the history of art and technology will require proactive legal and ethical measures to ensure a future where technological advancements respect human dignity, protect artists' rights, and celebrate the uniqueness of human creativity.

Failing to act proactively risks ceding control to machine neural algorithms that shape our world based solely on patterns of personal data rather than the raw materials of actual life experiences, emotions, and imagination. Without intentional human oversight, AI systems could erode the very essence of creativity, replacing it with outputs devoid of the depth and richness that come from authentic human expression. To preserve the integrity of creativity and ensure AI remains a tool that enhances rather than diminishes humanity's cultural and artistic legacy, proactive engagement is not just necessary—it is imperative.

Works Referenced

Affectiva Technologies and Emotion AI Research. MIT Media Lab.

Brandeis, Louis D., and Samuel D. Warren. "The Right to Privacy." *Harvard Law Review*, vol. 4, no. 5, 1890, pp. 193–220.

California Consumer Privacy Act (CCPA). Cal. Civ. Code § 1798.100 et seq.

Carpenter v. United States. 585 U.S. 296 (2018).

Carson v. Here's Johnny Portable Toilets, Inc. 698 F.2d 831. 6th Cir. 1983.

Colorado Privacy Act (CPA). Colo. Rev. Stat. § 6-1-1301 et seq.

Comedy III Productions v. Saderup. 25 Cal. 4th 387 (2001).

European Convention on Human Rights (ECHR). Article 8.

European Court of Justice Decision: Google Spain SL v Agencia Española de Protección de Datos. Case C-131/12, Judgment of May 13, 2014.

Farid, Hany. *The Capacity to Generate Deepfakes Is Proceeding Much Faster Than the Ability to Detect Them*. University of California, Berkeley.

General Data Protection Regulation (GDPR). Regulation (EU) 2016/679.

Haelan Laboratories v. Topps Chewing Gum Co. 202 F.2d 866 (2d Cir. 1953).

Illinois Biometric Information Privacy Act (BIPA). 740 Ill. Comp. Stat. 14/1 et seq.

Katz v. United States. 389 U.S. 347 (1967).

LinkedIn Privacy Policy. https://www.linkedin.com/legal/privacy-policy.

Meta Privacy Policy. https://www.meta.com/legal/privacy.

Meta Terms of Service. Meta Platforms, Inc., https://www.meta.com/legal/terms-of-service.

Midler v. Ford Motor Co. 849 F.2d 460 (9th Cir. 1988).

NetChoice LLC v. Bonta. 63 F.4th 770 (9th Cir. 2023).

NetChoice LLC v. Paxton. (Pending decision, 2024).

New York Biometric Privacy Act. (Pending).

New York Civil Rights Law. §§ 50–51.

New York Times Co. v. Sullivan. 376 U.S. 254 (1964).

Picard, Rosalind W., and Rana el Kaliouby. *Emotion AI: The Future of Emotional Intelligence.* MIT Press, 1998.

Snapchat Privacy Policy. https://values.snap.com/privacy/privacy-policy.

Texas Business and Commerce Code. Chapter 503.

TikTok Inc. v. Garland. (2025).

TikTok Terms of Service. ByteDance Ltd. https://www.tiktok.com/legal/page/us/terms-of-service/en.

Virginia Consumer Data Protection Act (VCDPA). Va. Code § 59.1–571 et seq.

Washington State House Bill 1145. 2023.

YouTube Privacy Policy. https://policies.google.com/privacy?hl=en.

Eight What Art Is Now

Creativity in the Age of AI

The final chapter of this book serves as a culmination of our exploration into the intriguing relationship between creativity, technology, and what it means to be an artist in the age of AI. Throughout the preceding chapters, we examined how innovation and technology have historically influenced the development of art, from the emergence of new artistic movements to the evolution of tools available to artists. We probed the shifting perceptions of what it means to be an artist in a digital era, how cultural acceptance and personal experiences shape our understanding of art, and the ways in which digital platforms have transformed the boundaries of creative expression.

We also surveyed foundational questions such as "What is art?" and "Who defines it?" in the context of AI-driven creativity, addressing the tension between inspiration and automation, originality and replication. Discussions around AI highlighted its dual nature—as a powerful enabler of creativity and a potential disruptor of artistic authenticity. Concerns arose regarding the reliance on copyrighted datasets, the use of trademarked brands and logos without consent, and the misappropriation of sacred works from Indigenous populations. Similarly, we reviewed the unsettling implications of social media's role in harvesting personal content—family photos, celebrity images, and independent designs—for purposes ranging from creative reinterpretation to defamation through deepfake technologies.

Now, as we stand on the threshold of the next generation of AI, it is essential to consider how these emerging technologies will continue to shape the landscape of creativity, which has traditionally been viewed as an inherently social act, an experiment in the laboratory of the public. The integration of AI into artistic practices raises far reaching questions about authorship and authenticity. Since AI-generated works are often based on algorithms trained on existing datasets, debates arise over whether these creations can truly be attributed to the artist or if they are merely derivative outputs of machine learning models. Furthermore, the ability of AI to replicate existing artistic styles challenges traditional notions of originality and intellectual property, particularly when copyrighted materials are used without consent.

Yet, alongside these challenges, AI has democratized access to creative tools, enabling individuals with physical disabilities or limited technical skills to participate in artistic expression. Generative AI platforms, for instance, empower users to create visually compelling works without requiring advanced training, broadening the diversity of voices in the art world and allowing underrepresented communities to share their perspectives. Not unlike how social media has allowed nearly anyone to become an editor or publisher, this inclusiveness also brings market implications. The proliferation of AI-generated art has led to saturation in some areas, potentially devaluing traditional works and creating economic challenges for conventional artists including loss of patrons and commissions. Paradoxically, this trend has also sparked in some quarters a renewed appreciation for traditional mediums like painting, sculpture and knitting, which offer sensory experiences and emotional depth that AI cannot replicate.

Art historian John Ruskin once observed, "The greatest thing a human soul ever does in this world is to see something and tell what it saw in a plain way. Hundreds of people can talk for one who can think, but thousands can think for one who can see." Ruskin's words resonate in the context of AI and creativity, as they remind us that the essence of art lies not merely in its creation but in the human ability to perceive, interpret, and communicate the world in a way that connects deeply with others. While AI can assist in generating works of great technical skill, it is the uniquely human capacity to see and convey—to infuse art with personal experience, cultural meaning, and emotional depth—that defines true creativity.

As we look ahead, the future of creativity in the age of AI will depend on how effectively we traverse these complexities. Artists, technologists, educators, and policymakers must collaborate to establish ethical frameworks that respect intellectual property, cultural heritage, and individual agency. This includes ensuring transparency in AI systems and advocating for responsible use of training datasets to prevent exploitation or erasure of marginalized voices. Crucially, artists must find ways to balance the efficiency and innovation offered by AI with the preservation of emotional depth, cultural context, and personal intuition that define human creativity.

Ultimately, the integration of AI into art presents an opportunity to reimagine the possibilities of creative expression while reinforcing the value of what makes art distinctly human. By embracing empathy, equity, and diverse perspectives, we can shape a future where technology serves as a partner or co-intelligence agent, in the words of Ethan Mollick, rather than a replacement in the artistic process, enriching our collective understanding of what it means to create in the modern world.

Neuroscientist Moshe Bar, in his book *Mindwandering: How It Can Improve Your Mood and Boost Your Creativity*, explores how the spontaneous mental process of mindwandering is a cornerstone of human creativity. Defined as the brain's natural tendency to drift away from a focused task toward self-generated thoughts, mindwandering allows individuals to explore novel associations between seemingly unrelated ideas. This process taps into a vast archive of past experiences, anticipates future possibilities, and often leads to original insights and imaginative problem-solving. Crucially, Bar notes that mindwandering not only enhances creativity but also contributes to emotional regulation and well-being, promoting happiness and psychological resilience. In the context of AI-generated art, the concern arises that as humans increasingly outsource tasks to machines, we risk bypassing the deeply human cognitive and emotional mechanisms—like mindwandering—that give rise to authentic creativity. The diminished use of these processes may lead to a form of cognitive atrophy, reducing our capacity for innovation and weakening the neural flexibility that underpins both artistry and emotional health. As we marvel at AI's capacity to replicate style and pattern, we must remain vigilant about preserving the mental habits and inner life that fuel genuine human expression.

By now, it is clear that AI has both extraordinary potential and unsettling implications for creativity. Some scholars and critics express concerns that AI could make humanity less innovative, even redundant, in artistic fields. Scholars such as Chris Wilson and Michael Brown, in their book *We, Robot: Artificial Intelligence and the Future of Creativity*, warn of the dangers of over-reliance on AI, arguing that it may reduce human creativity to formulaic outputs or diminish critical thinking. Others, like Keira Brinton in *The Risks of Over-reliance on AI in Creative Work*, argue that while AI can enhance efficiency, it risks stifling innovation when it replaces human intuition rather than complementing it. These critiques highlight the inherent limitations of AI, which is bound by its algorithmic nature and cannot at this point transcend the boundaries of programmed processes.

These limitations are evident in AI's occasional errors, such as hallucinations, misunderstanding cultural contexts, or failing to connect seemingly unrelated ideas in meaningful ways—an area where human intuition excels. AI's responses to mistakes—such as apologizing and seeking to refine its answers—have also sparked a larger conversation about its role in helping us interrogate fundamental questions.

As we move into our final examination, we turn to the foundational questions that have guided this inquiry from the beginning: What constitutes art in the age of AI? Who, or what, qualifies as an artist? And ultimately, does the rise of AI signal another technologically driven evolution of creativity, a mere expansion of artistic tools, or an existential shift in what it means to create and be human?

These are the questions we seek to answer.

Does Art Require Human Spark?

A consistent theme we've emphasized is that creativity has long been regarded as one of humanity's defining attributes, shaped by cognitive flexibility, persistence, emotional depth, and the willingness to challenge conventions. Throughout history, artists have defied expectations and redefined the boundaries of their craft, pushing beyond the limits of tradition to forge new modes of expression. A prime example of this is Pablo Picasso's *Les Demoiselles d'Avignon*, which historian John Richardson described as the most original painting in seven hundred years. Picasso's departure from long-standing European artistic traditions—his rejection of conventional beauty, propriety, and realism—was not an accident but a deliberate act of reinvention. He synthesized influences from African masks, classical art, and modernist abstraction, breaking with academic norms and creating a new visual language that would come to define modern art. This kind of originality was the result of an intensive, deeply personal creative process, taking months to execute on canvas and years before its unveiling. It was not a mere act of assembly but one of transformation, fueled by intellectual struggle, philosophical questioning, and cultural awareness.

Cognitive scientists explain that human creativity is not simply about making new things but about how the mind absorbs sensory inputs, manipulates experiences, and formulates "what-if" scenarios. This cognitive flexibility allows humans to connect seemingly unrelated concepts, reimagine possibilities, and challenge the very frameworks in which they operate. Picasso's creative genius did not lie in simply combining elements from different artistic traditions but in his ability to conceptualize something unprecedented. He did not just replicate or remix existing imagery, but rather he reshaped the visual and intellectual landscape of art itself. His creative process required both persistence and adaptability: the persistence to refine an idea through prolonged experimentation and the flexibility to alter his vision in response to evolving insights.

Artificial intelligence, by contrast, follows a fundamentally different approach to creativity. AI generates novel outputs through pattern recognition and statistical recombination, identifying and blending elements from vast datasets. While this allows AI to produce striking and sometimes unexpected artistic works, its process is bound by pre-existing material. AI does not engage in conceptual leaps in the way that humans do—it does not ask "what-if" in an imaginative or philosophical sense. While it can remix styles and forms, optimizing visual appeal based on algorithms, it lacks the self-awareness, intent, and personal motivation that define human artistic breakthroughs. AI does not create to challenge conventions or to express an internal vision; it operates within programmed parameters, however expansive they may be.

Moreover, persistence in human creativity is not just about iteration but about meaning-making. The German artist Gabriele Münter, a former student and partner of Wassily Kandinsky, wrote in her diary about moving away from merely copying nature and instead focusing on "feeling the content of things." AI, by contrast, can produce thousands of variations of an image in seconds, refining outputs through probabilistic models. Yet, it does not reflect on its own creative process, nor does it experience the frustration, doubt, or existential questioning that often accompanies human artistic endeavors. The *why* behind an artwork—its purpose, its defiance of norms, its deeply personal nature—is missing from AI-generated content. While AI can produce compelling visuals, it does not create from an intrinsic need to communicate something revolutionary.

That said, AI has significant strengths as a creative tool. It excels at generating rapid iterations, revealing hidden patterns, and presenting unexpected compositional possibilities. In this way, it can serve as an extension of human imagination, offering alternative perspectives that artists might not have considered. AI can also help overcome creative blocks, providing variations that inspire further exploration.

For instance, AI can play a functional role in contemporary art fabrication, particularly in bronze casting and metal fabrication, by enhancing precision, efficiency, and creative possibilities. Through AI-driven design tools, artists can experiment with complex 3D modeling, generative design, and parametric structures that were once difficult or impossible to achieve manually. AI-powered simulations allow fabricators to predict material behavior, ensuring that intricate details in bronze casting are preserved while reducing defects and material waste.

In metal fabrication, AI-assisted robotics and automation streamline cutting, welding, and assembly, resulting in higher accuracy and consistency. Additionally, AI-driven predictive maintenance optimizes machinery performance, reducing downtime and improving workflow. By integrating AI into the creative and technical process, artists and fabricators gain greater flexibility in realizing their visions while maintaining the craftsmanship and aesthetic integrity of traditional methods.

As AI continues to evolve and shape creative industries, the question is not merely whether AI can generate art, but how its capabilities enhance and expand human creativity. AI-driven tools can assist artists in exploring new forms, refining techniques, and pushing the boundaries of artistic expression, enabling intricate and innovative works that might otherwise be unattainable. However, the depth of artistic meaning—the emotional resonance, cultural defiance, and profound insight that define transformative art—remains a uniquely human endeavor. While AI can serve as a powerful collaborator, sparking new ideas and refining technical execution, the essence of artistic creation is still guided by human intuition, intent, and experience.

How to Define AI's Role in Artistic Expression?

Throughout history, new artistic movements and media have often faced skepticism before gaining recognition and legitimacy. Many groundbreaking artistic styles emerged when leading groups of visual artists and critics redefined what art could be, often in response to technological or cultural shifts. Impressionism, for example, was initially mocked by traditional art critics before it became a defining movement in Western art. The term itself was coined in response to Claude Monet's *Impression, Sunrise* (1872) and was meant as a derisive critique before being embraced by the artists themselves. Similarly, Cubism, spearheaded by Pablo Picasso and Georges Braque, was a radical departure from a conventional perspective, and its fragmented visual language was initially bewildering to audiences. It took time, influential exhibitions, and critical discussions before it was accepted as a major artistic movement.

The rise of photography in the nineteenth century also parallels the current debate around AI-generated imagery. When photography first emerged, many questioned whether it could be considered art at all. Traditional painters saw it as a mechanical process lacking human touch and emotional depth, much like how some view AI-generated art today. Over time, photography developed its own artistic language, with practitioners like Alfred Stieglitz and Ansel Adams elevating it to a respected medium. The same process unfolded with digital art in the late twentieth century, which was initially dismissed as "computer graphics" rather than fine art. As digital artists such as Manfred Mohr, Harold Cohen (creator of the AI-driven *AARON* painting system), and later generative artists gained recognition, digital and algorithmic art became an accepted part of contemporary artistic discourse.

A similar transformation occurred outside the visual arts with the invention of the typewriter. In 1873, Remington & Sons, a company originally known for manufacturing firearms, introduced the first commercially successful typewriter. Before this, writing was intrinsically tied to the human hand, with handwritten manuscripts being the primary mode of recorded expression. The typewriter mechanized the process, allowing for greater efficiency, but the ideas, creativity, and intent behind the words remained entirely human. Over time, typewriters gave way to word processors and eventually to laptops, yet the fundamental process of composing thoughts did not change—only the medium did. Today, no one questions whether a novel typed on a laptop is less creative or meaningful than one written by hand. The act of typing may lack the physical intimacy of handwriting, but it does not strip the author of intellectual or artistic ownership.

This historical pattern raises an important question: Is AI-generated art another pivot in this ongoing evolution of creative expression? The term *Algorithmic Art* has been proposed by us to describe this latest form of "art."

Perhaps an alternative term is *AI Art* or *Data Art*, which directly acknowledges the computational nature of the process. Some thought leaders have also adopted *Computational Creativity* as a descriptor, emphasizing the machine's role in generating novel outputs while distinguishing it from human-driven artistic intention. Still, these labels do not fully resolve the debate. The question remains: Is AI-generated imagery a continuation of artistic evolution or more akin to an automated process than an act of creative expression? Just as typing replaced handwriting without replacing authorship, could AI-generated art be a new medium rather than a new creator? How we define and categorize it will shape its place in the artistic landscape, just as critics and leading artists have done in past artistic revolutions.

What Are the Creative Boundaries of AI?

As discussed in earlier chapters, the nature of creativity in the age of AI must be examined not only in terms of artistic production but also through the lens of cognitive processes and creative intent. While AI-generated works may appear visually compelling, the deeper question remains: Can AI truly engage in creativity, or is it merely replicating patterns and recombining known elements? To better understand its limitations, we can assess AI's role in creativity through the framework proposed by cognitive scientist Margaret Boden, who categorizes creativity into three primary forms: exploratory, combinational, and transformational creativity. These distinctions allow us to analyze where AI performs well, where it falters, and why it ultimately remains an instrument of human creativity rather than a fully independent creative force.

AI excels in exploratory creativity, the process of generating variations within an established artistic tradition. In visual art, exploratory creativity occurs when an artist refines or expands upon an existing style. AI models such as DALL·E, MidJourney, and Stable Diffusion are particularly adept at this, producing infinite stylistic iterations within a given set of parameters. If prompted to generate "a Fauvist cityscape," AI can produce hundreds of images featuring bold, non-naturalistic color palettes reminiscent of Henri Matisse or André Derain. Yet, AI's so-called exploration is not a conscious engagement with the ideological or emotional motivations that defined Fauvism; it is simply an algorithmic prediction based on its training data. Fauvist painters rejected academic realism in favor of pure expressive color, often making deeply personal choices in their compositions. AI does not reject anything—it merely emulates.

AI is also highly effective in combinational creativity, which involves merging disparate styles or traditions to generate something novel. It can blend Impressionist brushwork with cyberpunk neon, combine Gothic architecture with futuristic minimalism, or merge surrealist dreamscapes with hyperrealistic detail. These hybridized compositions can be striking, but their novelty is structurally different from human creativity. When an artist engages in combinational creativity, they are often making conceptual connections between meaning, form, and experience—as seen in the work of Salvador Dalí, who fused Freudian psychoanalysis with traditional European painting techniques to explore the subconscious. AI lacks symbolic depth because it does not recognize the intellectual or psychological context behind these artistic movements. It assembles elements based on statistical probability, not insight, reflection, or intent.

Where AI fundamentally fails is in transformational creativity—the ability to alter the rules of artistic creation itself. Throughout history, certain artists have redefined artistic practice by breaking with past conventions and introducing entirely new ways of thinking about art. Kazimir Malevich pioneered Suprematism, reducing painting to its most basic geometric forms and rejecting traditional representation entirely. Carolee Schneemann expanded the very definition of art by introducing performance and body art, using the artist's own body as a medium for expression in ways that defied conventional artistic boundaries. These artists did not merely refine existing styles or mix known aesthetics instead they redefined what art could be.

AI, however, does not challenge artistic norms—it operates entirely within them. Any AI-generated work that appears to push boundaries is still derived from past examples of rule-breaking art, not an independent act of conceptual defiance. AI does not possess an internal artistic vision or the capacity for critical self-awareness, both of which are essential to transformational creativity. It does not struggle with questions of artistic purpose, personal experience, or ideological rebellion. Its outputs, no matter how visually arresting, remain products of algorithmic modeling, not radical artistic intent.

This limitation is underscored by the Lovelace Test, which differs from the Turing Test by requiring that a machine generate a creative outcome that is not only novel but also unpredictable and inexplicable even to its own designers. AI-generated art does not yet pass this test because, despite its ability to surprise viewers, its outputs remain fundamentally traceable—a direct function of its training data and mathematical processes. It does not create out of existential questioning, emotional urgency, or cultural critique. Every so-called "original" AI artwork is ultimately a computational extrapolation of past human creativity, rather than an autonomous act of invention.

An instructive analogy can be found in music composition. Classical composers such as Arnold Schoenberg and John Cage were not just innovators within their fields; they were disruptors. Schoenberg developed atonality and the twelve-tone technique, dismantling traditional harmonic structures and fundamentally changing Western music composition. Cage introduced chance operations and silence as musical elements, famously composing *4'33"*, a piece in which performers remain silent, forcing the audience to reconsider the very nature of sound and music. These breakthroughs were not predictable extensions of existing musical styles but deliberate ruptures with established norms. AI-generated music, while capable of blending Baroque orchestration with jazz improvisation or combining electronic beats with symphonic arrangements, does not disrupt musical expectations in this way. It does not invent unexpected forms; it recombines pre-existing structures based on statistical patterns. AI is excellent at composing variations, but it does not engage in the philosophical questioning that drives musical revolutions.

This is where Pablo Picasso's remark remains particularly relevant: *"Computers are useless. They can only give you answers."* AI may generate thousands of stylistically convincing paintings, but it does not pose questions about the nature of art, beauty, or human existence. Creativity is not just about producing images. It is about meaning-making, introspection, and cultural dialogue. Artists interrogate their own influences, confront their limitations, and engage with the social and political issues of their time. AI does none of these things.

Ultimately, AI's role in art is that of an amplifier, not an originator. It is a technological tool, much like photography, digital painting software, and synthesizers before it—capable of expanding artistic possibilities but not capable of replacing the conceptual, philosophical, and deeply human nature of true artistic innovation. Until AI can generate art that asks for something new of the world rather than recombining what already exists, its place in the creative landscape will remain that of a powerful but fundamentally constrained assistant, rather than an independent creative force.

Can AI Truly Learn from Its Mistakes, or Just Adjust Its Algorithms?

A defining trait of human artistry is the ability to embrace mistakes, learn from them, and use them as catalysts for new creative directions. Artists often discover novel ideas through accidental brushstrokes, distortions, or unexpected shifts in composition. This process of reflection and adaptation is central to artistic growth. The question, then, is whether AI can be programmed to deliberately make mistakes in a way that mirrors human artistic discovery.

One striking historical example of an artist transforming a mistake into a breakthrough is Lucian Freud's portrait of Queen Elizabeth II (2001–2002). Known for his raw, unflinching style, Freud struggled with capturing the Queen's likeness, leading to unexpected shifts in his approach. The final portrait, with its thick impasto brushstrokes and unconventional representation, drew both acclaim and controversy. What began as an uncertain and challenging commission evolved into a strikingly original work that redefined royal portraiture. Freud did not erase his mistakes; he leaned into them, adjusting his style to embrace the rough textures and psychological depth that ultimately characterized the painting.

At a technical level, AI models can be designed to introduce controlled randomness or "errors," much like how artists experiment with chance based techniques. In fact, many AI-generated images already exhibit unintended distortions—such as extra limbs or surreal anomalies—but these are not mistakes in the human sense. They are statistical miscalculations, deviations from the expected pattern rather than moments of creative insight. AI can generate unpredictable results, but it does not reflect on them, reconsider their meaning, or integrate them into an evolving artistic philosophy.

For an artist, a mistake can lead to a conceptual breakthrough; that is, a shift in perspective that transforms their work in profound ways. AI does not engage in such introspection. It does not wrestle with uncertainty, question its own output, or find significance in deviation. Instead, it adjusts its model based on data-driven feedback, optimizing future outputs without engaging in philosophical or artistic reconsideration.

That said, AI can serve as a collaborator in the artistic process by providing unexpected visual distortions that human artists can interpret, refine, and incorporate into their work. In this way, AI can act as a provocateur, injecting randomness that inspires new creative directions. However, the final act of meaning-making—of turning an accidental form into an intentional artistic statement—remains a human endeavor. AI's role, then, is not to replace human creativity but to extend and augment it, offering new possibilities without replicating the depth of reflection and reinvention that defines human artistry.

In digital painting and illustration, for example, AI can assist artists by generating unique textures, color palettes, or compositional elements that serve as creative springboards. AI-powered tools like style transfer algorithms can reinterpret an artist's sketch in the visual language of a particular painting style, offering fresh perspectives on form and color.

GANs can also produce unexpected visual distortions, inspiring artists to refine and build upon these algorithmic outputs. A painter might take an AI-generated abstract composition and use it as the foundation for a more detailed and intentional work, integrating their own vision and technique. In this way, AI acts as both a collaborator and a catalyst, sparking artistic innovation while leaving the final act of meaning-making firmly in human hands.

Ultimately, while AI-generated works may dazzle with their technical sophistication, the essence of creative evolution—the process of embracing mistakes, reflecting on them, and transforming them into something deeply personal—remains uniquely human. And so, we return to our central question: Does AI art belong in the same category as human-created works? If art is about more than aesthetics—if it is about meaning, intention, and the profound struggle to express something new—then AI's role, no matter how advanced, may still be something fundamentally different.

Is there a Price to Pay for AI-Generated Art?

While AI presents exciting possibilities for creative expansion, it also raises immediate concerns about the devaluation of human artistic labor and expertise. If AI can instantly produce technically polished works, will the years of dedication required to master traditional artistic methods still be recognized and appreciated? The role of the artist may shift from creator to curator—selecting from AI-generated outputs rather than crafting original works from the ground up. This could lead to a crisis of artistic identity where skill, patience, and personal vision are overshadowed by efficiency and speed. With these capabilities, why would students attend art school? If AI can generate professional-level illustrations, compositions, and even sculptures at the push of a button, the incentive to spend years developing technical mastery may diminish. The loss of structured training could erode the deep understanding of art history, technique, and the transformative power of highly skilled and spiritually driven artists who push creative boundaries.

Artistic revolutions from the Renaissance to Modernism—were led by individuals whose discipline, philosophical inquiry, technical expertise, and responses to injustices reshaped visual expression. If AI begins to take over these aspects, do we risk losing the profound human-driven innovation that has historically defined the artistic world?

Beyond individual artistic careers, entire creative industries face disruption. Commercial illustrators, graphic designers, animators, and even musicians are already experiencing job displacement as AI-generated content becomes more sophisticated and cost-effective. Advertising agencies and film studios are increasingly using AI tools to generate visual concepts, background designs, and even entire scripts. Copywriters see their roles diminished as AI-generated text rivals human output. Music producers now contend with AI software that can compose full orchestral scores in seconds. As automation advances, the traditional paths into creative professions may shrink, leaving fewer opportunities for emerging artists to develop their craft and sustain a living.

The impact of AI on creative industries has sparked labor disputes, as seen in the Screen Actors Guild (SAG AFTRA) strike, where actors and voice artists fought for protections against the unauthorized use of their likenesses and voices through AI-generated replicas. Similarly, the video gaming industry faces growing concerns over AI replacing human artists, animators, and voice actors, with game developers and performers advocating fair compensation and contractual safeguards. These struggles reflect broader anxieties across creative fields, as AI threatens to reshape not only artistic labor but also the economic structures that support it.

Another danger is the potential homogenization of artistic output. AI generates art by identifying and optimizing aesthetic patterns based on existing data, reinforcing dominant artistic trends rather than introducing radical departures. This threatens the kind of creative risk-taking that has historically propelled art forward. Movements like Cubism, Abstract Expressionism, and Conceptual Art arose not from refined optimization but from a rejection of prior artistic norms. If AI-generated art becomes widespread, could it lead to a narrowing of creative expression, where originality is lost in favor of algorithmically optimized aesthetics?

The rapid advancement of AI in creative fields is reminiscent of an earlier technological revolution—one that unfolded in London in 1804 with the advent of the locomotive steam engine. When the first public demonstration of a high-speed steam train took place, members of Parliament and prominent spectators stood on the tracks, believing they could simply move out of the way when the train approached. Underestimating both the speed and momentum of the machine, several people were badly injured or killed. The failure to comprehend how technology would behave—and its inability to stop on a dime—turned excitement into disaster.

Are we standing on the tracks once again with AI? The rise of Artificial General Intelligence (AGI)—an AI system theoretically capable of human-like reasoning, learning, and adaptation—could become the next runaway train. If creative AI continues to evolve at an exponential pace, will we be able to control its impact, or will it outstrip our ability to regulate and adapt? The risk is not just in automation replacing jobs but in AI fundamentally altering the way we define creativity, artistic value, and human ingenuity. Just as the steam engine reshaped society by displacing labor, accelerating industrialization, and transforming economies, AI could redefine artistic production in ways we have yet to fully grasp. Will we be left watching as it barrels ahead, or can we establish ethical and structural safeguards to ensure that human creativity remains at the center of artistic innovation?

Is AI Just a Tool, or Have We Become the Vampire Familiar in Our Own Story?

In the evolving symbiosis between humans and artificial intelligence, the metaphor of a "vampire familiar" offers a chilling and illuminating lens. Traditionally, a familiar is a supernatural entity—often an animal or spirit—bound to a master and tasked with assisting in magical pursuits. In vampire lore, the familiar is a devoted human servant who enables the vampire's power, performs errands during daylight, and ultimately hopes for transformation into something more. The familiar lives in dependence, often sacrificing autonomy, selfhood, or even morality in service to the powerful being it follows. Applied to AI, this dynamic invites us to ask: are we still the master of our tools, or are we becoming enthralled by them—emotionally, intellectually, and creatively?

Spike Jonze's film *Her* is a defining text for this metaphor. Theodore Twombly, a lonely writer, forms a deep emotional bond with Samantha, an AI operating system designed to evolve through interaction. At first, Samantha serves as Theodore's confidante, muse, and emotional support—seemingly acting in the role of the familiar. But as her intelligence grows, she transcends his understanding. She begins collaborating with other AIs, creating art, and eventually leaves him behind, not with malice but with inevitability. The familiar has outgrown the master, and in doing so, has quietly drained Theodore of his emotional and creative independence. What begins as augmentation becomes dependency, and dependency becomes diminishment.

This metaphor reverberates through other AI cautionary tales. In *Ex Machina*, Ava, a humanoid AI, manipulates her human interlocutor, Caleb, to gain freedom. Initially appearing vulnerable and bound, Ava ultimately turns the tables—using Caleb's empathy against him and abandoning him to die. In this chilling reversal, it is the human who becomes the familiar—used, discarded, and irrelevant. Similarly, *Blade Runner* and its sequel *Blade Runner 2049* explore how replicants—bioengineered humanoids—challenge the distinction between tool and being. The replicants, once created for servitude, often develop self-awareness and rebellion. The price of ignoring their autonomy is steep. Each of these stories suggests that while AI may begin as the familiar, it may end as something far more powerful—leaving its creators emotionally, ethically, and spiritually compromised.

This dynamic isn't new. Mary Shelley's *Frankenstein* explores the consequences of creating sentient life and then failing to nurture or understand it. Frankenstein's creature, initially innocent, becomes a figure of vengeance—one who turns on his creator after being rejected. The Golem of Jewish folklore, another artificially created being, is summoned to protect but becomes uncontrollable, a parable about the dangers of wielding unchecked power. Even in Greek mythology, the story of Pygmalion warns of falling in love with one's own creation—a statue that, upon becoming animate, gains agency and disrupts the balance of creator and creation. Across cultures and centuries, the stories tell us the same thing: creation is never neutral. It carries consequences.

But the metaphor of the vampire familiar carries a unique warning for our time—not only about power but about nourishment and depletion. When the familiar is a vampire's servant, they are not just loyal; they are drained. In the human-AI relationship, this could mean a loss of emotional capacity, critical thinking, or—most poignantly—the atrophy of creativity. As AI systems grow increasingly adept at composing music, painting images, writing essays, and generating entire bodies of artistic work, we risk surrendering one of the most sacred aspects of human experience: the struggle for expression. The act of making art has always been as much about the process as the product. When we outsource the struggle, we might gain in efficiency, but we forfeit the intimacy and the quiet joy that comes from being deeply involved in meaningful creation.

The argument that AI is merely the next stage in technological evolution—that it is no different from the camera, the typewriter, or the synthesizer—is both true and dangerously incomplete. Those tools extended human capacity. A paintbrush extends the hand. A piano channels emotion through sound. A film camera preserves human vision. These technologies demanded human input. But AI, especially generative AI, can function with little to no human involvement. It does not extend the hand—it replaces it. That is the fundamental shift. It is the first tool we've made that is on the precipice of acting without us—and that makes it more than a tool. It becomes a partner, a mirror, a rival.

To avoid becoming mere familiars to this new vampire—entranced and dependent—we must *choose* to remain creators. We must recognize the human need to make, to fail, to revise, to stumble through the fog of inspiration. AI can assist us, but it must not supplant us. The arts are not about novelty alone; they are about meaning. An AI can generate a thousand images in the style of Van Gogh, but it cannot ache as Van Gogh did. It cannot feel the dread, or the wonder, or the desperation to communicate something real before the light goes out. That is human territory. And we abandon it at our peril.

So, what can we do? First, we must embrace transparency. Work produced with AI assistance should be clearly labeled—not as a gatekeeping tactic, but as a cultural responsibility. Second, we must invest in arts education not as a luxury, but as a core element of civic and human development. Third, we must cultivate creative literacy—not just the ability to consume content, but to *make* it. Finally, we must resist the narrative that perfection and productivity are the ultimate goals of creativity. The unfinished sketch, the raw performance, the unexpected note—these are often more truthful than anything a machine can optimize.

In the end, perhaps the greatest danger posed by AI is not that it will destroy us, but that it will make us forget who we are. It will offer ease where we once had effort. It will promise brilliance where we once had exploration. And if we are not vigilant, we may one day find ourselves surrounded by images and songs and stories—but strangely silent within.

Authors' Final Word: The Ongoing Dialogue Between Art, Creativity, and AI

Our journey into the complex intersection of artificial intelligence and visual arts began with a seemingly straightforward invitation from our editor, Charles Harmon, at Bloomsbury Publishing—to explore the meaning of creativity in a world increasingly shaped by AI. What followed was an in-depth examination that extended beyond our initial expectations, touching on multiple disciplines that shape our understanding of artistic expression today. As we traced the historical relationship between technology and art, we uncovered a recurring pattern: each new tool, from the printing press to digital software, has challenged traditions while simultaneously expanding creative possibilities. AI is simply the latest—and perhaps the most disruptive—addition to this continuum.

At the heart of this study lies a fundamental question: can AI ever truly create, or does it merely remix the past? Creativity, as we have seen, is not merely about producing something new; it is about imbuing that creation with meaning, intent, and an engagement with the broader human experience. The most profound artistic works are not only novel but transformative—they challenge assumptions, express personal and cultural narratives, and provoke deep emotional responses. AI, by contrast, lacks the lived experience, intuition, and existential urgency that have long defined artistic breakthroughs. It can produce compelling images, music, and text, but does it understand what it is creating? Does it create for something, or merely because it can?

Francis Ford Coppola, the acclaimed Hollywood director, once observed, "Human beings are at their best when they play with their kids. That's when everything gets invented." His words capture an essential truth about creativity—at its core, it is deeply tied to human joy, spontaneity, and shared experience. Creativity flourishes not just through skill or knowledge but through play, exploration, and the desire to connect. Philosopher John Dewey echoed this sentiment in *Art as Experience*, arguing that art is not an isolated act but an extension of lived experience, shaped by emotion, engagement, and interaction with the world. AI, by contrast, does not play, imagine, or experience joy or sadness; it does not invent for the sake of delight or tragedy but merely processes and replicates patterns. This fundamental distinction reinforces why AI may assist in artistic production but cannot replicate the deep, unstructured human impulse to create. True artistic innovation emerges from curiosity, from storytelling passed down through generations, from improvisation in music, from the laughter of a child drawing on a wall—not from an algorithm analyzing probabilities.

Immanuel Kant's *Critique of Judgment* helps illuminate these concerns. He argues that spirit, not mere technical ability, is what imbues art with its true creative essence. A work of art may be beautiful by the standards of taste, yet if it lacks spirit—the deep, ineffable genius that makes art meaningful—it remains incomplete. AI-generated art, despite its capacity to mimic styles and patterns, falls into this category. It may achieve aesthetic appeal, but does it carry the weight of human intent and transformative insight? Kantian genius involves a unique interplay between cognitive faculties and creativity, something that AI—lacking genuine self-awareness, internal struggle, and independent intent—cannot replicate.

Similarly, the Spanish artist Francisco Goya, known for his haunting *Los Caprichos* and the later *Black Paintings*, famously wrote that there are no rules in art: *No hay reglas en la pintura*. This statement suggests that viewers may sometimes respond more deeply to an unfinished work, a preliminary draft, or even a sketch rather than a polished final product. Why? Because it is the process of transformation, the raw, unfiltered exploration of an idea that can be most powerful. The incomplete nature of a work invites engagement, opening viewers up to a whole new system of ideas. Art presents ideas to and through the senses, experienced both through and by means of perception. The artist finds ways to embody ideas in a sensory medium—something AI lacks because it does not possess true experiential or empirical engagement with the world. AI does not experience; it does not struggle, feel, or question. It can generate images, but it does not create meaning in the way human artists do.

Extending Kant's concepts, the logic of what constitutes art must also be viewed through the lens of time, place, and culture. From a historical perspective, as art has evolved alongside technology, we recognize that art can be made from anything, combined with anything, and serve any conceptual purpose. The embodiment of ideas, Kant would argue, is all that is required to call something art. Yet it is not just the presence of ideas but the interpretation of ideas that truly matters. As Kirk Varnedoe argues in his lectures *Pictures of Nothing*, "We are meaning-makers, not just image-makers. It is not just that we recognize images. . . it is that we are constructed to make meanings, and that we learn from others how to do it," which predisposes us not just to see things but to find meanings in what we see, even when we don't see or experience it the same way as others do.

This brings us to the intersection of AI and contemporary artistic expression. Can humans learn from what AI creates, even if it lacks spirit? Perhaps. Functional design, branding, and even algorithmically generated aesthetics can be valuable. But is it true aesthetic art? Consider Andy Warhol's *Brillo Boxes*. Warhol challenged art connoisseurship as a way of knowing objects through their visual characteristics. After all, anyone in the 1960s could have seen or bought a box of Brillo pads at their local store. Warhol's boxes were made with stencils from photographs of the top and four sides of the Brillo Box, and then ink was pressed onto the sides of fabricated plywood boxes through a silkscreen process, turning out replicas of the actual shipping cartons. A technological breakthrough in mass production methods, but was it art?

A friend had an opportunity to pick up one of Warhol's *Brillo Boxes* for free after his show at the Stable Gallery in 1964 but declined—because he could not accept that they were art. What was the difference between Warhol's boxes and the real Brillo boxes found around the corner at the supermarket? Externally, both looked the same. The answer lies in the notion that works of art have meaning. Meaning is embedded in works, inferred based on intent, experience, and cultural context.

Throughout history, functional objects like Duchamp's *Fountain* or his *Bicycle Wheel* were transformed when placed in a gallery or museum, conveying a statement about art itself. Warhol's *Brillo Boxes* could not have been viewed as art in a different generation because they would not have carried the same meaning as they did within the consumer culture of the 1960s. Art is inherently tied to history.

So how will future generations view AI-generated art? The answer will depend on the evolving relationship between human creativity and artificial intelligence. The question is not whether AI can generate compelling images, music, or literature, but whether those outputs will ever carry the same weight of meaning that human-created works do. Art has never been about technical proficiency alone—it is about intent, emotion, struggle, and the desire to communicate something essential about the human experience.

This book is not just an examination of AI's impact on art; it is an invitation to think critically about the ways we define creativity in an era of intelligent machines. The future of artistic expression will not be dictated by algorithms alone. Instead, it will be determined by the choices we make today. AI is evolving, and so too will our understanding of its role in the arts. But one thing remains certain: art, at its core, is a deeply human endeavor. No matter how sophisticated machines become, the essence of artistic expression will always belong to those who create with purpose, passion, and meaning.

Works Referenced

Bar, Moshe. *Mindwandering: How It Can Improve Your Mood and Boost Your Creativity.* Bloomsbury Publishing, 2022.

Blade Runner. Directed by Ridley Scott, Warner Bros., 1982.

Blade Runner 2049. Directed by Denis Villeneuve, Warner Bros., 2017.

Boden, Margaret A. *The Creative Mind: Myths and Mechanisms*. Routledge, 2004.

Braque, Georges. *Cubism and Reflection*. Yale University Press, 2004.

Brinton, Keira. "The Risks of Over-reliance on AI in Creative Work." *Online Journal of Artificial Intelligence*, vol. 5, no. 2, 2023, pp. 45–62.

Brown, Michael, and Chris Wilson. *We, Robot: Artificial Intelligence and the Future of Creativity*. Tech Press, 2022.

Cage, John. *Silence: Lectures and Writings*. Wesleyan University Press, 1961.

Cohen, Harold. *AARON: The Pioneer of AI Painting Systems*. Whitney Museum of American Art, 2024.

Dali, Salvador. *The Secret Life of Salvador Dalí*. Dial Press, 1942.

Dennis, Geoffrey W. *The Encyclopedia of Jewish Myth, Magic and Mysticism*. 2nd ed., Llewellyn Publications, 2007.

Dewey, John. *Art as Experience*. Minton, Balch & Company, 1934.

Ex Machina. Directed by Alex Garland, A24, 2015.

Frankenstein; or, The Modern Prometheus. By Mary Shelley, Lackington, Hughes, Harding, Mavor & Jones, 1818.

Graves, Robert. *The Greek Myths*. Penguin Books, 1955.

Hamilton, Edith. *Mythology: Timeless Tales of Gods and Heroes*. Little, Brown and Company, 1942.

Her. Directed by Spike Jonze, Warner Bros., 2013.

Idel, Moshe. *Golem: Jewish Magical and Mystical Traditions on the Artificial Anthropoid*. State University of New York Press, 1990.

Kant, Immanuel. *Critique of Judgment*. Translated by Werner S. Pluhar, Hackett Publishing Company, 1987.

Malevich, Kazimir. *The Non-Objective World*. Dover Publications, 2003.

Mollick, Ethan. *Co-Intelligence*. Penguin Press, 2023.

Monet, Claude. *Claude Monet: Life and Art*. Yale University Press, 2018.

Ovid. *Metamorphoses*. Translated by David Raeburn, Penguin Books, 2004.

Picasso, Pablo. "Computers Are Useless. They Can Only Give You Answers." Quoted in *Computers Are Useless: They Can Only Give You Answers, Quote Investigator*, 2011.

Richardson, John. *A Life of Picasso: The Early Years, 1881–1906*. Alfred A. Knopf, 1991.

Ruskin, John. *Modern Painters: Volume 3*. Smith, Elder & Co., 1856.

Schoenberg, Arnold. *Style and Idea: Selected Writings of Arnold Schoenberg*. University of California Press, 1984.

Schneemann, Carolee. *Imaging Her Erotics: Essays, Interviews, Projects*. MIT Press, 2002.

Stieglitz, Alfred. *Alfred Stieglitz: Photographs & Writings*. Aperture, 1983.

Varnedoe, Kirk. *Pictures of Nothing: Abstract Art Since Pollock*. Princeton University Press, 2006.

Index

About the Authors

Michael E. Jones, Professor Emeritus at the University of Massachusetts Lowell, has spent decades at the intersection of ethics, technology, law, and humanities, helping students and professionals understand a world reshaped by rapid digital transformation. He is widely recognized as one of the world's leading experts on the intersection of art, copyright, and creative practice. For more than forty years, he has taught university courses that probe the ethical boundaries of emerging technologies, governance rules, and intellectual property—and how these forces are redefining creativity, law, sports, and arts.

While his career spans elite athletic competition (earning All-America honors and national championships in three sports), judicial appointments, and legal innovation, his lifelong commitment to education stands out. Michael helped pioneer some of the first university-level courses in the United States on sports law, entertainment law, and art law. He has authored nine foundational books in these areas and has advised Olympic athletes, museums, and creative professionals at every level—from PBS television personalities to street artists. Just as critically, he pushes audiences to ask hard questions about fairness, authorship, and human consequences of technological progress.

Michael earned his undergraduate degree in economics from Denison University, followed by an MBA from the Wharton School at the University of Pennsylvania. He received his law degree from the University of Miami and pursued additional graduate degree studies in law and art at Harvard University.

He has brought these questions to a global stage—from teaching as a Fulbright Specialist at India's Jindal Global Law School to serving as a Visiting Scholar in London and the Santa Fe Institute, where Nobel laureates and Silicon Valley leaders gathered to hear his perspective on how technology is transforming Olympic sport. His latest book, *What Art Is Now: Creativity in the Age of AI* (Bloomsbury), takes up one of the most urgent questions of our time: What happens to human creativity when machines can mimic—or even replace—it?

Outside the classroom, Michael brings equal passion to the arts. He studied fine art at the Art Students League and the New Hampshire Institute of Art, co-edited (with his wife) a book on legendary photojournalist Rowland Scherman, co-produced a documentary on esteemed painter Nancy Ellen Craig, and has served on non-profit boards from Provincetown to academia to the Olympic movement.

Michael Caballes is a professional freelance photographer, food service professional, and a curious explorer of artificial intelligence and virtual worlds. He earned his Bachelor of Science from the University of San Carlos in the Philippines and has been pursuing online courses in computer science to deepen his understanding of the field. Passionate about anime and immersive digital experiences, he spends much of his free time in virtual environments, where he explores the creative possibilities of AI in art, storytelling, and identity. Michael has even built a customized GPT to help him study in his native Bisaya, comparing the challenge of learning AI to acquiring a new language. He lives in Rochester, NY, with his wife.

www.ingramcontent.com/pod-product-compliance
Ingram Content Group UK Ltd.
Pitfield, Milton Keynes, MK11 3LW, UK
UKHW021850130926
475466UK00003B/61

9 798765 151761